The Fun Seeker's Los Angeles

THE ULTIMATE GUIDE TO ONE OF THE WORLD'S HOTTEST CITIES

THE FUN ALSO RISES TRAVEL SERIES

Back Cover Photo Credits: Venice Beach (left) courtesy of Kenna Love /LACVB; Frank Gehry's Walt Disney Concert Hall (center) courtesy of Laphil.org; Rooftop Bar at The Standard Downtown (right) courtesy of Nadine Johnson, Inc.

30% postconsumer content. 

Distributed in the United States by National Book Network (NBN).

First Edition. Printed in the United States by Central Plains Book Manufacturing.

ISBN: 0-9666352-9-9

Credits

Executive Editor	Alan S. Davis
Editor	Peter Cieply
Book Design	DeVa Communications
Maps by	Reineck and Reineck
Production	Samia Afra
	Jo Farrell

About the Author

Jordan Rane is a former senior editor of *Escape* magazine and a former West Coast editor of *Travelocity* magazine. His work has appeared in *Backpacker*, *Islands*, *The Los Angeles Times*, *Maxim*, *Southwest Spirit*, and *Utne*. He was last seen in Los Angeles with his wife, son, and five cats.

GREENLINE PUBLICATIONS
Extraordinary Guides for Extraordinary Travelers
P.O. Box 590780
San Francisco, California 94159-0780

The Fun Also Rises Travel Series

The Fun Seeker's Los Angeles

The Ultimate Guide to One of the World's Hottest Cities

Jordan Rane

GREENLINE PUBLICATIONS

To Our Readers:

In 1998 I wrote and published *The Fun Also Rises Travel Guide North America*, followed in 1999 by *The Fun Also Rises International Travel Guide*. Together, these books covered the world's most fun places to be at the right time—from the Opera Ball in Vienna to the Calgary Stampede.

The success of these guides persuaded me of the need for a different approach to travel book publishing—*extraordinary guides for extraordinary travelers*. Greenline Publications was launched as a full-scale travel book publisher in December 2002, with ***The 25 Best World War II Sites: Pacific Theater***, the first book in the **Greenline Historic Travel Series**.

The Fun Also Rises Travel Series was introduced in 2003 with an updated version of the first book—now called ***The Fun Seeker's North America***. Like Ernest Hemingway's *The Sun Also Rises*, which helped popularize what has become perhaps the most thrilling party on earth (Pamplona's Fiesta de San Fermín, also known as the Running of the Bulls), **The Fun Also Rises** travel books take readers to the world's most fun places.

For the series, we have identified 21 cities worthy of five-star ratings for fun. Greenline will be releasing original, single-destination guides for each of these cities, including Las Vegas, New York, San Francisco, London, and Athens.

Greenline's guiding principle is simple: Never settle for the ordinary. We hope that a willingness to explore new approaches to guidebooks, combined with meticulous research, provides readers with unique and significant travel experiences.

Please let me know if our guides fail to meet your expectations in any way. To reach us, or for updated information on all Greenline books, please visit our website at www.greenlinepub.com.

Wishing you extraordinary travels,

Alan S. Davis
Publisher

Table of Contents

How to Use This Book

***The Fun Seeker's* Los Angeles** takes a selective approach to the city that saves you days of figuring out what to see, where to go, and which freeway exit to take. You'll be taken beyond the obvious tourist traps and into the heart—or hearts—of this multifaceted city. First, we'll key you in to **City Essentials**, travel tips for getting to and around Los Angeles, and provide you with a **Cheat Sheet** filled with savvy tips, trivia, and the very least you need to know about this town.

Next you'll find **The Perfect Los Angeles**, a compilation of *The Fun Seeker*'s "best" picks for hot and happening restaurants, spas, beaches, golf courses, studio tours, shopping experiences, and other attractions.

Then, while most guidebooks are organized geographically, *The Fun Seeker's Los Angeles* offers a unique approach to exploring the city: **The L.A. Experience**, five different ways to explore L.A., each focused on a different theme. Each experience is outlined in a quick overview, followed by a detailed three-day itinerary that gives you insider tips on where to be when for maximum fun. Following that, you'll find in-depth reviews of all the best hotels, restaurants, bars, theatres, and attractions related to that particular experience (these listings appear in bold in the itineraries).

We've customized five different Los Angeles Experiences—*Classic Hollywood, New Hollywood, Hipster L.A., Coastal L.A.*, and *Downtown & About L.A.*, so you can go wherever a mood takes you with ease.

• Long before The Hollywood Wax Museum opened and Ozzy Osbourne's name was emblazoned on the Walk of Fame, the place called Hollywood lived up to all its hype. It was the entertainment industry's ground zero, a celebrity playground of theaters, drinking holes, and hotel suites that served regulars like Clark Gable, Carole Lombard, and Humphrey Bogart. Several reinventions later, Hollywood and its ritzier satellites like Beverly Hills still offer glimpses of its illustrious past. You'll find these Golden Era locations in **Classic Hollywood**.

• On to Hollywood's illustrious present. Need a good place to power-lunch? Or the right bar to pretend to close a picture deal and create a false buzz? Mythical Hollywood rolls out a brand new red carpet for itself every few years. From industry-magnet hotels to the latest celebrity hangouts and VIP studio tours, here's a borderless roadmap for Greater Hollywood's latest reinvented itself—the **New Hollywood**.

• Searching for young, hip, artsy, in-the-know scenes filled with people nearly as cool as you are? Casting for *Swingers II* and *III* is in session right here. The tastiest cocktails from Hollywood to Silverlake, a golf course you can breeze through with a hangover, and a hotel with just the right amount of attitude and shag carpet—you'll find all this and more in **Hipster L.A.**

• For those who need solid proof that Los Angeles is actually on the water, **Coastal L.A.** lets you get acquainted with that massive chunk of sunny waterfront. Hit the nicest beaches, get some surfing lessons, meet a family of gray whales, dine in style, and check into a room overlooking the waves.

• In Los Angeles on business? Who says you have to act like it the whole time? When the meeting adjourns, the convention's over, and the tie and name tag come off, you can get a lot more action and culture out of this town than free HBO and a decent night's sleep. From Downtown galleries and historic sights and Pasadena's top spas and fairways to some of the city's best retreats and culinary finds, **Downtown & About L.A**. packs some off-hours L.A. punch into your next business trip.

After all that, if you find yourself weaving on the freeway or shopping for screenplay software, it's clearly time to get out of town for a day. Check out **Leaving Los Angeles**, a collection of day and overnight trips to great escapes like Catalina Island, Disneyland, Laguna Beach, and Palm Springs.

Finally, check your travel dates with **The L.A. Calendar**, the short list of the hottest happenings in the city throughout the year. And for quick reference, you can find in **The L.A. Black Book** all of the important addresses and phone numbers you'll need (along with their page numbers in the theme chapters and "best" lists).

Key to Pricing Symbols

Hotel symbols indicate each hotel's best non-suite double room price per night.

$ = Up to $199
$$ = $200 to $299
$$$ = $300 to $399
$$$$ = $400 and up

Restaurant symbols indicate average cost of one entrée; nightclub and attraction symbols indicate cover or entry fee.

$ = Up to $19
$$ = $20 to $29
$$$ = $30 to $39
$$$$ = $40 and up

Acknowledgments

An entire life could be spent writing a guidebook on a place as vast, varied, and remarkable as Los Angeles. Tempted as I was, I couldn't free up that much time. So I'm forever grateful to those friends, colleagues, and strangers who generously lent their hours, enthusiasm, expertise, and influence, to support the cause. They're all living proof that people do actually return your calls in this town.

A round of thanks goes to Carol Martinez at the Los Angeles Convention & Visitors Bureau, Leron Gubler and Ana Martinez-Holler at the Hollywood Chamber of Commerce, and Michael Robinson at the Beverly Hills Conference & Visitors Bureau for helping out in the early days and for passing along several good leads.

Many thanks to Philip Ferentinos, Tony Hoover, Daniel Lumbrera, and Eric Lynxwiler for their eye-opening reintroductions to the city. And to Annie Crenshaw, Joseph Oskey, Mark Segal, and Mike Simon for their valuable input. Among their many fine deeds, Charles, Rebecca, and Margaret Rannells were my first hosts and guides in L.A. and lent me a Thomas Guide when I most needed one. Thanks to anyone else over the years who, as it turns out, provided an important service by suggesting some bar, restaurant, beach, trail, gallery, theatre, or hole-in-the-wall spot that ended up in these pages. Special thanks to publisher Alan Davis and the Greenline Publications team for making this project fly, and to editor Peter Cieply, whose respectful and meticulous work came at the right time.

I'd walk five hundred miles and write a guidebook on Reno for Jemma, who makes it all worthwhile—and Jackson, who's never too young to know that he does too.

Jordan Rane

A special thanks to those who helped guide me to the very best that Los Angeles has to offer: Paul Davis;, Didi and Jeff Fine; Dennis, Florence and Lisa Forst; Gloria and Jim Hassan; and John and Holly Nuckols.

Alan S. Davis

Publisher and Executive Editor

Introduction

Los Angeles: What It Was, What It Is

Welcome to Los Angeles. By that, we mean welcome to that vast county in Southern California comprised of a half-dozen area codes, 21 freeways, 75 miles of coastline, 88 independent cities, 300 museums, a half-million strip malls, and a gazillion straight days of sunshine per year (give or take). Welcome to this Los Angeles, and only this Los Angeles. Other Los Angeleses—like Los Angeles, Texas (pop. 140), a little spot near San Antonio that adopted the name in 1923 as an unsuccessful promotional stunt, or Los Angeles, Chile, an eight-hour drive south of Santiago and no doubt a very nice place to visit, but some other time perhaps—are beyond the scope of this book.

Everyone has an opinion about Los Angeles, especially those who've never actually been here. If L.A. was Chicago, Des Moines, or Tampa, it might care what people who've never actually seen it have to say about it. But L.A. is too wrapped up in itself to return those calls. It's too busy being the entertainment capital of the world, speaking in 86 different tongues, making fashion statements, fusing Vietnamese and Salvadorian cuisines, erecting famous art galleries and music halls, sipping iced lattes in the dead of winter and cocktails from plastic cups at Skybar, remembering the riots, reserving a patio table in Beverly Hills, reading bad spec scripts on the treadmill, cruising Sunset Boulevard, admiring the Playboy Mansion, wobbling into Venice Beach on rollerblades, roaming through tidepools in Malibu, hiking in the Santa Monica Mountains, watching car chases on sublimely lame local news channels, and welcoming about 25 million satisfied visitors each year. Los Angeles isn't trying to be rude. There's just no time to respond to all the jealous hate mail. Plus, life is short (especially with the Big One still out there).

Close to four million people inhabit the city of Los Angeles, with its crazy-legs borders running in various directions from the tip of the San Fernando Valley to the cliffs of San Pedro. Ten million people fill out Los Angeles County, which stretches from Malibu and Santa Monica (at its western borders) through Beverly Hills and Hollywood to Burbank and Pasadena (in the Valley), and as far south as Long Beach, and includes a patchwork quilt of several dozen other cities you'll probably never visit. Four neighboring counties belong to the greater Los Angeles area, which in itself constitutes the world's tenth largest economy and has a higher population density than all

El Pueblo de Nuestra Señora la Reina de los Angeles del Río Porciúncula was founded on September 4, 1781. In time, the city would be known simply as Los Angeles.

but three states in the entire country. How did a semi-arid desert without a decent natural water supply get so hot?

It all started humbly enough when a small racially-mixed band of farmers was dispatched by Spanish missionaries to settle a piece of land by a river about ten miles south of the Mission San Gabriel Archangel. On September 4, 1781, what was surely the longest-named small city in the world was founded in the area that is now Downtown L.A.—El Pueblo de Nuestra Señora la Reina de los Angeles del Río Porciúncula (population 44). In time, the city would come to be known simply as Los Angeles.

Over the next century of change, a combination of booms, bumper crops, land grabs, and engineering feats would transform this isolated farming pueblo into a Big American City. Among the first to stake their claim in the early 1800s were the rancheros, a prosperous group of newly independent Mexican landowners shipping cattle hides to the eastern U.S. and selling beef to a soaring population of gold miners in Northern California. Their fortunes would change radically after the U.S.–Mexican War (1846–1848), when land rights were reviewed and land was largely expropriated by the U.S. government. The arrival of a railroad connecting Los Angeles to the East Coast coincided with the planting of some orange trees in the area. Soon Southern California's sagging economy was back in business, the area swiftly becoming the nation's top orange producer. In the 50 years leading up to 1900, Los Angeles' population would balloon from barely 1,000 to more than 100,000.

L.A. soared into twentieth century prosperity with the discovery of oil and a burgeoning industry led by L.A.'s first oil baron, Edward L. Doheny. The opening of the Panama Canal would turn young San Pedro Harbor (now part of the nation's busiest cargo terminal) into a bustling port. Of course, none of this desert basin's wild success could have been sustained without the biggest civic coup in L.A. history. In 1904, Los Angeles water bureau superintendent William Mulholland found the city's badly needed solution to its water supply woes, 250 miles north in the snowmelt-rich Owens Valley. Land was snatched up on false pretenses (ostensibly for a cattle farm), and soon an enormous aqueduct project was underway. Nine years, 24.5 million dollars, and one con job later, water from the Owens Valley was being siphoned into the thirsty jaws of its metropolis neighbor to the south. Problem solved. Case closed.

Nice weather, easy filming conditions, and safe distance from Thomas Edison's Patent Wars back east fostered L.A.'s first fledgling movie business around the same time the water started flowing. The pioneers of this trade were ragtag peddlers cranking out silent shorts, taking only the occasional bullet in the lens—Edison's collection agents' warnings for dodging patent royalty payments. A bona fide movie industry of studio moguls, directors, and celebrities soon followed, churning out the first flicks, turning the name of its small community headquarters—Hollywood—into a major brand, and selling tickets to watch scenes being shot on the Universal lot (long before the Back To the Future ride was installed). The world's most glamorous industry—The Industry, as it would come to be called—had arrived, and its calling card has been L.A.'s biggest marketing banner ever since.

What hasn't Los Angeles seen over the last century? Earthquakes, brush fires, mudslides, race riots, and trials-of-the-century have periodically shaken this city to its roots. And what roots they are. Huge territorial expansions and an influx of people from more than 140 countries have turned greater L.A. into a sprawling microcosm of the world. The summer Olympics have been here twice (that's at least once more than anyplace else). The Dodgers and Lakers have come, the Rams and Raiders have gone (along with O.J.). The Queen Mary has parked herself in Long Beach Harbor and opened three restaurants and a hotel. Disneyland is just down the road. If you've come to L.A. to see Fabio or Lassie's star on the Hollywood Walk of Fame, well, that's just fine, because they are

Hollywood's pioneers were ragtag peddlers churning out silent shorts and dodging Thomas Edison's patent royalty collectors. The world's most glamorous industry had arrived.

Welcome to the six area codes, twenty-one freeways, seventy-five miles of coastline, eighty-eight independent cities, three hundred museums, and half-million strip malls that make up the Los Angeles area.

here. The entertainment industry is L.A.'s best known and most fluid backdrop, moving with effortless ease between the silver screen, the patio at Spago, and the lobby at Shutters. But the rest of Los Angeles—a goliath among the world's major cities—is out there too, under the same warm sun and twinkling satellites, using the same pinched water supply, resisting anything close to a cohesive definition.

Los Angeles loves the term "reinvention," but a city this size can change only about as fast as a big ship turns—slowly and significantly. If you haven't been here in a while, places like Hollywood and Venice Beach will look brighter and cleaner; if it's your first time, they may look like they could use a good scrubbing. Undeniably, the place is changing, most recently from multimillion-dollar revitalization efforts that have given us the Hollywood & Highland complex, the Kodak Theatre, the Grove at the Farmers Market, and a new-and-improved and safer Ocean Front Walk. Downtown Los Angeles is now grander, hipper, and more inviting with the Walt Disney Concert Hall, the STAPLES Center, and the Rooftop Bar at The Standard Hotel. First-timers may still see it as an eerily sequestered place, but Downtown is filled with history and history in the making.

So, once again, welcome to Los Angeles. And by that we mean welcome to an inexhaustible number of experiences that this city-within-a-county-within-an-area offers visitors (or locals who can pretend to be visitors in a place this large and varied). Challenges await you, like trying to digest a cheese-drenched enchilida at El Coyote, trying to bar-hop without having to fill up your gas tank, or trying to accept that the grumpy little dwarf sitting at the table across from you is in fact Jean Claude Van Damme. But most experiences will leave you craving more, and the best are here between these covers. Have fun.

WELCOME TO

Fabulous

LOS ANGELES

GREATER LOS ANGELES

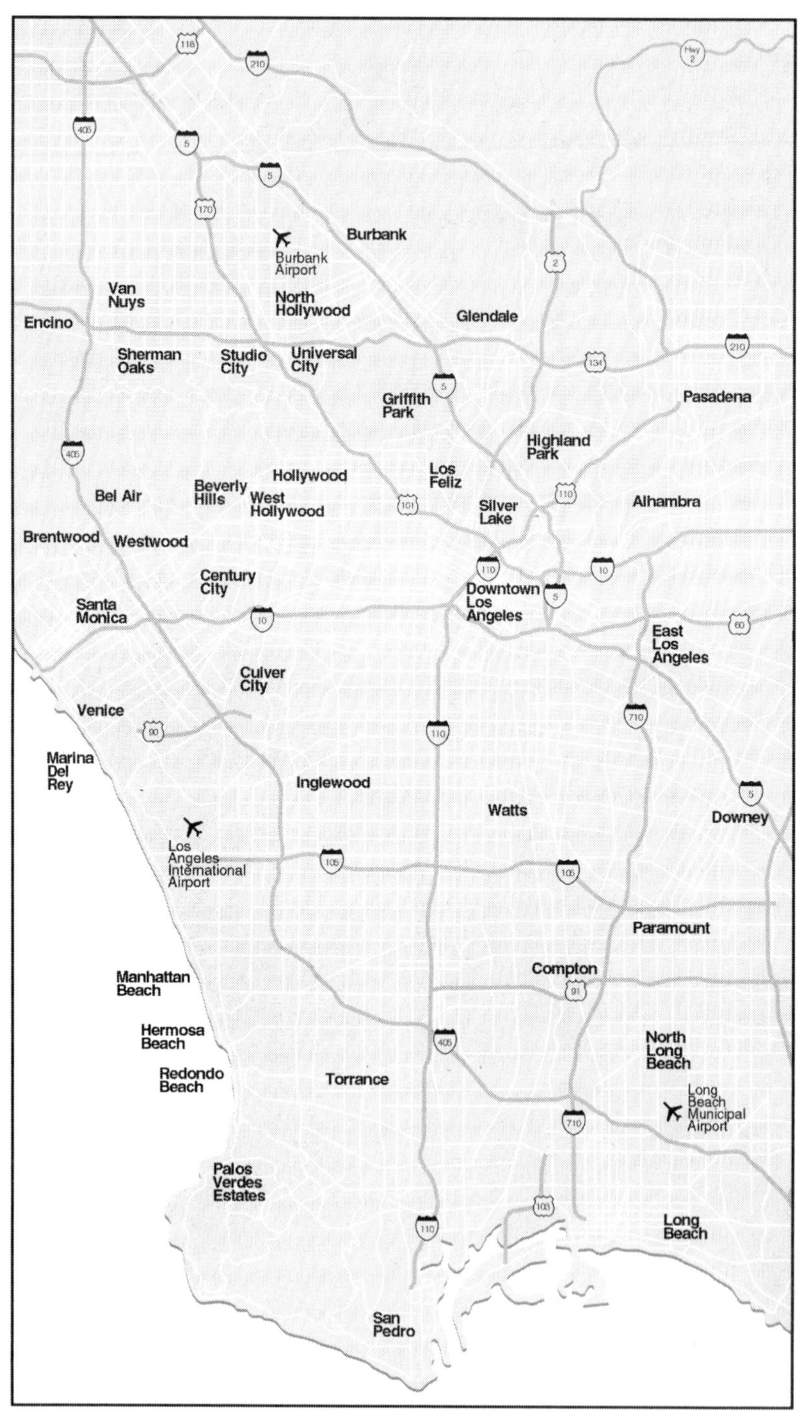

Hit the Ground Running

If you've never been here before—or even if you live here—the Los Angeles area can seem overwhelming. Which freeway takes you where? Which mountains are those? And by the way, what season is it? If you want to make like a native, you need to know the basics. Here are most of the facts and figures, including our Cheat Sheet, a quick-reference countdown of vital infromation that'll help you feel like an instant Angelino.

City Essentials

Getting To Los Angeles

By Air: Los Angeles International Airport (LAX) 1 World Way, Los Angeles, 310-646-5252 www.lawa.org/LAX

Flying Times to L.A.

Chicago:	4 hours
Honolulu:	5 hours
Las Vegas:	1 hours
London:	11 hours
Miami:	5 hours
New York:	6 hours
San Francisco:	1.5 hours
Seattle:	2.5 hours
Tokyo:	10 hours
Washington, D.C.:	5.5 hours

Better known as LAX, Los Angeles International Airport ranks among the world's five busiest airports, with more than 50 million passengers and nearly 2 million tons of cargo passing through annually. Eight domestic terminals (Terminal 8 is inside Terminal 7) and one international terminal are arranged in a double-tiered U-shape with curbside baggage check-in available on the upper/departure level and baggage claim on the lower/arrival level. Clearly marked shuttle and courtesy van stops are also on the lower level in front of each terminal. Amenities include a first-aid station in the Tom Bradley International Terminal, a 48-port cyber cafe in Terminal 4, free shuttle service between terminals on LAX's "A" Shuttle, and plenty of food and beverage options ranging from McDonalds and Starbucks to California Pizza Kitchen and Wolfgang Puck's. LAX's grooviest venue is the space-age Encounter Restaurant (310-215-5151), perched in the historic Theme Building complex between the terminals. Travelers Aid of Los Angeles (310-646-2270) operates several booths throughout the airport.

Located right on the coast between El Segundo and Marina del Rey, LAX is an easy commute to Santa Monica or the South Bay beach communities. Traffic allowing, Hollywood and downtown are each about a 30-minute drive.

Several smaller airports serve Greater Los Angeles (see box). Burbank-Glendale-Pasadena Airport is closest to Universal Studios in the heart of the San Fernando Valley. Long Beach Municipal Airport serves Long Beach and upper Orange County. John Wayne Airport in Orange County is the closest airport to Disneyland. Ontario Airport is 35 miles east of downtown Los Angeles, serving the Inland Empire and neighboring counties of Riverside and San Bernardino.

Airlines Serving Los Angeles International Airport

Air Canada (888-247-2262, www.aircanada.ca) Terminal 2

Air France (800-237-2747) Tom Bradley International Terminal

Alaska Airlines (800-252-7522, www.alaskaair.com) Terminal 3

America West (800-235-9292, www.americawest.com) Terminal 1

American Airlines (800-433-7300, www.americanairlines.com) Terminal 4

American Trans Air (800-435-9282, www.ata.com) Terminal 3

British Airways (800-247-9297, www.british-airways.com) Tom Bradley International Terminal

Continental Airlines (800-525-0280, www.continental.com) Terminal 6

Delta Air Lines (800-221-1212, www.delta.com) Terminal 5

Frontier Airlines (800-432-1359, www.frontierairlines.com) Terminal 3

Hawaiian Airlines (800-367-5320, www.hawaiianair.com) Terminal 2

Japan Airlines (800-525-3663, www.japanair.com) Tom Bradley International Terminal

Midwest Express Airlines (800-452-2022, www.midwestexpress.com) Terminal 3

Northwest Airlines (800-225-2525, www.nwa.com) Terminal 2

Qantas (800-227-4500, www.qantas.com.au) Tom Bradley International Terminal (arrives at Terminal 4)

Singapore Airlines (800-742-3333, www.singaporeair.com) Tom Bradley International Terminal

Southwest Airlines (800-435-9792, www.southwest.com) Terminal 1

United Airlines (800-241-6522, www.united.com) Terminal 6, 7, & 8

US Airways (800-428-4322, www.usair.com) Terminal 1

Virgin Atlantic Airways (800-862-8621, www.fly.virgin.com) Terminal 2

Airport Shuttle Service

Several shuttles offer 24-hour door-to-door service from LAX, making a few stops along the way. Fares are often cheaper than taxis. For groups of three or more, taxis are a better bet. Typical fares from LAX are: Downtown $15; Hollywood $20; Santa Monica $20; Pasadena $25. Add $10 for each additional passenger.

Airport Express	310-645-8181	800-311-5466
Metropolitan Express	310-417-5050	800-338-3898
SuperShuttle	310-782-6600	800-258-3826
Prime Time Shuttle	310-342-7200	800-733-8267

Additional Airports in the Los Angeles Area

Burbank-Glendale-Pasadena Airport, 2627 N. Hollywood Way, Burbank
818-840-8840, www.burbankairport.com

John Wayne Orange County Airport, 19051 Airport Way N., Anaheim
949-252-5200, www.ocair.com

Long Beach Municipal Airport, 4100 Donald Douglas Dr., Long Beach
562-570-2678, www.lgb.org

Ontario International Airport, Terminal Way, Ontario
909-937-2700, www.lawa.org/ont

By Car: Los Angeles is accessed by several major highways.

Driving to L.A. by Car

From	Distance (mi)	Time (hr)
Chicago	2,050	34
Las Vegas	270	4.5
New York	2,790	47
Omaha	1,560	26
Phoenix	370	6
San Diego	120	2
San Francisco	380	6.5
Seattle	1,141	19

From the North: I-5 is the straightest (and ugliest) shot through central California's San Joaquin Valley, entering the San Fernando Valley and passing downtown L.A. en route to San Diego. For a more scenic but longer drive, US-101 winds along the Coast Ranges from San Jose, accessing San Luis Obispo and Santa Barbara before entering Ventura County, Hollywood, and the highway's terminus in downtown L.A. The scenic Pacific Coast Highway (also known as PCH or Hwy. 1) traces the Big Sur Coast, entering L.A. through Malibu and connecting with I-10 East in Santa Monica.

From the South: I-5 leads into Downtown L.A. from San Diego and Orange County. I-405 splits from I-5 at the southern end of Orange County, running through L.A.'s Westside before re-connecting with I-5 at the top of the San Fernando Valley.

From the East: I-10 begins in Jacksonville Florida, passes through downtown L.A., and curves north into PCH at the beach in Santa Monica.

By Train: Amtrak (800-USA-RAIL, www.amtrak.com) enters and leaves Los Angeles from downtown's Union Station (800 N. Alameda St.). Trains pulling into this classic Mission-style building include the Coast Starlight, heading down the West Coast from Seattle through Portland and Oakland; the Pacific Surfliner, offering 11 daily round-trips from San Diego and carrying on to Santa Barbara and San Luis Obispo in the north; the Southwest Chief, starting in Chicago and cutting through Kansas City and the Midwest; the Sunset Limited, leaving from Orlando Florida on a two-day milk run through the Deep South and Southwest.

Getting Around Los Angeles

By Car: In theory, it's possible to get around Los Angeles without a car. It's also something that most visitors wouldn't dream of doing. A basic knowledge of the main freeways and streets (see later in this chapter) is invaluable. So is a Thomas Guide for Los Angeles and Orange Counties (complete indexed street map) if you're planning on spending much time here. Speed limits, unless otherwise posted, are 35 mph on city streets and 65 mph on freeways. Rush hour is generally from 7 a.m.–10 a.m. and 3–7 p.m. Accidents clogging up the freeways can be avoided by tuning into traffic updates reported every 6–10 minutes on the AM stations KNX 1070 and KFWB 980. Freeway carpool lanes can be a huge time-saver, but don't risk a $271 fine if you're driving alone. Street parking is easy and relatively safe in many areas of the city and far more difficult in congested parts of Downtown and permit-only neighborhoods close to all the action. Keep a stash of quarters and small bills handy. City-run lots in Beverly Hills, Santa Monica, and West Hollywood usually offer two free hours of parking during the day and low hourly rates thereafter. In the restaurant districts, valet parking is convenient, ubiquitous, and a service commonly used like a public lot in Los Angeles. Rates range anywhere from $3 to $10.

Rental Cars

All major rental car companies offer complimentary shuttle service to offices just outside the airport. Courtesy phones are available in the arrival areas.

Alamo (310-649-2242 / 800-462-5266, www.goalamo.com)

Avis (310-646-5600 / 800-230-4898, www.avis.com)

Budget (310-642-4555 / 800-527-0700, www.budgetrentacar.com)

Dollar (800-800-3665, www.dollarcar.com)

Enterprise (310-649-5400 / 800-325-8007, www.enterprise.com)

Hertz (310-568-5100 / 800-654-3131, www.hertz.com)

National Car Rental (310-338-8200 / 800-227-7368, www.nationalcar.com)

Thrifty (310-645-1880 / 800-847-4389, www.thrifty.com)

High-End

Beverly Hills Rent-a-Car (310-337-1400 / 800-479-5996, www.bhrentacar.com)

Independent

Rent-A-Wreck (310-826-7555 / 800-995-0994, 1233 W. Pico Blvd., West L.A.)

Directions from LAX: To Santa Monica and the other northern beach communities, follow Sepulveda Blvd./Hwy. 1 north to Lincoln Blvd./Hwy. 1. To Manhattan Beach and the South Bay, take Sepulveda Blvd./Hwy. 1 south. To Beverly Hills, West Hollywood, and Hollywood, take Century Blvd. west to I-405 north and exit Santa Monica Blvd. east. For an alternate route north (especially useful during rush hour), take La Cienega Blvd. To Downtown or Pasadena take Sepulveda Blvd. south to I-105 east to I-110 north.

By Train: Metro Rail (213-626-4455/800-266-6883, www.mta.net) offers four lines connecting a large portion of Greater Los Angeles. The Blue Line runs north-south between Downtown and Long Beach. The Green Line runs east-west between Norwalk and Redondo Beach. The Red Line is L.A.'s subway, running northwest from Downtown through Hollywood to Universal City and North Hollywood. The recently opened Gold Line runs northeast from Downtown to Pasadena. Metrolink (800-371-5465, www.metrolinktrains.com) is a commuter train system connecting downtown's Union Station with neighboring Orange, Riverside, San Bernardino, and Ventura Counties.

By Bus: Relying on the bus to see L.A. is a bit like relying on the breast stroke to tour Venice, Italy. That said, you can cheaply get around on one. A network of 200 bus lines covers L.A., mainly for carless local commuters. Contact the Metropolitan Transportation Authority (MTA) for maps, timetables, and passes (213-626-4455, www.mta.net). The Cadillac of L.A. bus services is Santa Monica's Big Blue Bus (www.bigbluebus.com, 310-451-5444), which offers clean, efficient service throughout the Westside. DASH (808-2273 (no area code needed), www.ladottransit.com) offers 25-cent rides all over the downtown area from dawn to dusk.

Taxis

Taxis are an afterthought in Los Angeles. You'll find them at the airport, at stands throughout the city, or if you call, but don't expect to hail one from the street. Base fares usually start at $2–$2.50 and cost about $1.50 per mile. Carriers from LAX usually charge a flat-rate, typically $15 (Manhattan Beach), $25 (Santa Monica, Beverly Hills, Hollywood, Downtown), $45 (Burbank/Pasadena). Companies servicing the airport include:

Beverly Hills Cab	323-469-6611	800-273-6611
Independent Taxi	323-666-0050	800-521-8294
United Taxi	323-653-5050	800-411-0303
Yellow Cab	310-412-8000	800-200-1085

Emergency

Call 911 for the police, fire department, ambulance, and paramedics. Cellular call boxes dot the side of L.A. freeways for all emergencies. 24-hour emergency rooms operate at Cedars-Sinai Medical Center (8700 Beverly Blvd., Los Angeles, 310-423-3277), UCLA Medical Center (10833 Le Conte Ave., Los Angeles, 310-825-9111), and St. John's Health Center (1328 22nd St., Santa Monica, 310-829-5511). Sav-on (800-627-2866) and Rite Aid (800-748-3243) pharmacies are spread throughout the city. Extended pharmacy hours can be found at the Sav-on in West L.A. (24-hours, 3010 S. Sepulveda Blvd., 310-478-9821), Rite Aid in Westwood (until midnight, 1101 Westwood Blvd., 310-209-0708), and Horton & Converse in West L.A. (until 2 a.m., 11600 Wilshire Blvd., 310-478-0801). The Los Angeles Traveler's Aid Society (310-466-2270) is part of a national nonprofit organization helping travelers in need. Hotlines: Poison Hotline 800-876-4766; Rape/Domestic Violence 213-626-3393; Suicide Crisis Line 310-391-1253.

Weather

A touch of fog in the summer. A dash of rain in the winter. Nearly 300 days of at least partial sunshine annually and no humidity. Smog aside, it really is a lovely day just about every day in Los Angeles. While spoiled locals may moan about "June Gloom" (mild overcast skies in early summer) or the "Santa Anas" (warm winds in early fall), travelers won't find much to complain about weather-wise in L.A. during any season—or what passes for a "season" here. August and September are the hottest months. January and February are the coolest and rainiest, though T-shirts are commonly worn in the winter. Desert rules apply in the evenings when temperatures can plummet as much as 40 degrees at any time of year. Cool breezes keep the coast about 10–15 degrees cooler than the rest of the city. It's hottest in the valleys, which

Monthly High and Low Temperatures

Month	Fahrenheit	(Celsius)
January	66°/48°	(19°/09°)
February	67°/50°	(19°/10°)
March	69°/51°	(21°/11°)
April	71°/54°	(22°/12°)
May	73°/56°	(23°/13°)
June	77°/60°	(25°/16°)
July	82°/63°	(28°/17°)
August	83°/64°	(28°/18°)
September	82°/63°	(28°/17°)
October	78°/59°	(26°/15°)
November	73°/53°	(23°/12°)
December	68°/49°	(20°/09°)

frequently hit the triple digits in the summer. Ocean temperatures are generally colder than on the east coast, barely reaching 70 degrees in the heart of summer and plunging into the low-50s in the winter.

Attire

This may be Southern California but it's also the high desert. Layering is key. Pack all the bathing suits, shorts, T-shirts, and sunglasses you want, but make sure to include a light jacket and some reasonably warm clothes for those cool summer evenings. Warmer clothing is required in the winter, when you can see your breath at night. Wear sunscreen. Even on the rare cloudy day, the rays are strong.

Los Angeles is obsessively style conscious, and otherwise as relaxed or done-up as you want to make it. Casually hip is the usual dress code. Jeans and a funky shirt (and don't forget the right shoes) may be the uniform here, but they're the right sort of jeans and the right sort of shirt—and dry-cleaned just so. Jackets, ties, and traditional formal-wear are rarely required, and will more likely stick out than blend in. Don't panic if you feel at all out of place. You're in the right city to modify your wardrobe.

Media

The Los Angeles Times (www.latimes.com) is one of the most widely read and respected newspapers in the country. The thick-as-a-book Sunday edition includes "Calendar," a current city-wide entertainment and listings guide. *LA Weekly* (www.laweekly.com) is the city's largest free weekly entertainment publication, published every Thursday. *Los Angeles Magazine* (www.lamag.com) is L.A.'s monthly glossy, with a mini dining guide in the back of each issue.

Radio Stations (a selection)

FM Stations

88.1 KKJZ Jazz
89.3 KPCC National Public Radio
89.9 KCRW NPR/Eclectic
91.5 KUSC Classical
92.3 KHHT R&B Oldies
93.1 KCBS Rock Oldies
93.9 KZLA Country
94.7 KTWV Smooth Jazz
95.5 KLOS Rock
96.3 KXOL Spanish
97.1 KLSX Talk
98.7 KYSR Mainstream Rock
100.3 KKBT Urban Contemporary
101.1 KRTH Oldies
102.7 KIIS Top-40
104.3 KBIG Adult Contemporary
105.1 KMZT Classical
105.9 KPWR Dance
106.7 KROQ Rock

AM Stations

570 KLAC Jazz Standards
640 KFI Talk
710 KSPN ESPN Sports
790 KABC News/Talk
980 KFWB News/Traffic Reports
1070 KNX News/Traffic Reports
1150 KXTA Fox Sports/Talk

General Information for Visitors

Los Angeles Convention and Visitors Bureau, 685 S. Figueroa St., Los Angeles, 213-689-8822, www.lacvb.com. L.A.'s main visitors' hub offers city maps, calendars, TV taping listings, amusement park discounts, friendly advice, and round-the-clock information on the events hotline (same telephone number). Open Mon.–Fri. 8 a.m.–5 p.m. Sat. 8:30 a.m.–5 p.m.

Beverly Hills Convention and Visitors Bureau, 239 South Beverly Dr., Beverly Hills, 310-248-1015, www.beverlyhillscvb.com

Hollywood Chamber of Commerce, 7018 Hollywood Blvd., Hollywood, 323-469-8311, www.hollywoodchamber.net

Pasadena Convention and Visitors Bureau, 171 South Los Robles Ave., Pasadena, 626-795-9311, www.pasadenacal.com

Santa Monica Convention and Visitors Bureau, 1400 Ocean Ave, Santa Monica, 310-393-7593, www.santamonica.com

West Hollywood Convention and Visitors Bureau, 8687 Melrose Ave., Suite M-38, West Hollywood, 310-289-2525, www.visitwesthollywood.com

Party Conversation and Other Useful Facts

- Hiking to the Hollywood sign in Griffith Park is now illegal, after a series of stunts transformed the fifty-foot white letters into "Ollywood," during the Iran-Contra hearings, and "Hollyweed" by some dope activists.

- A state-wide smoking ban can get you fined $100 and booted out of a Los Angeles bar for lighting a cigarette.

- The Getty Center cost more than $1 billion to build. Admission is free.

- The worst thing you can do during rush hour is get on the 405 freeway. When heading north from LAX, take La Cienega Boulevard instead.

- Los Angeles smog warnings have been reduced by 80% in the last 25 years—but breathing is still healthier by the coast.

- Griffith Park is the largest city park in the country, and is nearly five times the size of New York's Central Park. Spread across 4,107 acres, it contains a zoo, a museum, an observatory, the historic Greek Theatre, three golf courses, and miles of hiking and horseback trails.

- The first two neon signs in the U.S. were purchased and hung at a Los Angeles car dealership in 1923.

- L.A.'s Red Line subway system runs 17.4 miles and cost $4.5 billion, making it the most expensive and mismanaged subway ever built per mile.

- Los Angeles, the country's second biggest sports market, hasn't had an NFL team since the Raiders and Rams bailed in 1995.

- Migrating gray whales can be spotted off the L.A. coast between December and April.

- You can still be a contestant on *The Price Is Right.* Send a self addressed stamped envelope specifying dates to CBS Television City, 7800 Beverly Blvd., L.A., CA 90036. Or call 323-575-2458.

The Cheat Sheet

The Very Least You Ought to Know About L.A.

If you're going to hang out here, you better know something about the place. Here's a countdown of the ten most essential facts and factoids you need to keep from looking like a *turista*. There will be a quiz.

Ten Neighborhoods

Beverly Hills has pretty much been home to the rich and famous since the coining of the term. Its downtown fashion district, the Golden Triangle, is one of the world's easiest places to max out several platinum cards in one spree. Highlights include Rodeo Drive, the Museum of Television & Radio, and the Polo Lounge at the Beverly Hills Hotel.

Burbank's sedate east San Fernando Valley location is the unlikely headquarters for some of the world's largest studios and recording companies, including Walt Disney Productions, Warner Bros. Studios, and NBC Studios.

Downtown is where the whole L.A. thing got started a few centuries ago. Bursting with history and history-in-the-making, it's home to the new Walt Disney Concert Hall, the Staples Center, Chinatown, the Museum of Contemporary Art—and, yes, that mandatory grove of bank towers.

Hollywood is simultaneously hip, seedy, and occasionally glamorous. You'll find old Tinseltown chestnuts here like the Egyptian and Chinese theatres, tourist traps like the Walk of Fame and the Wax Museum, bright new additions like the Kodak Theatre, and enough bars to keep you hopping.

Malibu's 25 miles of sunny shoreline boasts some of the best surfing and sand-lazing spots in (and out of) the city. Backed by the rugged Santa Monica Mountains National Recreation Area (and fronted by its share of celebrity mansions), Malibu is home to several state parks and beaches including Leo Carillo State Park and Zuma Beach.

Manhattan Beach is where the Beach Boys spent a few endless summers before the rents went up. Now a yuppified mecca for surfers, rollerbladers, volleyball studs/babes, and investment bankers, this South Bay charmer boasts a fine patch of sand and easy access to the area's party headquarters next door in Hermosa Beach.

Pasadena is L.A.'s influential neighbor to the north and the cultural center of the San Gabriel Valley. Its many famous sites include the Huntington Botanical Gardens, the Norton Simon Museum, the Pasadena Playhouse, and the Rose Bowl. Downtown Pasadena also has a hip small-town feel (if that's not an oxymoron) that can offer a nice break from the L.A. buzz.

Santa Monica is L.A.'s most time-honored (and televised) beach community—a thriving city in its own right offering first-class dining, shopping, and fun-seeking right on the coast. Highlights include the Third Street promenade, the Santa Monica Beach promenade, Montana Ave., Bergamot Station, and its popular next-door-neighbor, Venice Beach.

Silver Lake is the place where—along with its flanking neighborhoods Los Feliz and Echo Park—L.A.'s hipper, artsier Eastside crowd distinguishes itself with alternative music venues, retro lounges, backroom galleries, out-of-the-way cafes, wacky stores, and a smattering of architectural masterpieces by historic big guns Frank Lloyd Wright and Richard Neutra.

Westwood, home of UCLA, is about as college-town as it gets in Los Angeles. Westwood boasts the city's most impressive supply of big, loud movie theatres, with their share of red carpets during premiere nights.

Nine Streets

Hollywood Blvd. runs east from Laurel Canyon through downtown Hollywood, merging with Sunset at Hillhurst Ave. in Los Feliz.

La Brea Ave. runs north from I-10 to Hollywood.

La Cienega Blvd. runs north from the LAX area to West Hollywood.

Mulholland Dr. straddles the Hollywood Hills from Hollywood to I-405.

Santa Monica Blvd. runs west from Hollywood/Downtown to Ocean Ave. in Santa Monica.

Sunset Blvd. runs west from Silver Lake/Downtown to Pacific Coast Highway in Pacific Palisades.

Ventura Blvd. runs along the south end of the San Fernando Valley from Universal City to Woodland Hills.

Western Ave. bisects the city, running south from Hollywood/Griffith Park to San Pedro.

Wilshire Blvd. runs west from Downtown to Ocean Ave. in Santa Monica. Crosses Santa Monica Blvd. in Beverly Hills.

Eight Performing Arts Venues

Greek Theatre This historic open-air venue has hosted summer concerts of rock, pop, jazz, classical, world music, and comedy for more than 70 years. Season runs May–October.
2700 N. Vermont Ave., Griffith Park 323-655-1927, www.nederlander.com

Hollywood Bowl One of the largest outdoor amphitheaters in the world, hosting concerts of all genres under the stars from July–September.
2301 N. Highland Ave., Hollywood 323-850-2000, www.hollywoodbowl.org

Kodak Theatre The new home to the Oscars ceremony as well as to concerts, dance, dramas, and musicals.
6801 Hollywood Blvd., Hollywood & Highland, Hollywood 323-308-6300, www.kodaktheatre.com

The Music Center of Los Angeles The Music Center of Los Angeles is comprised of three venues (along with the new Walt Disney Concert hall, below). The Ahmanson Theater produces musicals, comedies, and dramas and hosts Broadway productions; the Mark Taper Forum is a regional theatre that focuses on new plays; the Dorothy Chandler Pavilion is home to the acclaimed Los Angeles Opera.
135 N. Grand Ave., Downtown 213-628-2772, www.taperahmanson.com, www.losangelesopera.org

Pantages Theater A classic Art Deco hall that primarily hosts touring productions of Broadway musicals and plays.
6233 Hollywood Blvd., Hollywood 323-468-1700, www.nederlander.com

Pasadena Playhouse Once the official State Theatre of California, the Playhouse is now a year-round regional theatre producing a variety of plays, comedies, and musicals.
39 S. El Molino Ave., Pasadena 626-356-7529, www.pasadenaplayhouse.org

Walt Disney Concert Hall The new Frank Gehry–designed concert hall, home to the L.A. Philharmonic and the Master Chorale.
111 S. Grand Ave., Downtown 213-628-2772, www.musiccenter.org/wdch

The Wiltern A legendary concert venue for pop and rock concerts.
3790 Wilshire Blvd., Los Angeles 213-388-1400, www.thewiltern.com

Seven Sports Teams

Los Angeles Avengers Arena Football League, 310-788-7744
www.laavengers.com

Los Angeles Clippers NBA Basketball, 310-426-6031
www.clippers.com

Los Angeles Dodgers Major League Baseball, 323-224-1448
www.dodgers.com

Los Angeles Galaxy Major League Soccer, 310-630-2200
www.lagalaxy.com

Los Angeles Kings NHL Hockey, 888-546-4752
www.lakings.com

Los Angeles Lakers NBA Basketball, 310-426-6031
www.lakers.com

Los Angeles Sparks WNBA Basketball, 310-426-6031
www.lasparks.com

Six Freeways

I-5 The Golden State Fwy. runs northwest from Downtown into the Valley; the Santa Ana Fwy. runs southeast from Downtown into Orange County.

I-10 The Santa Monica Fwy. runs west from Downtown to Santa Monica; the San Bernardino Fwy. runs east from Downtown to San Bernardino.

I-110 The Harbor Fwy. runs south from Downtown to San Pedro, runs north from Downtown to Pasadena.

I-405 The San Diego Fwy. runs north from the LAX area to I-5 in the Valley and south from LAX to I-5 in Orange County.

US-101 The Hollywood Fwy. runs northwest from Downtown to North Hollywood; Ventura Freeway continues northwest from North Hollywood to Santa Barbara.

Hwy. 1 The Pacific Coast Highway (or PCH) hugs the Los Angeles (and California) coast merging at various points with several roads and freeways.

Numbers to Drink by:

2: A.M. When most bars close.

21: That's how old you have to be to drink in Los Angeles. And, just so you know, we've seen people with gray sideburns carded here.

Five Area Codes

213 Downtown L.A.

310 Beverly Hills to Santa Monica and the South Bay

323 Hollywood and West Hollywood east of La Cienega Blvd.

626 Pasadena

818 San Fernando Valley

Four Retail Centers

The Beverly Center 8500 Beverly Blvd., Los Angeles
310-854-0070 www.beverlycenter.com

Hollywood & Highland 6834 Hollywood Blvd., Hollywood
323-460-6003, www.hollywoodandhighland.com

Third Street Promenade Third St. (Broadway to Wilshire) Santa Monica
310-393-8355, www.thirdstreetpromenade.com

The Grove 189 The Grove Dr., Los Angeles
323-900-8000, www.thegrovela.com

Three Theme Parks

Disneyland 1313 S. Harbor Blvd., Anaheim
714-781-7290, www.disneyland.com

Six Flags California 26101 Magic Mountain Pkwy, Valencia
661-255-4100, www.sixflags.com

Universal Studios Hollywood 100 Universal City Plaza, Universal City
818-508-9600, www.universalstudios.com

Two Sports Stadiums

Dodger Stadium 1000 Elysian Park Ave., Los Angeles, 323-224-1448

STAPLES Center 1111 S. Figueroa St., Downtown, 213-742-7340

One Time Zone

Los Angeles runs on Pacific Time (in case you were uncertain what that body of water was). That's three hours earlier than New York.

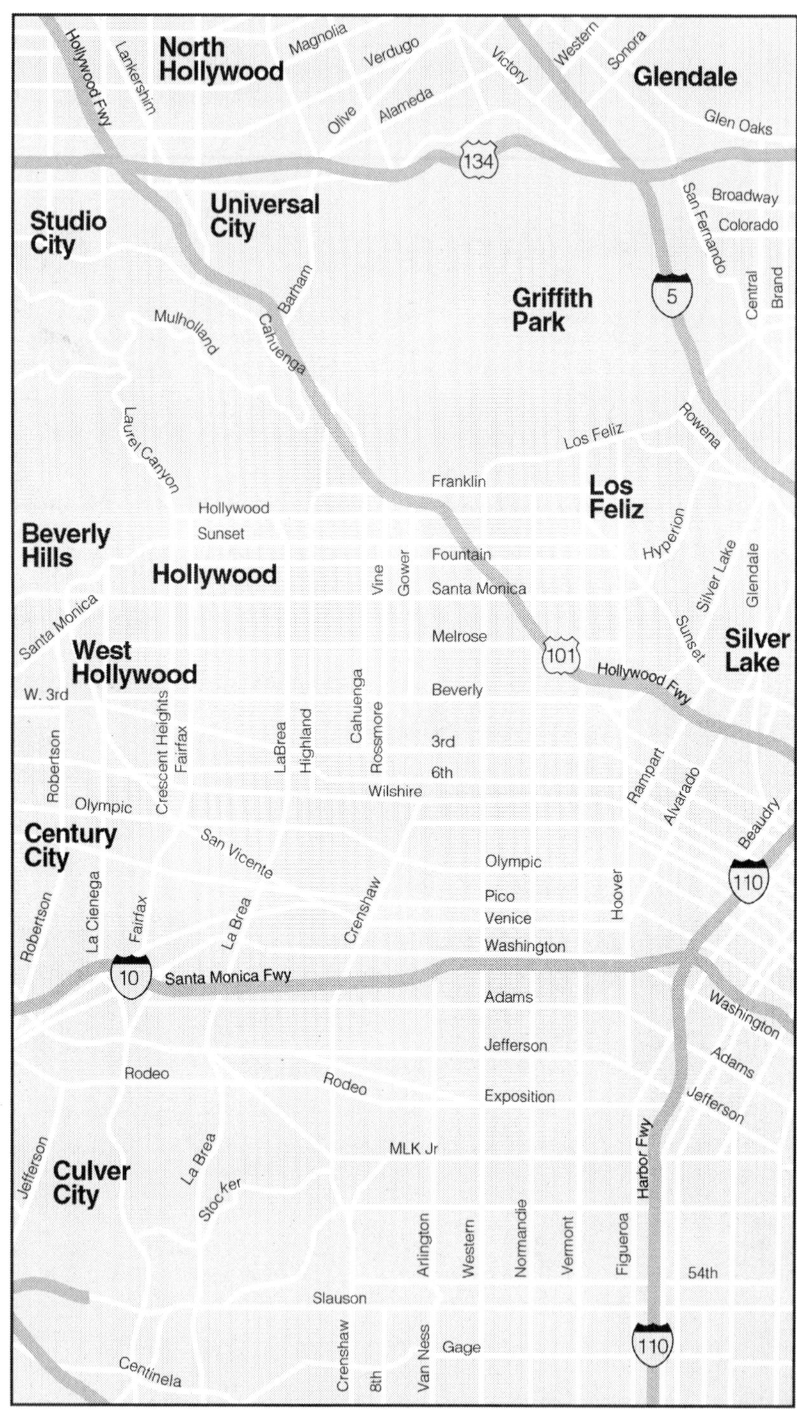
North Hollywood
Glendale
Studio City
Universal City
Griffith Park
Los Feliz
Beverly Hills
Hollywood
West Hollywood
Silver Lake
Century City
Culver City
Hollywood Fwy
Lankershim
Magnolia
Verdugo
Victory
Western
Sonora
Olive
Alameda
Glen Oaks
134
Broadway
San Fernando
Colorado
5
Central
Brand
Barham
Mulholland
Cahuenga
Laurel Canyon
Los Feliz
Rowena
Franklin
Hollywood
Sunset
Fountain
Vine
Gower
Santa Monica
Hyperion
Silver Lake
Glendale
Santa Monica
Melrose
Sunset
101
Hollywood Fwy
W. 3rd
Beverly
Crescent Heights
Fairfax
LaBrea
Highland
Cahuenga
Rossmore
3rd
6th
Wilshire
Robertson
Olympic
Rampart
Alvarado
Beaudry
San Vicente
Olympic
110
Robertson
La Cienega
Fairfax
La Brea
Crenshaw
Pico
Venice
Hoover
Washington
10
Santa Monica Fwy
Adams
Washington
Jefferson
Adams
Rodeo
Rodeo
Exposition
Jefferson
Harbor Fwy
MLK Jr
Jefferson
La Brea
Stocker
Arlington
Western
Normandie
Vermont
Figueroa
54th
Slauson
Crenshaw
8th
Van Ness
Gage
110
Centinela

The Perfect Los Angeles

When you're on vacation, you don't want a city with all its little flaws and inconveniences, you want the perfect city. You want the hottest, hippest, funnest, best places to be, and you want them now. We've taken the guesswork out of hotspotting and present to you the best of L.A., the most up-to-the-moment What-When-Where-and-Whys for all of L.A.'s premium draws, from celebrity restaurants to celebrity graveyards, right here, right now.

Always-Trendy Tables

In a city where of-the-moment restaurants go in and out like the tide in Santa Monica Bay, it takes some serious staying power to captivate L.A.'s fickle dining audiences for longer than ... I'm sorry, what were you saying? I wasn't listening.... Um, well, rest assured, these places should still be piping hot when you get there.

Asia de Cuba

8440 W. Sunset Blvd., West Hollywood, 323-848-6000

The Draw: Like the rest of its home, the Mondrian hotel, this chic Asian-Latin fusion eatery is a magnet for the sort of done-up Hollywood fanfare that led you to this part of town. Great $15 cocktails, and the oxtail spring rolls rise to the occasion, too.

The Scene: Awash in creamy whites, the dining room seats a mix of stylish industry folk, even more stylish eye candy, and hotel guests admiring excellent views of the city. A quieter, leafier scene is out on the glassed-in patio.
Open daily for breakfast 7–11 a.m.; lunch 11:30 a.m.–3:30 p.m.; dinner Mon.–Thurs. 5:30–11:30 p.m., Fri.–Sat. 5:30 p.m.–1 a.m., Sun. 5:30–10:30 p.m. $$

Hot Tip: Reserve well in advance for weekends. (Sorry, eating here doesn't get you in to Skybar—see p. 108).

Linq

8338 West Third St., Los Angeles, 323-655-4555

The Draw: One of L.A.'s top fusion restaurants also boasts one of the liveliest, loveliest bar scenes in town. Eat, drink, and gape all night at this classy one-stop-shop.

The Scene: No, you're not color blind. A suffusion of black marble and white lacquer, glass and mirrors, and halogen and candlelight establishes a monochrome palette through three sleek, mini dining rooms, with a busy raised bar at the front.
Open daily 6 p.m.–1:30 a.m. $$

Hot Tip: For a warmer ambience, request a fireside table. Dessert? The walnut and banana tart with malted-milk sauce is a definite winner.

Spago

176 N. Cañon Dr., Beverly Hills, 310-385-0880

The Draw: Everyone who's watched the Oscars knows Spago. It's the flagship of über-chef Wolfgang Puck's culinary empire and one of L.A.'s most defining dining scenes.

The Scene: Power lunchers, industry players, stars, and a medley of 90210 types gather in this boldly designed wood, marble, and tile dining room and out on the fountained patio shaded by a couple of imported century-old olive trees. The menu is playfully indefinable, including sashimi, risotto, wienerschnitzel, and strudel.
Open for lunch Mon.–Fri. 11:30 a.m.–2:15 p.m., Sat. noon–2:15 p.m.; dinner Sun.–Thurs. 5:30–10 p.m., Fri.-Sat. 5:30–11 p.m.) $$$

Hot Tip: Everyone wants a patio seat, but for action-packed views into the open kitchen, ask for the back tables inside.

Art Spaces

L.A.'s appetite for high art never seems to exhaust its stock—unlike, say, the water supply. A wellspring of neighborhood art enclaves, public exhibits, and private galleries big and small helps prevent this town from being completely desiccated by soulless production studios. When you need a serious art fix, start here.

Bergamot Station

2525 Michigan Ave., Santa Monica, 310-829-5854

The Draw: Sharing grounds with the Santa Monica Museum of Art, this complex of local galleries has swiftly become the city's most dynamic one-stop art hop.

The Scene: The seven-acre property retains some funkiness from its years as an abandoned industrial site. More than 30 galleries provide a living, breathing art scene for painters, sculptors, jewelry designers, photographers, and other creators. *Open Tues.–Sat. 11 a.m.–6 p.m. (most galleries).* Free.

Hot Tip: When everything starts to look the same, it's time for a break at The Gallery Café. Tasty specials change daily.

Museum of Contemporary Art (MOCA)

250 S. Grand Ave., Downtown, 213-626-6222

The Draw: L.A.'s most important modern art forum offers rotating contemporary exhibits plus permanent works by Jackson Pollock, Robert Rauschenberg, Diane Arbus, and Mark Rothko, among others.

The Scene: The building itself is one of MOCA's most impressive examples of modern art, with its labyrinth of cylindrical and pyramidal-shaped galleries burrowed into Downtown's Bunker Hill.
Open Tues.–Sun. 11 a.m.–5 p.m., Thurs. until 8 p.m. $

Hot Tip: Admission is free all day Thursday. Entrance to the main facility also includes admission to MOCA's Downtown satellite facility, the Geffen Contemporary (152 N. Central Ave.).

Norton Simon Museum

411 W. Colorado Blvd., Pasadena, 626-449-6840

The Draw: Easily overlooked in the Getty's shadow, the Norton Simon houses what most consider to be the greater art collection. One of the world's most astonishing single-collector accumulations includes galleries full of impressionist masterpieces, Asian works spanning two millennia, and sculptures by Henry Moore, Rodin, and Diego Rivera, among others.

The Scene: More than 50,000 square feet of gallery space, brightened by a recent Frank Gehry renovation (to the tune of six mil), and some nice gardens. *Open daily 12–6 p.m. except Fridays (until 9 p.m.) and Tuesdays (closed).* $

Hot Tip: The Norton's award-winning audio tours highlight more than a hundred works in whatever order you choose to see them.

Beaches

With so much sun-baked coast, the question is, where do you dive in? L.A.'s 75-mile stretch of surf has it all, from secluded coves and lonely tide pools to beach towns full of longboarder dudes and volleyball babes. You can pedal for 20 miles along Santa Monica Bay or park on a towel in Malibu. Here are some good places to get wet.

Manhattan Beach

End of Manhattan Beach Blvd., Manhattan Beach

The Draw: Hard-to-please visitors cheer up when taken to this swell yuppie backyard in the South Bay. "Now, this is California..."

The Scene: Former squatters like the Beach Boys would gasp at the rents down here these days, but otherwise it's still Endless Summer, a mecca for surfers, volleyball exhibitionists, rollerbladers, and bikini chasers. If you wove together all the blond hair on this sunny strand, it would reach Jupiter.

Hot Tip: For a lively happy hour, head one beach community south and take your pick of the bars on the Hermosa Strand.

Venice Beach

Ocean Front Walk at 27th St., Venice

The Draw: At least once in your life, you have to visit Ocean Front Walk—a carnival of sun-damaged artists and performers, palm readers, homeless chiropractors, open-air weight lifters, incense hucksters, circle drummers, hoop dreamers, freaks, exhibitionists, voyeurs, and people on various wheeled contraptions.

The Scene: See above. If you were here ten years ago, you'll be impressed by the ace clean-up job. If not, the place may seem like it could use a cleaning.

Hot Tip: Tourists and locals alike seem too preoccupied with the Walk to notice Venice's excellent three-mile beach sitting wide open beyond it. Stretch out and pretend you're alone in Cancún.

Zuma Beach

30050 Pacific Coast Highway, Malibu

The Draw: Malibu seems a bit disappointing until you reach Zuma, its best full-service beach. Even Santa Monica residents gladly drive 20 miles to this patch of cleaner water and whiter sand.

The Scene: Three miles of towel space with excellent facilities, lifeguards, volleyball courts, and some good wave activity. Families, surfers, biceps, and bikinis—lots of fun for everyone.

Hot Tip: Lose the weekend crowds by following the surfers to Zuma's quieter north end or heading south to Westward Beach, near Point Dume (which is even quieter). Save six bucks by parking for free on Pacific Coast Highway (that's PCH in local parlance).

Celebrity-Owned Restaurants

Any restaurant worth its sea salt in L.A. has some kind of celebrity connection, no matter how remote (George Clooney ordered the prik king, Cameron Diaz loves the chicken mole, Sean Connery used the restroom), but only a handful of hot restaurants actually have big star investors. If you're searching for real star power, head to these celebrity-owned joints.

Ago

8478 Melrose Ave., West Hollywood, 323-655-6333

The Draw: The most happening trattoria in West Hollywood. Robert De Niro and the brothers Weinstein of Miramax (among others) own a piece of this Italian eatery, run by executive chef Agostino Sciandri.

The Scene: Warm up at the front bar, abuzz with movie-biz types and dressed-to-kill industry fawns. Graduate to the perfectly lit split-level dining room or the heated outdoor patio for upscale classic Tuscan fare, priced for its clientele.
Open for lunch Mon.–Fri. noon–2:30; dinner Mon.–Fri. 6–11:30 p.m., Sat. 6–11:30 p.m., Sun. 6–10:30 p.m. $$

Hot Tip: Chef's specialty: Bistecca alla fiorentina—a 22-ounce Angus T-bone steak prepared in the wood-burning oven.

Dolce

8284 Melrose Ave., West Hollywood, 323-852-7174

The Draw: At press time, this chic new Italian restaurant co-owned by young Hollywood stallion Ashton Kutcher was the place to dine among stars like Ashton, girlfriend-du-jour Demi Moore, and their cohorts.

The Scene: A slick room, heavy on the leather and marble, lined with spacious booths, a bar backlit with a row of flames, and an enclosed patio. The classic Italian menu is secondary to the scene but does hold up.
Open nightly 6 p.m.–2 a.m. $$

Hot Tip: Sample smaller bites (in the $6–$9 range) by requesting Dolce's Enoteca tasting menu. Hang out for DJ nights Thursdays through Saturdays starting at 10 p.m.

Madre's

897 Granite Dr., Pasadena, 626-744-0900

The Draw: You may not see owner Jennifer Lopez at this hot new addition to Pasadena's dining scene, but she's for sure sat in at least a few of these chairs.

The Scene: The formal main dining room suggests old-school Havana with lace tablecloths, fine china, and enough chandeliers to open a lighting store. Cuisine is Latin with a distinct Cuban accent.
Open Tues.–Sun. 11 a.m.–3 p.m. and 5–11 p.m. $$

Hot Tip: Madre's offers live Latin music Thursdays through Saturdays after 9 p.m.

Cheeseburger and Pie

You'd think America's favorite lunch combo would be easy enough to get right. For a great burg, there's always the double-double at In-N-Out or the soulful version at Mo Better Meatty Meat Burger, the behemoth at Zigs, or the $20 hamburger and fries at The Ivy. And for a splendid slice of coconut custard pie, you can count on Du-Pars. But for the whole shebang all in one place, check out these class acts.

The Apple Pan

10801 W. Pico Blvd., West L.A., 310-475-3585

The Draw: The most distinguished burger joint in Los Angeles is a shoebox on the Westside that's launched many imitators but never a real competitor.

The Scene: A horseshoe-shaped counter with a line behind it. Two robotic waiters work their half of the room almost telepathically, pouring soda and ketchup, refilling your coffee, and repeating which pies have just been baked, over and over again.
Open Tues.–Thurs., Sun. 11 a.m.–midnight, Fri.–Sat. 11 a.m.–1 a.m. $

Hot Tip: Avoid the weekday lunch rush. Don't ask, just order the hickory burger.

Chaya Venice

110 Navy St., Venice, 310-396-1179

The Draw: The finest ten-dollar cheeseburger in town somehow ended up on the lunch menu at this trendy Pan-Asian restaurant on the Venice/Santa Monica border. Ten ounces of top sirloin adorned with white cheddar, spicy mayo, and—the *sine qua non*—chutney. The apple and mixed berry cobbler à la mode will have to suffice as pie. And it will.

The Scene: The crowds at this stylish East-meets-West joint are artsy Venice types with enough coin to eat here.
Open Mon.–Fri. 11:30 a.m.–midnight, Sat. 5 p.m.–midnight, Sun. 5–10 p.m. $

Hot Tip: Come back for sushi "happy hour," every day from 5–7 p.m.

Pie 'N Burger

913 E. California Blvd., Pasadena, 626-795-1123

The Draw: Not much has changed over the last 40 years at Pasadena's favorite burger joint. Lovingly created burgers are still spiked with homemade Thousand Island dressing. Sodas are hand-mixed from syrup and soda water. Pies are made right here.

The Scene: One Formica counter and a few token tables. Regulars are a motley crew with one thing in common: The wait staff has their orders memorized.
Open Mon.–Fri. 6 a.m.–10 p.m., Sat. 7 a.m.–10 p.m., Sun. 7 a.m.–9 p.m. $

Hot Tip: Unless you're a true French-fry glutton, the half order is plenty for one person.

Classic Hotel Bars

Nothing against frying your eardrums in a crowded bar with a sweaty glass of Jack and Coke in your hand, but occasionally it's nice to sit down and drink like—well, a grown-up. When an oak-paneled imbibing den with boys-club leather armchairs and rows of 8,000-year-old single-malt scotches beckons, here are our gold, silver, and bronze choices.

The Bar at Hotel Bel-Air

701 Stone Canyon Rd., Bel-Air, 310-472-1211

The Draw: Bel-Air's neighborhood bar. Must we explain further?

The Scene: If you're the Duke of York, some big producer, Nancy Reagan's neighbor, or you're pretending to be some combination of the above for the evening, you're in the right place. A clubby, refined setting with a wood-burning fireplace, comfy leather chairs, a humidor, and gallons of rare port on the menu.
Open Sun.–Thurs. 11 a.m.–12:30 a.m., Fri.–Sat. 11 a.m.–1:30 a.m.

Hot Tip: House pianist Antonio Castillo de la Galla arrives at around 8 p.m. Tues.–Sat. to tickle the ivories.

Club Bar at The Peninsula Beverly Hills

9882 S. Santa Monica Blvd., Beverly Hills, 310-551-2888

The Draw: Today's generation of industry schmoozers congregate at this premium bar as routinely as yesteryear's mucky-mucks gathered at the Polo Lounge.

The Scene: As impeccably tasteful as everything else at The Peninsula. Brass sconces, red leather chairs, California birch paneled walls, vintage booze, and a perceptible scent of Hollywood agents in the air. Somehow it's still more warm than stuffy in here. *Open Mon.–Sat. 1 p.m.–1 a.m., Sun. 1 p.m.–midnight*

Hot Tip: Try the Millionaire Margarita: double reserve Cuervo tequila, 150-year-old Grand Marnier, Cointreau, and fresh lime juice.

Gallery Bar at the Millennium Biltmore Hotel

506 S. Grand Ave., Downtown, 213-624-1011

The Draw: Passing through the hotel's frescoed galleria into this prohibition-era lounge is about the grandest old drinking experience you'll be finding downtown.

The Scene: Gold walls with headshots of Lucille Ball and friends smiling at you, red leather chairs and stools, cherubs floating above a burnished granite bar, and a mixed white-collar crowd of local Downtowners and conventioneers.
Open daily 4 p.m.–2 a.m.

Hot Tip: For a notch of rowdiness with your next highball, head to the hotel's Grand Avenue Sports Bar.

Classic L.A. Museums

We're talking about places that in some shape or form define this city more than the usual dinosaur bones. There are too many to list—the Museum of Tolerance, the Peterson Automotive, the Gene Autry, the Southwest, and the Museum of Jurassic Technology, to name a few. Topping our charts are these essentials.

The Getty Center

1200 Getty Center Dr., Los Angeles, 310-440-7300

The Draw: The complex itself is an obvious masterpiece. L.A.'s grandest architectural feat took more than 14 years and a billion dollars to build. Van Gogh's Irises plus a huge portion of the J. Paul Getty collection are featured in this hilltop edifice.

The Scene: 16,000 tons of imported Italian travertine marble, assembled high above the Sepulveda Pass (and 405 freeway), with five interconnected pavilions, a bright courtyard, lovely gardens, and sweeping views of the coast.
Open Tues.–Thurs. & Sun. 10 a.m.–6 p.m., Fri.–Sat. 10 a.m.–9 p.m. Free.

Hot Tip: Parking at the Getty lot is first-come, first-served and busiest at midday. A free shuttle operates from the overflow lot two miles south of the museum on the northwest corner of Sepulveda Blvd. and Constitution Ave. Book ahead for lunch or dinner at the museum's elegant restaurant (310-440-6810).

Hollywood Entertainment Museum

7021 Hollywood Blvd., Hollywood, 323-465-7900

The Draw: Any museum on Hollywood Blvd. without wax statues deserves a medal. Here's a surprisingly fun, earnest, hands-on look at the world of show biz. In this town, what could be more edifying?

The Scene: Part memory lane, part off-lot studio tour. Highlights include a series of interactive sound and special effects exhibits and original sets from *Star Trek* and *Cheers*.
Open 11 a.m.–6 p.m., closed Wednesdays during the winter. $

Hot Tip: Visit the museum gift shop for props used and clothes worn by the stars.

Museum of Television & Radio

465 N. Beverly Dr., Beverly Hills, 310-786-1000

The Draw: The Beatles on Ed Sullivan. The first moon landing. Your favorite *Rhoda* episode. Come to this outstanding media library to enjoy anything that's gone on in front of a TV camera or radio microphone over the last eight decades.

The Scene: A stark Richard-Meier–designed building in downtown Beverly Hills, stocked with a database of more than 100,000 radio and television programs, and with comfy private consoles for private viewing/listening.
Open Wed.–Sun. noon–5 p.m. Free (suggested donation $10).

Hot Tip: If you're not fussy about what you watch, selections are also screened regularly in the facility's two main theaters.

Ethnic Dining

An encyclopedia could be written on the many cuisines of the world in Los Angeles, with a special section for all those outstanding hole-in-the-wall restaurants that are far better than their strip mall locations imply. But that's another book. For great dining atmospheres as well as wonderful out-of-this-continent food, these savory spots are sure to satisfy.

Crustacean

9646 Little Santa Monica Blvd., Beverly Hills, 310-205-8990

The Draw: The next best thing to eating like royalty in French-Colonial Vietnam is dining at this family-run Euro-Asian celebrity magnet in the heart of Beverly Hills.

The Scene: Bamboo gardens, a waterfall, and a glass-covered koi pond walkway leading into the dining room. Good evening, Vietnam!
Open for lunch Mon.–Fri. 11:30 a.m.–2:30 p.m.; dinner Mon.–Thurs. 5:30–10:30 p.m., Fri.–Sat. 5:30–11:30 p.m. $$$

Hot Tip: Order a dish from the Secret Kitchen, featuring the An family's heavily-guarded recipes.

Dar Maghreb

7651 W. Sunset Blvd., Hollywood, 323-876-7651

The Draw: After a multicourse feast of lamb, couscous, b'stilla, and other Moroccan specialties at this little palace in Hollywood, you may never need to eat again.

The Scene: Like a set design from *The Arabian Nights*, with knee-high tables, seat cushions, and robed servers swooping in with a huge prix-fixe meal that you eat with your hands.
Open Mon.–Fri. 6–11 p.m., Sat.–Sun. 5:30–11 p.m. $$$

Hot Tip: Bring a stack of one-dollar bills for the belly dancer, who performs every night between 7 and 11 p.m.

Nonya

61 N. Raymond Ave., Pasadena, 626-583-8398

The Draw: Acquaint your palate with Nonya's distinctive pan-Asian cuisine—a delicate blend of Chinese, Indonesian, and Malaysian influences. An outstanding newcomer in downtown Pasadena.

The Scene: The Asian garden–style dining room is a study in good feng shui, with rich dark woods, flickering candles, high ceilings, groves of potted bamboo, and a koi pond.
Open for lunch Sun.–Fri. 11:30 a.m.–2:30 p.m.; dinner Sun.–Thurs. 5–10 p.m., Fri.–Sat. 5–11 p.m. $

Hot Tip: Warm up with traditional Asian cocktails at the bar during happy hour, Monday through Friday 4–7 p.m.

Fashion Districts

L.A. is one of the world's most style-conscious cities, and is either a shopper's wildest fantasy or worst nightmare, depending upon stupid stuff like budget and self-control. For life beyond Macy's and Banana Republic, walk your platinum card down these top fashion blocks.

Montana Avenue

From Seventh St. to 17th St., Santa Monica

The Draw: Hardcore shoppers on the Westside may warm up at the Santa Monica Promenade, but they really exercise their right to spend money at this upscale shopping district on the edge of Brentwood.

The Scene: Nearly a dozen tree-lined blocks of top designers' fashions, trendy boutiques, happening galleries, hot home-furnishing stores, cool cafes, and yoga studios.

Hot Tip: Hit Montana Ave.'s two biggest sidewalk sales: the third Saturday of May and the first Friday of December.

Rodeo Drive

Between Wilshire Blvd. and Santa Monica Blvd., Beverly Hills

The Draw: Definitely not the bargains. These three blocks of Italian designers ateliers, French boutiques, and world-class jewelers are about as famous and hilariously high-end as a power-fashion zone can get.

The Scene: The cobblestoned Two Rodeo plaza and The Rodeo Collection complex (421 Rodeo Dr.) are the major "malls" along this tree-lined row of top-tier names, including Armani, Cartier, Dior, Gucci, Tiffany, Vuitton, ... You get the picture.

Hot Tip: Window-shopping is free. Avoid Sundays, when many stores are closed and the camera-toting tourist crowds are heaviest.

Sunset Strip

Between La Cienega Blvd. and Doheny Dr., West Hollywood

The Draw: L.A.'s flashiest boulevard of bars, nightclubs, and comedy stages is also a material world of designer's boutiques, sex shops, and music megastores.

The Scene: Tourists and rich/famous/stylish/kinky locals are drawn to a mishmash of showrooms including Virgin Megastore (8000 Sunset Blvd.), Tower Records (8801), Hustler Hollywood (8920), and a range of big names like Nicole Miller, Oliver Peoples, Billy Martin's, Kenneth Cole, and Butler & Wilson, all based in and around Sunset Plaza (8600-8700).

Hot Tip: For more hot designers, continue your spree about a mile south on Robertson Ave. (between Beverly and Third St.).

Golf Courses

You don't have to be a celebrity or an unemployed actor to enjoy a beautiful day on the green in Los Angeles. With so many open-to-the-public courses spread across town, the only hurdle you face at the better ones is booking a weekend slot after 4 a.m. Reserve as far in advance as you can at these top fairways.

Brookside Golf Course

1133 Rosemont Ave., Pasadena, 626-796-0177

The Draw: The most sophisticated championship course open to the public in Pasadena, and a distinguished former host to the Los Angeles Open.

The Scene: Pasadena's lush Arroyo Seco grounds, home of the Rose Bowl, provide a lovely backdrop. Pros and well-heeled amateurs flock to the Koiner course, a 7,037-yard, par 72 endurance test designed by Bobby Bell.
Open daily 6 a.m.–7 p.m. $$$$

Hot Tip: Brookside's E.O. Nay course (or "Course Two") is a thousand yards shorter and easier to book.

Rancho Park Golf Course

10460 W. Pico Blvd., Los Angeles, 310-838-7373

The Draw: Everyone wants to golf in Beverly Hills, where there aren't any courses. Geographically, this 6,681-yard, par 71 (there's also a 9-hole, par 3 course) is as near as it gets. If you can take the crowds, it's one the best courses in the City Parks system.

The Scene: A deceivingly challenging 18 holes with numerous treelines and lots of hilly terrain. Arnold Palmer once took a 12 on the last tee.
Open daily until sundown. $$

Hot Tip: To reserve a time, you must first obtain a City Parks golf card (213-473-7055). The other option—showing up that day and putting your name on the course's waiting list—is always a crapshoot.

Wilson/Harding Golf Courses

4730 Crystal Springs Dr., Griffith Park, 323-664-2255

The Draw: Angelenos have been carting their clubs to this reliable and well-stocked pair of par 72s in Griffith Park for the past 80 years.

The Scene: Side-by-side on the eastern edge of the largest municipal park and urban wilderness in the U.S., Wilson and Harding (6,947 and 6,536 yards) also offers a 50-tee double-decked driving range, four practice putting greens, two pitching and chipping greens, and a well-appointed clubhouse.
Open sunrise to sunset. $$

Hot Tip: Weekend tee times should be arranged in advance by getting a reservation card from the pro shop or by calling the City of Los Angeles Golf and Tennis Reservation Office (213-473-7055).

Graveyards of the Stars

It gets tiresome waiting at all of those alleged celebrity hangouts for someone better than Judd Nelson or Ice-T to enter the room. Stargazing in these final resting grounds, on the other hand, is a sure thing. Please be respectful.

Hollywood Forever Cemetery

6000 Santa Monica Blvd., Hollywood, 323-469-1181

The Draw: Formerly called Hollywood Memorial Park, the new name suggests a field of golden-era legends that still love an audience, and the helpful management here is happy to support that cause. Famous interred include Cecil B. DeMille, Douglas Fairbanks (Sr. and Jr.), Alfalfa (Carl Switzer) and Darla (Hood) from *The Little Rascals*, Clifton Webb, and, in a mausoleum of his own, Rudolph Valentino.

The Scene: The grounds are more than a century old, and it shows. It's still the most respectable plot in workingman's Hollywood, with two giant mausoleums, an interesting assortment of moldering headstones, and a lake. Get oriented with a detailed map of the grounds, available in the flower shop by the front gate.
Open Mon–Fri. 7 a.m.–7 p.m., Sat.–Sun 7 a.m.–5 p.m.

Hot Tip: Every other Saturday night during the summer and on other special nights (e.g. Halloween), Cinespia screens oldies on the marble outer wall of Valentino's mausoleum. BYO bottles, blankets, and picnic dinner (www.cinespia.org).

Holy Cross Cemetery

5835 W. Slauson Ave., Culver City, 310-670-7697

The Draw: Bing Crosby, Rita Hayworth, Bela Lugosi, John Candy, John Ford, and Sharon Tate, among others.

The Scene: Large, tasteful grounds hiding down in lower Culver City, dotted with waterfalls, ponds, and peaceful grottos.
Open daily 8 a.m.–6 p.m.

Hot Tip: If you haven't had your fill of famous headstones, check out Hillside Memorial, a few blocks south. Guests there include Al Jolson, Jack Benny, and Michael Landon (6001 Centinela Ave., 310-641-0707).

Westwood Village Memorial Park

1218 Glendon Ave., Westwood, 310-474-1579

The Draw: Marilyn Monroe.

The Scene: Norma Jean's headstone steals the show in this tiny two-acre cemetery hiding behind some office towers on Wilshire Blvd., but the impressive supporting cast includes Eva Gabor, Jack Lemmon, Walter Matthau, Carol O'Connor, Natalie Wood, and the unmarked graves of Roy Orbison and Frank Zappa.
Open daily 8 a.m.–sundown

Hot Tip: To ensure that this tiny place stays public-friendly, park on the street or in the lot across the road, and leave the video camera in the trunk.

Guided Tours

You can board a Hollywood cattle-call bus and chug up to the Playboy Mansion any hour of the day. A good guided tour, on the other hand, is an indispensable window on L.A. in its myriad shapes, forms, and fetishes. These tours have heart. They have soul. They have character. They have drinks. Well, at least one of them does.

Los Angeles Conservancy Walking Tours

523 W. 6th St., Suite 826, Downtown, 213-623-2489

The Draw: L.A.'s most earnest walking tours are run by a nonprofit organization dedicated to preserving and restoring the city's historic architectural landmarks. Volunteer guides lead a variety of excellent Saturday morning Downtown walks for less than the price of a movie.

The Scene: The Broadway Theaters tour is a runaway favorite, showcasing the ornate remains of Movietown's first Main Street (before Hollywood Blvd. took over in the '20s). Other walks include close-ups of Union Station, the Biltmore Hotel, and Little Tokyo, as well as focus tours like "Art Deco" and "Marble Masterpieces." $

Hot Tip: Book in advance for Last Remaining Seats, a Conservancy-organized June festival of classic screenings in the old theaters along Broadway.

Los Angeles Neon Tour

Museum of Neon Art, 501 W. Olympic Blvd., Downtown, 213-489-9918

The Draw: Board an open-air double-decker bus at the Museum of Neon Art (MONA) for an evening exploration of L.A.'s coolest, brightest neon signs.

The Scene: Three dozen people rolling through Downtown, midtown, Chinatown, and Hollywood, questing for neon and picking up various cultural and historical tidbits along the way. Drinks and snacks are served at a reception at the museum. $$$$

Hot Tip: Book well ahead, and bring a sweater for those cool evenings. Tours run from April through October. A second tour in the neon-rich San Fernando Valley is planned.

Red Line Tours

6773 Hollywood Blvd., Hollywood, 323-402-1074

The Draw: This small outfit runs knowledgeable walking tours around Hollywood and Downtown, getting you inside places the buses can't. Microphoned guides equip guests with volume-controlled headsets, so you can walk, look, and listen at the same time.

The Scene: The 75-minute Inside Historic Hollywood Tour roams through the heart of Hollywood Blvd., getting you up to speed on the area's multimillion-dollar revival and dipping into several historic theatres and hidden landmarks along the way. $

Hot Tip: Customized and extended walks can be arranged with some advance notice.

Hikes

See those hills out yonder? Stretching from Malibu to Downtown, they comprise one of the world's largest urban recreation areas—a 150,000-acre swath of parkland that can transport you from concrete jungle to secluded canyon trail with the twist of a car key. When nature calls, these popular hiking retreats always answer.

Point Mugu State Park

9000 Pacific Coast Hwy., Malibu, 818-880-0350

The Draw: La Jolla Valley Loop Trail at Point Mugu is one of the most rewarding ten-milers in the western Santa Monica Mountains, featuring secluded peaks, gorgeous ocean vistas, and rare indigenous grasslands.

The Scene: From the Ray Miller trailhead, take the La Jolla Canyon Trail to the La Jolla Valley Loop Trail. Small seasonal waterfalls, oak groves, and bursts of sage, lavender, and spring wildflowers greet you along the way. It's moderately strenuous but crowd-free.

Hot Tip: Near the junction of these two trails, La Jolla Valley Camp provides piped water, restrooms, and oak-shaded picnic tables. Bag a few more miles and higher vistas on this day-hike by cutting west from the Valley Loop Trail to the Mugu Peak Trail.

Runyon Canyon Park

North of Franklin Ave. (at Fuller), Hollywood, 213-485-5111

The Draw: A quick and easy retreat in the Hollywood Hills, and one of the more reliable spots in the city to run into stars walking their dogs.

The Scene: Early, before work, or late in the afternoon, the main entrance at Fuller is a convention of randy canines waiting for the leashes to come off. From here, it's a two-mile loop up and down a chaparral-covered hill with a nice payoff view of the entire city on a clear day.

Hot Tip: Closed at sundown. Enter from the park's quieter north entrance at Mulholland Drive for a quick scramble up Indian Rock to Runyon's highest point.

Temescal Gateway Park

15601 Sunset Blvd., Pacific Palisades, 310-454-1395

The Draw: A favorite spot in Topanga State Park for Westsiders, who turn off their cellphones and check out for a few hours here.

The Scene: Enter the parking lot from Sunset at Temescal Canyon Road. Follow either the Temescal Ridge Trail or the Temescal Canyon Trail (they form a five mile loop up a moderate to steep grade) into an oasis of seasonal waterfalls, rocky outcrops, and sweeping coastal views.

Hot Tip: Bring your own water, and watch out for poison oak (leaves grow three to a stem and each leaf contains three leaflets, which look like small oak leaves).

Hotel Pools

L.A. is full of hotel pools, but only a few of them are destinations unto themselves. Walk onto these rareified pool decks and an undeniable feeling of "I Have Arrived" washes over you. Whether or not you can swim is irrelevant.

Beverly Hills Hotel & Bungalows

9641 Sunset Blvd., Beverly Hills, 310-276-2251

The Draw: The most exalted waterfront in Beverly Hills. If you need a few names, Katharine Hepburn, Raquel Welch, Faye Dunaway, and Ringo Starr all waded here (though not together). Also, many of the bad movies you saw 20 years ago got greenlighted somewhere in the shallow end.

The Scene: Surrounded by palms and manicured grounds, the competition-size outdoor pool comes with a Jacuzzi, pool cafe, neat rows of traditional green-and-white striped lounge chairs, and those storied cabanas—21 of them in all.

Hot Tip: All cabanas are not created equal here. Spring the extra 50 bucks for the lower cabanas, which are larger and offer poolside convenience. They're available to registered guests for the bargain price of $175 per day.

Millennium Biltmore Hotel-Los Angeles

506 S. Grand Ave., Downtown, 213-624-1011

The Draw: One of the city's few indoor pools that's worth getting out of the sun for. This Art Deco beauty tucked away in the Biltmore basement has been Downtown's most refined splash for more than 75 years.

The Scene: The Pompeii-themed room is decked in blue-and-ivory tiles, ornate columns, and shiny brass rails. The water is an unwavering 80 degrees. Add a health club complete with fitness room, wet steam, sauna, Jacuzzi, and an on-call massage therapist—and you can skip your date with the beach today.

Hot Tip: Not a guest here? Just fork over 15 bucks and the place is yours.

Mondrian

8440 W. Sunset Blvd., West Hollywood, 323-650-8999

The Draw: It's the holy grail of pools on the Sunset Strip and the centerpiece of the Mondrian's chic club, Skybar.

The Scene: A stunning infinity pool surrounded by teak decking, a bevy of cozy lounge beds, and a sweet panoramic view of the city. The demographic is usually a mix of bikini-clad Eurotrash, power-lunchers from nearby Asia de Cuba, and gawkers like yourself.

Hot Tip: If you can get in here before 8 p.m., the doorman and velvet rope at Skybar are behind you.

Late-Night Eats

When it seems like everyplace serving decent grub in L.A. must've closed about four hours ago, a closer look reveals an amazing assortment of kitchens working the after-last-call shift with gusto. In a pinch, there's always the 24-hour Hollywood Denny's (7373 Sunset Blvd.), but these late-night shrines hit the spot in an only-in-L.A. way.

Canter's

419 N. Fairfax Ave., Los Angeles, 323-651-2030

The Draw: Come to this Fairfax district landmark for an around-the-clock bowl of matzo-ball soup and a thick pile of corned beef on rye, served by grandmas in Keds.

The Scene: Little has changed since the first bagels came out of the oven in 1931. Old brown booths, seasoned staff, and a few odd personal touches like an autumnal scene on the ceiling. After midnight, there's a decent chance you'll see someone relatively famous here.
Open 24 hours daily $

Hot Tip: For dicey live music with your kishka, head to the row of tables next door in the Kibitz Room.

Du-Pars

12036 Ventura Blvd., Studio City, 818-766-4437

The Draw: The one place where piping hot pancakes smothered in butter and syrup may add years to your life. Don't bother opening the unnecessarily large menu. Coffee and a tall stack, please.

The Scene: An intriguing cross-section of life-forms in the Valley, quietly hunching over brown counters and booths. Matronly wait staff treats you like someone better than the lush you are.
Open Sun.–Thurs. 6 a.m.–1 a.m., Fri.–Sat. 6 a.m.–4 a.m. $

Hot Tip: The other Du-Pars branch, worth circling on your map, is at the Farmers Market (3rd & Fairfax, 323-933-8446).

Sanamluang Café

5176 Hollywood Blvd., Hollywood, 323-660-8006

The Draw: Great noodle dishes and curries are served almost until sunrise at this savory Thai stop between the bars in Hollywood and Silverlake.

The Scene: The bright, no-frills room and frantic cooking noises in the back are like a good shot of caffeine. Thai teens breaking curfew and tattooed musicians graze on curried noodles and sip Thai iced tea, like the rebels they are.
Open daily 10 a.m.–4 a.m. $

Hot Tip: Two words: General's Noodles.

Meet Markets

Looking for that special someone to test your latest lousy pick-up line on and maybe spend the rest of your life or at least the night with? Los Angeles is filled with bars to indulge in that sport. That said, we know you're way too discriminating to be chasing strangers in any old watering hole...right?

Circle Bar

2926 Main St., Santa Monica, 310-450-0508

The Draw: A recent makeover turned this former dive into one of Santa Monica's top lounges and best reasons not to schlep all the way out to Hollywood. The new regulars here all shower and have teeth, but the place remains a welcome respite from the rest of Santa Monica's BananaRepublicked-up Main Street.

The Scene: The room is done up in those faux-Orient reds and blacks that still draw 'em in. A young Westside crowd preys on each other here nightly.
Open nightly 9 p.m.–2 a.m. $

Hot Tip: DJs spin rock on Tuesdays, dance mixes Wednesdays, and trance on Sundays.

Daddy's

1610 N. Vine St., Hollywood, 323-463-7777

The Draw: Maybe because not too long ago it used to be a stylish supper club, this Hollywood hipster bar maintains a dark, sexy vibe that the drinking closets and kitsch-shops one block over on the Cahuenga corridor can't quite match.

The Scene: A 20- and 30-something crowd of viable partners rubs against the bar. Cozy ottomans and low-tabled booths hug the opposite wall for close conversations and gentle groping.
Open Mon.–Sat. 8 p.m.–2 a.m., Sun. 9 p.m.–2 a.m. (No cover charge.)

Hot Tip: When you reach the "quieter drink" stage, head to The Well (6255 W. Sunset Blvd.), an equally sleek but toned-down version of Daddy's run by the same owners.

Jones Hollywood

7205 Santa Monica Blvd., West Hollywood, 323-850-1727

The Draw: One of West Hollywood's slickest alternatives to roaming up and down Sunset looking for action. A good-looking crowd of industry types hides out here to drink martinis and swap phone numbers.

The Scene: The room's outer shell of banquettes reminds you that this dark, stylish place is half-restaurant. But all the action is up a few steps at the bar, where capable drink-mixers and a good jukebox warm up pairs of future bedmates.
Open Mon–Fri. for lunch noon–4:30 p.m.; cocktails only 4:30–7 p.m.; nightly 7 p.m.–1:30 a.m. (No cover charge.)

Hot Tip: Jones is one of the better spots to order food at 1:30 a.m. Try the thin crust pizza and save the nightcap for the Formosa, across the street.

Best

Movie Theatres

In the town that invented the whole movie-watching pastime, you can bet there are some fine places to drop ten bucks and sit in the dark for a few hours. L.A.'s top movie theaters range from Westwood premiere palaces and ornate Hollywood relics to indie landmarks that still host Saturday-at-midnight *Rocky Horror* screenings. Here are some of our favorites.

Egyptian Theatre

6712 Hollywood Blvd. Hollywood, 323-466-3456

The Draw: Hollywood's first major movie house doesn't draw mobs of tourists like its younger sister, Grauman's Chinese Theatre. But the eclectic range of screenings in this revived theatre, the new home of the American Cinematheque, is far more impressive.

The Scene: Hieroglyphics, sphinx-heads, and ancient Egypt–style columns line the forecourt. The main auditorium is new and improved, with sliding walls that reveal some of the theatre's original structure. $

Hot Tip: For the full experience, book a guided afternoon tour of the theatre. All regular screenings are in the evening.

Mann's Village Theatre

961 Broxton Ave., Westwood, 310-248-6266

The Draw: This huge movie premiere site is one of the few reasons people schlep out to Westwood Village these days. Of several excellent movie theatres in the neighborhood, it's the oldest, the largest, and the loudest.

The Scene: Outside is the famous FOX tower, a 73-year-old landmark. Inside are polished marble floors, 1,400 cushy seats full of UCLA students, and a sound system to suit them. $

Hot Tip: Forget popcorn. Buy half a dozen warm cookies across the street at Diddy Reese (926 Broxton Ave.) and sneak 'em in under your trench coat.

Silent Movie Theatre

611 N. Fairfax Ave., Los Angeles, 323-655-2520

The Draw: Charlie Chaplin, Mary Pickford, Douglas Fairbanks, and the rest of the pre-talkie gang perform nightly in this revived old venue, which hails itself as "the last fully operational silent cinema in America."

The Scene: An intimate auditorium featuring live pre-show organ music and a cappuccino bar upstairs. Feature films are usually preceded by *Felix the Cat* and other classic cartoon shorts. $

Hot Tip: Regular showtimes are Tues.–Sat. at 8 p.m. Sunday matinees (1 p.m.) are popular, so come early.

Music Venues

The Hollywood Bowl, the Greek Theatre, The Jazz Bakery, The Baked Potato, Sixteen-Fifty, The Viper Room, The Palace, The Mayan, The Garage, The Knitting Factory, McCabe's, The Mint, The Joint, The Whiskey A Go Go...L.A. is a great place to work out your eardrums (and that's not even counting the new Disney Hall). For sheer popularity, variety, and volume, these three live music venues are good places to start.

House of Blues

8430 W. Sunset Blvd., West Hollywood, 323-848-5100

The Draw: Okay, so it's part of a corporate chain and not quite as legendary as some old roadhouse down the street where The Doors once played. It's still the best place on the Strip to hear an actual concert.

The Scene: The crowd in this cartoonish tin barn varies as much as the lineup of artists who play here. Great sound and lighting, a comfortable-sized floor, bars all around, and a restaurant upstairs serving tasty Cajun-themed grub.
Open nightly 5–11 p.m., concert hours vary; Sunday brunch, two seatings: 10 a.m.–noon or 1–3 p.m. $

Hot Tip: If your nights are already booked, come to the Sunday Gospel Brunch for—well, live gospel music and a buffet feast.

Spaceland

1717 Silver Lake Blvd., Silver Lake, 213-833-2843

The Draw: L.A.'s top underground music venue for the past decade. Spaceland features bands that won't be headlining at the Greek this summer—everything from cutting edge alternative and fringe punk to Bangles reunion concerts.

The Scene: Cheap drinks, low covers, and no pretensions. It's all about heavy bands, high volumes, and one of the city's most devoted local fan bases. There's a funky lounge upstairs and a smoking room in the back.
Open nightly 8 p.m.–2 a.m. $

Hot Tip: Monday is one of the wildest nights, featuring local talent and no cover.

Troubadour

9081 Santa Monica Blvd., West Hollywood, 310-276-6168

The Draw: West Hollywood's beloved rocker shrine has hosted a ton of famous musicians and local bands over the last 50 years. And the beat goes on.

The Scene: While everything else changes in this neighborhood, the Troub is basically the same old earsplitting sweatbox it's always been—though its metal emphasis has eased a bit. A stage, a floor, a VIP balcony, a pair of bars plastered with 8x10s, and a palpable sense of history. All ages welcome.
Open nightly 8 p.m.–2 a.m. $

Hot Tip: Free concerts on Mondays.

Best Nightclubs

With so many openings, closings and frantic name changes happening all the time, it's hard to keep track of Los Angeles's blurry nightclub scene. In the meantime, these young and slightly older winners haven't lost their steam or—dare-we-say-in-L.A.—loyal followings.

The Conga Room

5364 Wilshire Blvd., Los Angeles, 323-938-1696

The Draw: The place is big and beautiful, the salsa bands sizzle, and part-owners J-Lo and Jimmy Smits add a dollop of star power.

The Scene: Outside, it's dead. Upstairs, it's L.A.'s pounding take on Havana. Head to the main ballroom where a heavy orchestra plays for a done-up crowd who know their salsa moves. Warm up on the ground floor with a plate of paella and round of mojitos in the club's bright restaurant, La Boca del Conga Room.
Open Wed.–Sat. 7:30 p.m.–2 a.m. $

Hot Tip: Come at 8 p.m. for a one-hour dance lesson. You may need it here, and it's free with regular admission.

Deep

1707 N. Vine St., Hollywood, 323-462-1144

The Draw: Deep is what you get when imagination collides with raunchiness—and a few million bucks of reno money—on the corner of Hollywood and Vine. Presto: the neighborhood's darkest, lustiest go-go scene.

The Scene: The deeper in you go, the more you think Larry Flynt must have a hand in this. Get your bearings in the main bar area. Then venture into an erotic maze with a glass cube dance floor, dozens of one-way mirrors, and a trio of hired club dancers simulating positions that—you have to see for yourself.
Open Tues.–Sat. 7 p.m.–2 a.m. $

Hot Tip: Beat the steep weekend cover by reserving a table.

Ivar

6356 Hollywood Blvd., Hollywood, 323-465-4827

The Draw: Dress for the occasion and you'll have a chance of getting into this trendy new behemoth in the heart of Hollywood. There's room for about a thousand people, all drawn to one of best DJ lineups in the city.

The Scene: Measuring in at 14,000 square feet, Ivar's vast postmodern landscape includes four bars, a dazzling orange-colored lounge, a large outdoor smoking patio, five VIP rooms, and a pounding dance floor.
Open Wed.–Sat. 9:30 p.m.–2 a.m. $

Hot Tip: Get there early to get in. Thursday night features house and trance. All other evenings are a steady groove of dance and hip hop.

Of-the-Moment Dining

Is there a more vital pursuit in L.A. than checking off an "in" restaurant while it still tops the charts? It's not just the food or the scene or the manic reviews spread throughout every important magazine that's drawn you here. It's all of the above—with the caveat that, like celebrity marriages, the sizzle can't last forever, no matter how divine it seems at first. Get to these places while they're hot.

Grace

7360 Beverly Blvd., Los Angeles, 323-934-4400

The Draw: As warm and inviting as champagne bubble bath, this high-class New American newcomer is leading Beverly Blvd.'s latest dining renaissance with a creative menu from renowned local chef Neal Fraser and a whole lotta buzz.

The Scene: There's nothing pretentious about the casually elegant dining room bathed in earth tones and furnished with comfy banquettes—except perhaps the foodies and industry VIPs debating over whether to have the bacon-wrapped saddle of rabbit or the tenderloin of wild boar.
Open Tues.–Thurs. 5:30–11 p.m., Fri.–Sat. 5:30 p.m.–midnight, Sun. 5:30–10 p.m. $$

Hot Tip: The Dungeness crab salad should be on the city's Top Ten Appetizers list.

Paladar

1651 Wilcox Ave., Hollywood, 323-465-7500

The Draw: Sip house-special mojitos and chow down on shredded flank steak with plantains or yucca mash at Hollywood's most happening Cuban restaurant and lounge—unless Vin Diesel is hosting another private party here.

The Scene: '50s Havana meets 21st-century Hollywood in this small, slightly surreal space adorned with Cubanesque steel-grill room partitions, lacquered tobacco leaves on the wall, and lots of young, hip eye candy.
Open Mon.–Fri. 11:30 a.m.–11 p.m., Sat.–Sun. 5:30–11:30 p.m. $

Hot Tip: After dinner, the party migrates next door to Nacional, one of Hollywood's hottest new clubs.

White Lotus

1743 Cahuenga Blvd., Hollywood, 323-463-0060

The Draw: From the producers of the Sunset Room comes this slick new Asian-fusion restaurant. Start with sashimi and a page of premium sake in the dining area and follow the crowd to the venue's adjoining VIP-studded nightclub scene.

The Scene: Under twin white canopies, you'll find a pulsing sushi bar and professional scenesters eating duck leg confit or Thai bouillabaisse on a fountained patio adorned with Buddha statues.
Open Tues.–Sat. 6 p.m.–2 a.m., last dinner reservation is at 10:30 p.m. $$

Hot Tip: Dining here also gets you into the club. People eat fashionably late—book for 10 p.m.

Places to Rent Wheels

There's always a white Sentra with your name on it, but in L.A. it's only natural to crave a more rousing ride. Not just because of all the driving you'll be doing, rolling along the coast, down Rodeo Drive, and through the mountains. Not just because Benzes, Hummers, and heritage Mustangs flank you at every stoplight. There are many reasons to drive in style in Los Angeles, and the lameness of a Sentra is the least of them.

Beverly Hills Rent a Car

9220 S. Sepulveda Blvd., Los Angeles, 310-337-1400

The Draw: A yellow Lamborghini Diablo? There may be one more in the back. SoCal's best-known provider of luxury and exotic automobiles wouldn't dream of embarrassing you at the Spago valet.

The Scene: Bentleys, Ferraris, Hummers, Jags, Land Rovers, Porsches, Vipers, and some older Eldorados.

Hot Tip: The imaginative "economy" line starts with a PT Cruiser or an Infinity G20.

EagleRider

11860 S. La Cienega Blvd., Los Angeles, 310-320-3456

The Draw: The only thing that beats a nice drive in Southern California is a nice drive with a Harley humming between your calves. If you know how to operate "the American Dream," this place is your launch pad—one of the best-known motorcycle rental companies in the country.

The Scene: Electra Glides, Road Kings, Sportsters. Pick your own shiny Harley at this nice-sized fleet by the airport. Helmets, jackets, and accessories are all available here too.

Hot Tip: If you want some company, Eaglerider's guided tours cover the entire country.

Rent-A-Wreck

12333 W. Pico Blvd., West L.A. 310-826-7555

The Draw: If Steve McQueen came back as an L.A. tourist, he'd take this backwoods rental counter over Enterprise any day of the week. Dave Schwartz's original Rent-A-Wreck location, run by the owner himself, is full of the usual new cars and vintage classics you haven't driven or seen in decades.

The Scene: What's your pleasure? A '66 Mustang convertible, a '68 Cadillac Coupe de Ville, a '70 Oldsmobile Cutlass? Choose from T-Birds, Skylarks, and Ford Woody Station Wagons that'll make the trip to Santa Barbara.

Hot Tip: Don't let the slightly out-the-way location in West L.A. deter you. Rent-A-Wreck offers 24-hour pick-up and drop-off service from LAX every day of the week.

Power Lunches

Throughout history, very important people have been required to Do Lunch in very important places. It just comes with the job. If you fit the mold (or want to practice) L.A.'s cross-section of power lunch spots runs the gamut. Meat and potatoes, lobster bisque, or pickled herring? Take your pick and look at who's sitting right over there.

Barney Greengrass

9570 Wilshire Blvd., 5th Floor, Beverly Hills, 310-777-5877

The Draw: See some famous faces over matzo brei and whitefish salad at this imported New York deli on the top floor of Barneys.

The Scene: A deli that's fashionable enough for weight-deprived actresses who want to grab a bite between shoplifting sprees. Great views of Beverly Hills from the outdoor terrace and a dependable cast of recognizable regulars.
Open Mon.–Wed. 8:30 a.m.–6 p.m., Thurs.–Fri. 8:30 a.m.–7 p.m., Sat. 9 a.m.–7 p.m., Sun. 9 a.m.–6 p.m. $

Hot Tip: The specialty is the smoked fish—sturgeon, salmon, whitefish, sable—all flown in from the Big Apple. If you're looking for the traditional Naugahyde deli with waitresses who call you "honey," Nate 'n' Al's is just up the street (310-274-0101).

The Grill on the Alley

9560 Dayton Way (Wilshire Blvd.), Beverly Hills, 310-276-0615

The Draw: For the quintessential Who's-Who lunch rush, look no further. Steaks, chops, martinis, strawberry shortcake, and other corporate American comfort food, served in the presence of Hollywood's chieftains.

The Scene: If you just got bumped from that open table, it's probably because David Geffen or his equivalent just walked through the door. Dinner (seven days a week) is also a scene in this dignified and clubby dining den.
Open Mon.–Thurs. 11:30 a.m.–11 p.m., Fri.–Sat. 11:30 a.m.–midnight, Sun. 5–9 p.m. $$$

Hot Tip: Reservations are always recommended. We recommend the chicken pot pie.

The Ivy

113 N. Robertson Blvd., Los Angeles, 310-274-8303

The Draw: Celebrities who need some quick paparazzi coverage, along with a pricey chopped salad or designer meatloaf, have been trained to take a seat on the front patio of this genteel New American staple.

The Scene: Recognized by its white picket fence and its valet-spun turnstile of Bentleys and Hummers (and from several movie cameos, most memorably, *Get Shorty*), this cottagey setting is ground zero for midday Hollywood schmoozers.
Open Mon.–Fri. 11:30 a.m.–10 p.m., Sat.–Sun. 10:30 a.m.–10 p.m. $$$

Hot Tip: For the full experience, request a seat on the front patio. For the same menu (and less of a scene) by the sea, try the Ivy at the Shore (see p. 148).

Presidential Suites

Is dropping ten grand on a room wasteful? The Aga Kahn, the Windsors, George W. Bush, and various other honorees who don't pick up the tab would say No, it is not. If you fall into this general category, these pinnacles of L.A. luxury are the places to celebrate and dispense freely your good fortune. (The standard rooms in all these hotels are also pretty wonderful.)

The Peninsula Beverly Hills, Peninsula Suite

9882 S. Santa Monica Blvd., Beverly Hills, 310-551-2888

The Draw: The most spectacular living quarters, for only $3,000 a night, in what is often called L.A.'s finest hotel.

The Scene: More than 2,000 square feet of palatial living space, overlooking the hotel's fountained front courtyard. The Peninsula Suite includes two spacious bedrooms, a dining room for ten, and a living room with a fireplace and a baby grand.

Hot Tip: For all Peninsula rooms, check-out time is a full 24 hours from whenever you checked in. The grandest of 16 self-contained units on the property is the two-story Peninsula Villa (also $3,000 a night).

St. Regis Los Angeles, Presidential Suite

2055 Avenue of the Stars, Century City, 310-277-6111

The Draw: Hands down L.A.'s most presidential suite—and the only room in town designed with the assistance and approval of the U.S. Secret Service. Ronald Reagan was the first guest here, and every U.S. President since then has checked in. You can too, for a mere 10 Gs a night. Can we see some I.D., please?

The Scene: The whole top floor of this luxury 30-story property, offering 7,300 square feet of living space, done up in Asian American–fusion decor. Three bedrooms, five bathrooms, private elevator access, a formal dining room and kitchen, and L.A.-wide vistas from the Pacific to Downtown.

Hot Tip: Travelers on a tighter budget can rough it by reserving half of the penthouse for a fraction of the cost. The West wing is only $5,500; the East wing is just $4,500.

Shutters on the Beach, Presidential Suite

1 Pico Blvd., Santa Monica, 310-458-0030

The Draw: $2,500 a night gets you a Presidential Suite at L.A.'s best beachfront hotel. Lots of famous guests stay here, and if you opt for the seventh-floor Presidential (others are on the second and third floors) they'll all be sleeping where they belong—beneath you.

The Scene: Fifteen hundred square feet with a full-sized living room and fireplace, kitchen, marble bathroom, and—count 'em—three balconies with front-row ocean views.

Hot Tip: These go fast during the high season (April–September). Shorter notice reservations are easiest to book between November and January.

Rides on a Harley

Forget Sturgis and Daytona. V-twin nirvana is rumbling all around you in greater Los Angeles on a lazy Sunday afternoon—up and down the coast, through winding canyons, and between forested peaks. Rent a custom Fatboy or Softail at EagleRider (see p. 54.) or Route 66 Riders (4161 Lincoln Blvd. Marina del Rey, 310-578-0112). Then leave the crowded freeways and cocooned drivers in the dust on any of these liberating runs.

Angeles Crest Highway

Take Route 2 north, from Hwy. 210 into the San Gabriel Mountains.

The Draw: Climb 8,000 feet into the San Gabriel Mountains, with tremendous views of greater L.A. from the Mt. Wilson cutoff.

The Scene: A dramatic introduction to the Angeles National Forest's 650,000-acre wilderness of chaparral and pine-covered peaks. Experienced riders only.

Hot Tip: Save this ride for the summer months and dress for the altitude. Fill up before entering the forest reserve, where there are no gas stations.

Bouquet Canyon to Lake Castaic

Take US5 N to Lyons Ave. west. Go left on San Fernando Rd., which becomes Bouquet Canyon Rd. Take a left on Spunky Canyon Rd.; right on San Francisquito Canyon Rd.; left on Elizabeth Lake Rd.; and left on Lake Hughes Rd. to Castaic Lake State Recreation Area.

The Draw: Another rewarding ride through Angeles National Forest, west of Antelope Valley, to Lake Castaic—home of L.A.'s annual Love Ride (in November).

The Scene: Lots of easy cruising through the quiet lake country of Bouquet Canyon. As car-free as it gets.

Hot Tip: Burgers and live music are waiting for you at the Big Oaks Lodge (33101 N. Bouquet Canyon Rd. 661-296-5656).

Mulholland Highway

Take Pacific Coast Highway about 30 miles west from Santa Monica to Mulholland Highway. Hang a right into the hills.

The Draw: Not to be confused with Mulholland Drive (straddling the Hollywood Hills further east) this scenic artery through the secluded canyons above Malibu is a chrome convention on weekends.

The Scene: Miles of breezy straightaways along PCH lead to a winding ride through the green valleys and brown cliffs of the northwestern Santa Monica Mountains. If you've got the time, you can take it all the way from Malibu to Woodland Hills in the Valley.

Hot Tip: Stop in at the Rock Store (30354 Mulholland Hwy, 818-889-1311) for a cheeseburger and beer with every other biker on the planet.

Romantic Dining

What's your idea of a perfect spot for gazing lovingly into each other's eyes? By the ocean? In the hills? On a candlelit patio bursting with bougainvillea? Roscoe's Chicken and Waffles? However you define romance, L.A. has the table set. These top picks cost less than couple's therapy—and leave a better taste in your mouth.

Il Cielo

9018 Burton Way, Beverly Hills, 310-276-9990

The Draw: Sharing an evening at this intimate Italian hideaway is like a quick honeymoon in Positano, without leaving Beverly Hills. Beautifully prepared dishes and traditional wines from "the Boot" live up to one of L.A.'s most fanciful dining settings.

The Scene: The homey interior exudes romance, with a fireplace, frescoed ceilings, and private rooms. But for the real deal, reserve a table under the stars in the front courtyard or on the rear garden patio.
Open lunch Mon.–Sat. 11 a.m.–3 p.m.; dinner 6–11 p.m. $$$

Hot Tip: As desserts go, is there a greater aphrodisiac than rose crème brûlée with candied rose petals on a bed of white chocolate and raspberry sauce?

The Little Door

8164 W. Third St., Los Angeles, 323-951-1210

The Draw: Stick up an old wooden door that's just a little too small. Behind it, build a solid reputation as L.A.'s most transporting French-Med Never Never Land. Of course everyone wants to pay through the teeth to see for themselves.

The Scene: The door opens onto a startling garden courtyard full of young, fah-bulous guests and French waiters hauling blackboard lists of the dessert specials.
Open Sun.–Thurs. 6 –10 p.m., Fri.–Sat. 6–11 p.m.; Sun. brunch 11 a.m.– 3 p.m. $$$

Hot Tip: Reserve early, and provide a good-sounding reason (anniversary maybe?) for a patio table. The crunch of deuces inside at the back is great for eavesdropping, but otherwise is a squeeze.

Restaurant at Hotel Bel-Air

701 Stone Canyon Rd., Bel-Air, 310-472-1211

The Draw: This Cal-French Eden is one of L.A.'s top restaurants and also its most Shangri-la–like fine dining scene.

The Scene: Set on a refined acreage with real swans (in the lake, not on the menu), Bel-Air's artful rendition of the great outdoors is out on the terrace—a medley of azaleas, bougainvillea, camellias, and some distinguished guests you'll probably recognize.
Open daily for breakfast 7–9:30 a.m.; lunch 12–2 p.m.; dinner 6:30–9:30 p.m.; Sun. brunch 11 a.m.–2 p.m. $$$

Hot Tip: If you can't make it for dinner, consider Sunday brunch. Want more privacy? Reserve your own private dining area, called "Table One."

See-and-Be-Seen Bars

Sure, you can cut the attitude with a knife, but that's at least partially why you showed up. What's a weekend in L.A. without throwing yourself into the exhilarating mix of terse doormen, aloof bartenders, Hollywood gentry and Valley pretenders, and Eurotrash? After enough overpriced cosmopolitans, it all makes sense. You got in, dammit, and that's all that matters.

Barfly

8730 W. Sunset Blvd., West Hollywood, 310-360-9490

The Draw: Make it past the velvet rope (and the ironic "welcome" mug shot of Charles Bukowski) to join the throng at this flagship of hip hype and dressed-to-the-nines glitz on the new Sunset Strip.

The Scene: Red velvet, candlelight, and fruity martinis everywhere. A young, chic, beautiful crowd—at least while your eyes are still adjusting to the dark.
Open Mon.–Sat. 7:30 p.m.–2 a.m.

Hot Tip: Try not to be over 30 years old. Come with a dinner reservation if you want to outfox the doorman.

Rooftop Bar at The Standard Downtown

550 S. Flower St., Downtown, 213-892-8080

The Draw: Leave it to The Standard to turn the roof of an abandoned Superior Oil building in the financial district into one of L.A.'s loftiest hotspots. Finally there's a reason to be Downtown at 2 a.m.

The Scene: The pool, the panoramas, the rad DJ rotation, the candyapple-red bar, the eight-buck beers, the Hollywood hipsters—it's all here. Come early to snag some "me" time in the vibrating space-pod waterbed cabanas. (Yes, you read that right.)
Open daily 11 a.m.–2 a.m.

Hot Tip: Showing up on a weeknight saves you a twenty-dollar cover and the lethal post–7 p.m. weekend lines.

Skybar

8440 W. Sunset Blvd., West Hollywood, 323-848-6025

The Draw: So what if the A-list has slipped to A-minus at this holy grail of exclusive poolside bars? It's still Skybar.

The Scene: Young, beautiful people paying big bucks to drink out of plastic cups on the Mondrian hotel's pool deck. The views (of all kinds) are pretty sensational.
Open daily 11 a.m.–2 a.m.

Hot Tip: If you're a hotel guest, walk right in. If not, get here before 8 p.m. when the doorman shows up.

Spas

Why are there so many spas in Los Angeles? Because people here are totally stressed out. Never mind that they're lounging at cafes drinking iced lattes on warm Tuesday afternoons in February. Stay here long enough and you'll need to get steamed, rinsed, wrapped, and twisted into a pretzel, preferably at one of these one-of-a-kind spas.

Beverly Hot Springs

308 N. Oxford Ave., Los Angeles, 323-734-7000

The Draw: An oilman struck hot mineral water at this unlikely sybaritic site. It now houses L.A.'s only natural thermal baths, offering steamy soaks, scrubs, and shiatsus.

The Scene: A traditional Korean-style spa, adorned with rock waterfalls and a soothing soundtrack of chimes, hissing steam, and easy-listening Brahms. Treatment rooms are only semiprivate, but after a few minutes that won't matter.
Open daily 9 a.m.–9 p.m.

Hot Tip: Shiatsus and deep-tissue massages last just under an hour, so make it a double. Call ahead to find out about frequent promo specials.

Ole Henriksen Face/Body

8622-A W. Sunset Blvd., West Hollywood, 310-854-7700

The Draw: Run by a famous Beverly Hills skincare guru, homespun treatments like "Effleurage Massage with Mango and Cocoa Butter" and "Dry Brush Exfoliation and Swedish Massage with Anti-Cellulite Formulation" are designed to whip your epidermis into shape.

The Scene: Glowing candles light this lovely facility in Sunset Plaza. Japanese shoji doors glide open and closed between treatment rooms. Multistep body treatments take guests through a series of herbal washes, mineral scrubs, tropical rain rinses, and cranial massage.
Open Mon. 8 a.m.–5 p.m., Tues.–Sat. 8 a.m.–8 p.m., Sun. 9:30 a.m.–4:30 p.m.

Hot Tip: Don't leave Henriksen's before doing penance with a viciously divine salt scrub.

Spa Mystique

2025 Avenue of the Stars, Century City, 310-551-3251

The Draw: The crown jewel of the Century Plaza Hotel's recent $70-million reno is this 35,000-square-foot spa, stocked with more than 30 private treatment rooms and the Westside's largest menu of Asian-style health, relaxation, and beauty services.

The Scene: A feng shui expert was on call during the design of this elegant two-story building, which includes a pair of Japanese furo pools, a meditation garden, a salon and cafe, a state-of-the-art fitness center, and pleasantly sedated guests milling around in kimonos.
Open daily 8 a.m.–9 p.m.; last treatment is at 7 p.m.

Hot Tip: Nonguests, use the valet service at the side entrance on Constellation Blvd.

Steakhouses with Atmosphere

Elite chains like Ruth's Chris, Arnie Morton's, and The Palm, and newcomers like Mastro's and Porterhouse Bistro are way up there of course, but a classic steakhouse should also have an entrenched sense of place—as though the town came afterward. These veteran chop shops win for their L.A. auras and damn good steaks.

Dan Tana's

9071 Santa Monica Blvd., West Hollywood, 310-275-9444

The Draw: This beloved Italian restaurant has been moonlighting as an A-list steak place for almost 50 years. But none of the Tom Jones–era regulars will laugh at you for ordering pasta instead of cow and steak fries. Not to your face, at least.

The Scene: Red leather booths, checkered table cloths, suspended Chianti bottles, a crowd of Goodfellas planted on bar stools, and a maitre d' named Jimmy. The place is relaxed enough to have a TV set above the tiny bar and Jerry West's Laker jersey on the wall.
Open daily 5 p.m.–1 a.m. $$

Hot Tip: There's one steak on the menu, the New York Strip. You just have to decide whether it'll be the 12- or 16-ounce.

Musso & Frank Grill

6667 Hollywood Blvd., Hollywood, 323-467-7788

The Draw: Hollywood's oldest restaurant doesn't look a day over 84. The moment you walk in, you'll see that you haven't come here just for the steak—which is still pretty good.

The Scene: Red leather, mahogany, chandeliers, and inebriated ghosts everywhere, including some of the waiters. If *The Shining* had been set in a Hollywood restaurant, this would've been the location.
Open Tues.–Sat. 11 a.m.–11 p.m. $$

Hot Tip: Vegetarians can come for breakfast (flannel cakes) or lunch (Bloody Marys).

Pacific Dining Car

1310 W. 6th St., Downtown, 213-483-6000

The Draw: Almost as old as Musso's, this round-the-clock class act is best known for its USDA Prime Eastern corn-fed, dry-aged, mesquite-grilled beef and its Russian novel–sized wine list.

The Scene: The rail-car theme comes and goes once you're past the front bar entrance. After that it's a hushed ambience of cozy booths and high-backed chairs.
Open 24 hours daily. $$$

Hot Tip: Great happy hour spreads include ribs, wings, and shrimp. PCD #2 is now open in Santa Monica (2700 Wilshire Blvd., 310-453-4000).

Studio Tours

Hollywood studios have been inviting people in for a peek since the silent era, when Universal boss Carl Laemmle came up with the idea of selling bleacher seats on the back lot during shoots. (Eggs were sold separately.) While most studios opt to stay out of the public eye (Paramount being the latest to shut its gates, for security reasons), a handful of tours are still offered by some of the most famous studios in the biz.

NBC Studios

3000 W. Alameda Ave., Burbank, 818-840-3537

The Draw: You've stared at their product in the box for long enough. It's time to step behind the scenes at the Burbank headquarters to see how it's done.

The Scene: The 70-minute walking tour roams through wardrobe, makeup, and set construction departments. There are some nifty hands-on demos in the sound and FX rooms, plus possible visits to the *Tonight* show and *Days of Our Lives* sets.
Tours depart regularly 9 a.m.–3 p.m. weekdays, plus weekends during the summer. $

Hot Tip: For free tickets to the *Tonight* show with Jay Leno, be at the NBC ticket counter well before 8 a.m., or request in advance by mail (NBC Tickets, 3000 W. Alameda Ave., Burbank, CA 91523).

Universal Studios Hollywood

100 Universal City Plaza, Universal City, 818-622-3801

The Draw: Famous for its theme park, Universal Studios is also, of course, a blockbuster film factory. Hiding behind all those rides is the world's largest movie and television studio.

The Scene: The standard 45-minute Studio Tour is basically an overrehearsed warmup for the park. The more personal VIP Experience Pass is pricey ($135), but provides two hours on the lot and far more behind-the-scenes access.
VIP Tours depart daily, generally on the hour between 9 a.m. and noon. $$$$

Hot Tip: VIP treatment also includes four privileged hours in the park (i.e. cut to the front of every line). Reserve at least a week in advance (818-622-5120).

Warner Brothers Studios

4301 W. Olive Ave., Burbank, 818-972-8687

The Draw: A refreshingly candid and unstaged tour in one of Hollywood's oldest, most famous movie and television studios.

The Scene: Small groups board a studio tram and are whisked all over the hundred-acre lot, visiting historic sets, prop warehouses, wardrobe departments, Foley rooms, and sound stages of prime time shows when the cameras aren't running.
Tours depart weekdays on the half hour between 9 a.m. and 3 p.m. $$$

Hot Tip: Warner's Deluxe Tour (Wednesdays only, at the moment) is twice as long and includes lunch.

Sushi

Delicate slabs of raw fish are about as prevalent in Los Angeles as 72 oz. steaks are in Amarillo, Texas. If you're just looking for a quick California roll and a few morsels of yellow tail, sushi bars are everywhere. On the other end of the spectrum, the most discriminating sashimi-scenesters will be treating themselves to these top picks.

Katana

8439 W. Sunset Blvd., West Hollywood, 323-650-8585

The Draw: From the producers of the very hot Sushi Roku chain comes this even hotter show-stealer on the Sunset Strip.

The Scene: Perched in the beautiful Piazza del Sol building (with fellow tenants Miramax), Katana's front patio and stylish redwood and steel candlelit interior draws industry types and in-the-know yuppies for sushi specials and robatayaki skewers. A crew of busy chefs always finds time to yell cheerful greetings and farewells to incoming and outgoing guests.
Open Sun.–Mon. 6–11 p.m., Tues.–Wed. 6–11:30 p.m., Thurs.–Sat. 6 p.m.–12:30 a.m. $$

Hot Tip: Drinks and sushi selections are $5 during happy hour (Mon.–Fri. 5:30–7 p.m.). For a show with dinner, dine in front of the open-flame grill at the robata bar.

Koi

730 N. La Cienega Blvd., Los Angeles, 310-659-9449

The Draw: At present, Koi is among the trendiest and most stylish tributes to raw fish in the city, boasting an inventive, Cal-inflected menu and an enviable A-list of regulars.

The Scene: A quartet of earth-toned dining areas filled with young, beautiful people drinking premium sakes out of bamboo cups and ordering from a diverse menu of sushi, tempura, and far-out signature dishes like Alaskan king crab legs with garlic-butter sauce. There's a sleek lounge, a candlelit bar, and an outdoor patio with a fireplace.
Open for lunch Mon.–Fri. 11:30 a.m.–2:30 p.m.; dinner Mon.–Thurs. 6:30–11 p.m., Fri.–Sat. 6:30 p.m.–midnight, Sun. 6:30–10 p.m. $

Hot Tip: Make weekend reservations fashionably late (not before 9 p.m.) at least a few days in advance. Try the Koi Yellow or Koi Blue, the restaurant's specialty sake martinis.

Matsuhisa

129 N. La Cienega Blvd., Los Angeles, 310-659-9639

The Draw: Innovative sushi master Nobu Matsuhisa runs what many foodies continue to call the best restaurant in the city.

The Scene: Surprisingly casual. There's very little to look at besides some posters on the wall and the odd celebrity in jeans and a T-shirt sitting across the room.
Open Mon.–Fri. for lunch 11:45 a.m.–2:15 p.m.; dinner daily 5:45–10:30 p.m. $$$

Hot Tip: Just say "*omakase*" (chef's choice) and let Nobu's talented disciples spare you the hassle of choosing from more than 100 possible dishes.

Theme Bars

Would you like a manicure or henna tattoo with that beer? How about a friendly reminder that "only you can prevent forest fires" with your vodka tonic? If it's just a cocktail you're after, there are a million stools you can sit on. But those who crave a chaser of good, hard kitsch with that flaming toasted marshmallow beverage will be better served in these three altogether wackier drinking atmospheres.

Beauty Bar

1638 Cahuenga Ave., Hollywood, 323-464-7676

The Draw: When you need a drink but just have to get your nails done, it's one-stop shopping at this ode to kitsch and '60s beauty school glamour on Hollywood's Cahuenga Corridor.

The Scene: Retro salon decor includes hair-styling chairs, a row of hood dryers against the wall, and the faintest whiff of hair spray in the air. Bartenders mix cocktails called Platinum Blonde and Prell. A manicurist is on duty.
Open Sun.–Wed. 9 p.m.–2 a.m., Thurs.–Sat. 6 p.m.–2 a.m.

Hot Tip: Forking over ten bucks for a drink gets you a free manicure Thursdays and Fridays after 6 p.m. and Saturdays 8–11 p.m. Henna tattoos are available on weekends.

The Bigfoot Lodge

3172 Los Feliz Blvd., Atwater Village, 323-662-9227

The Draw: The only hipster lounge in L.A. where you can come in from the cold and warm up with a brewski next to an animatronic raccoon sitting on a tree stump.

The Scene: A great outdoors motif runs wild in this big fake-log room furnished with stuffed owls, a big stone hearth, and a giant Smokey the Bear at the front entrance.
Open nightly 8 p.m.–2 a.m.

Hot Tip: Favorite specialty drinks include the flaming Toasted Marshmallow (Stoli vanilla, butterscotch liqueur, Frangelico, half & half, and an ignited Bacardi-dipped marshmallow) and the minty Girl Scout Cookie (crème de menthe, Irish Cream, and half & half).

Good Luck Bar

1514 Hillhurst Ave., Los Feliz, 323-666-3524

The Draw: This trend-setting singles lounge in Los Feliz takes the Far East theme about as far as it can go. Maybe farther.

The Scene: Between walls as red as Mao's Little Book is every clichéd piece of "Old China" decor, from paper lanterns, bamboo stools, barmaids with chopsticks in their hair, dragons on the ceiling, and an opium-den–styled back lounge to a last-call gong. After a few Singapore Slings and Hendrix tunes, it all feels very authentic somehow.
Open nightly 7 p.m.–2 a.m.

Hot Tip: The house special is The Good Luck—Amaretto, Midori, juice, and milk.

Unusual Shopping Experiences

You can get anything in Los Angeles. Anything. Beyond the city's swirling sea of boutiques and bookshops, retro furniture warehouses and vintage clothing closets, ginseng counters and sex toy stores, the following places truly cement L.A.'s reputation as a consumerist society run amok.

Necromance

7220 Melrose Ave., Los Angeles, 323-934-8684

The Draw: The Gap lasted only a few years on the Melrose Strip. Not so for Necromance, purveyor of dog skulls, cast monkey arms, mounted insects, and other "curios".

The Scene: A skeleton and some occult hardcovers dangle in the front window, along with a posting stating "All unattended children will be sold to medical research facilities." Inside, it's like an old lady's knitting room, but with bones everywhere. *Open Mon.–Sat. noon–7 p.m., Sun. 2–6 p.m.*

Hot Tip: Don't bring the kids. If you need a Partridge Family lunch box to carry your animal parts, check out Off the Wall antiques (7325 Melrose), one block west.

Skeletons in the Closet

1104 N. Mission Rd., Downtown, 323-343-0760

The Draw: Only in L.A. will you find a souvenir shop at the County Coroner.

The Scene: Best buys at this second-floor office in the Coroner's administrative building (autopsies are in the building next door), include beach towels with chalked-out body outlines, boxer shorts labeled "Undertakers," toe tag keychains, skeleton-head business card holders, and an assortment of T-shirts and mugs labeled "Coroner." *Open Mon.–Fri. 8:30 a.m.–4:30 p.m.*

Hot Tip: Don't enter the building next door.

Soap Plant/Wacko

4633 Hollywood Blvd., Los Feliz, 323-663-0122

The Draw: Classic kitsch, odd knickknacks, hygiene products that definitely aren't Proctor & Gamble, literature not carried by Borders, candy bars you've never heard of, and so much more.

The Scene: Shelves of natural soaps, cosmetics, and unique literature (including a "Snakes of the World" coloring book for the kids) is in the front. Wacko is the store's weirder half in the rear, for Davey and Goliath dolls, a foot-long Homer Simpson Pez dispenser, and an inflatable palm tree. Is it all starting to make sense? *Open Mon.–Wed. 11 a.m.–7 p.m., Thurs.–Sat. 11 a.m.–9 p.m., Sun. noon–6 p.m.*

Hot Tip: Check out the La Luz de Jesus Gallery in the back for the occasional dazzling pop art exhibit.

Views of L.A.

On a smoggy day, gazing down over Los Angeles from the Hollywood Hills might make you want to write a sympathy card to your lungs. So save that drive up to Griffith Park Observatory for a crisp afternoon when the sky can be distinguished from the ocean and the freeways. If you can't wait that long, these three unique perspectives of L.A. are always redeeming in their own ways.

Catalina Island

20 miles SW of Los Angeles (see p. 189).

The Draw: Gazing at Los Angeles from this getaway 20 miles offshore erases all the city's buildings and highways from view, leaving behind the hills, mountains, and sweeping coast. Here's what L.A. looked like when the dinosaurs were here.

The Scene: A charming island retreat that's as removed from the hustle of the city as it appears. Several trails from the port town of Avalon lead up to the best vistas of the Southern California coast.

Hot Tip: First you need to get here. Hop a ferry to Avalon from Long Beach or San Pedro with Catalina Express (310-519-1212).

Heli USA

16303 Waterman Dr., Van Nuys, 818-994-1445

The Draw: Make like a local traffic reporter and launch yourself above L.A. in a helicopter for the best bird's eye view of the city.

The Scene: Heli USA's standard tour is the Hollywood/Skyscraper Flight—a 30-minute aerial tour covering the Hollywood Hills, the Getty Center, Universal Studios, Beverly Hills, and Downtown.

Hot Tip: Add some air time along the coast on the City of Angeles Flight. Another option includes limousine pickup service from your hotel and a special Destination Dinner Flight to either Santa Monica Airport's Typhoon or LAX's Encounter restaurants.

Mulholland Drive

Between U.S. 101 and I-405

The Draw: Gaze down over the Los Angeles flats on one side and the San Fernando Valley on the other from this famous road that wends its way through the Hollywood Hills.

The Scene: Winding past mansions and celebrity estates, Mulholland Drive straddles the Hollywood Hills and Santa Monica Mountains for more than 20 miles. There are several turnoffs and lookout points between U.S. 101 and Coldwater Canyon.

Hot Tip: Come at night for the best city lights show. Keep your eyes on the road.

The L.A. Experience

You've only got three days to squeeze the maximum fun out of L.A. Where do you begin? That depends on which L.A. you're looking for. We've prepared five itineraries that will keep you hopping from dawn 'til —um, dawn. The Classic Hollywood itinerary is recommended for a Friday–Sunday schedule; the rest are Thursday–Saturday itineraries geared toward scenesters who know that the weekend starts early. But whether you're looking for the golden days of Hollywood or the golden sands of Malibu, we've got you covered. Fasten your seatbelts, it's going to be a fun ride.

Classic Hollywood

Despite its fickle and faddish nature, Hollywood has roots. Some of them are even older than Robert Evans and deeper than Steven Spielberg's pockets. Hollywood has bungalows where Marilyn Monroe cavorted, barstools where Bogart wobbled, theatres where Kate Hepburn attended premieres, and tables where Spencer Tracy ate Welsh rabbit. Gone are the Brown Derby, Pickfair, the Garden of Allah, and countless other classic haunts. A 24-hour Denny's now occupies the site of the first Hollywood stage set, at Sunset and Gower. But surprisingly, not all the great locations have been beaten down into strip malls and parking lots. Look closely (ignore that Josh Hartnett poster), and you'll notice that many pieces of Tinseltown's glorious past are still breathing—thriving even, with a recent wave of multimillion-dollar restoration efforts. If you're jonesing for the mythic glamor of Movieland, it's time for a Classic Hollywood fix.

Classic Hollywood: The Itinerary

Three Great Days and Nights

Your Hotel: **Beverly Hills Hotel & Bungalows**

Morning: Start with a hearty breakfast and some gourmet coffee at the Beverly Hills Hotel's Fountain Coffee Shop. Guests, famous and not, have been planting themselves on these *pink stools* since the '40s.

Then into Classic Hollywood proper. Begin your tour of duty at the fabled corner of *Hollywood and Vine*. Stroll along the star-studded **Hollywood Walk of Fame**, trying not to collide with others staring down at the more than 2,000 name plaques lining the sidewalk. Leaf through old movie and TV scripts at **Book City**, where you can also find unique Hollywood memorabilia. Check out Zsa Zsa Gabor's underpants at **Frederick's of Hollywood Lingerie Museum**, and carry on to see props from *Ben Hur* or *Your Show of Shows*, an authentic *Star Trek* set, and other industry artifacts at the **Hollywood Entertainment Museum**. Check out Hollywood's biggest makeover at the new **Hollywood & Highland** retail and entertainment complex, or take a tour of the **Kodak Theatre**, the grand new home of the Academy Awards.

If you want an expert to take you for a spin around the neighborhood, **Red Line Tours** supplies earphones and plenty of enlightening and lively commentary on their guided walk through the heart of *historic Hollywood*. Along the way, you'll get inside some of the area's most cherished landmarks.

Afternoon: You have a couple of classic options for a leisurely lunch. Have a bite at the revived **Pig 'n Whistle**, a favorite post-premiere *hangout of stars* of the 1930s and '40s. Or, across from the Warner lot (your next destination), is the **Smoke House**, a classic '40s-era steakhouse that's been frequented by generations of stars and execs. The savory hickory-smoked steaks are still excellent and the famous fluorescent garlic bread is brighter than ever.

Head over the hill to **Warner Brothers Studios** in Burbank for a two-hour VIP tour that won't disappoint. You'll get lots of Hollywood history plus *behind-the-scenes glimpses* of one of L.A.'s oldest, most famous movie and television lots.

Pay your respects at the **Hollywood Forever Cemetery**, where *Rudolph Valentino*, Douglas Fairbanks, and a number of other Golden Era legends are still drawing fans. Be sure to drive past the storied gates of **Paramount Pictures**, the last major studio standing in Hollywood.

Evening: Enjoy drinks and *fine views* above Hollywood at **Yamashiro**, a palatial Japanese restaurant where silent movie stars once held private soireés. (Stick to cocktails, though, and take a pass on the pricey, merely average eats). Window seats in the front lounge can fill up fast at sunset, so try to get here before 6 p.m.

Then, for dinner, roll back down the hill for nostalgic meat 'n' martini dining at Hollywood's oldest restaurant, **Musso & Frank Grill**. (The chops at **Dan Tana's**, another *landmark steakhouse* in nearby West Hollywood, may edge out Musso's.) As far as Classic Hollywood goes, this big oak-and-leather–bedecked establishment, with its cadaverous waiters and former regulars like Charlie Chaplin, William Faulkner, and the brothers Warner, is beyond reproach. Or head to **Miceli's**, Hollywood's landmark Italian restaurant, where you can hear *waiters croon* Sinatra over linguine and cheap Chianti.

If time permits, check out the film and video offerings presented by the *American Cinematheque* at the restored **Egyptian Theatre**, Hollywood's first major movie house. Less discriminating cinephiles can catch the usual Hollywood fare at **Grauman's Chinese Theatre**, after a stroll through the forecourt, studying the hand and shoe sizes of John Wayne, Norma Talmadge, and nearly 200 other immortal stars.

End your day with a nightcap or two at one of Hollywood's most famous *watering holes*, the **Formosa Café**, where celebs have been getting loaded since 1925.

Morning: Hey, you're staying in a nice joint—take advantage of it and fuel up with room service. Then head out on a meandering *drive through the Hollywood Hills* to check out some famous old residences. A good map is essential in this labyrinth. (In a pinch, get copies of the Thomas Guide pages for the Hills from the concierge. They've been asked before.) Here are a dozen doors to get you going; don't knock—they've all moved: 915 Foothill Drive (Frank Sinatra); 508 Palm Drive (Marilyn Monroe and Joe DiMaggio); 1000 Roxbury Drive (Lucille Ball); 1011 Cove Way (Rock Hudson); 9966 Beverly Grove (Cary Grant); 1158 Tower Road (Spencer Tracy); 1085 Summit Drive (Charlie Chaplin); 1143 Summit Drive (Douglas Fairbanks and Mary Pickford's "Pickfair" site); 1151 Summit Drive (Sammy Davis Jr.); 1436 Bella Drive (Rudolph Valentino's "Falcon Lair"). Include a visit to the manicured grounds at historic **Greystone Park & Mansion**, a grand 20-acre Beverly Hills estate open to the public during the day.

Golfers can opt out and spend a morning on the green at **Rustic Canyon Golf Course**, one of the top *new fairways* in Southern California, set in a beautifully preserved valley.

Afternoon: For today's lunch, order one of the famous *chopped salads* at **La Scala**, a Beverly Hills institution for nearly 50 years. Or indulge in a great meatloaf sandwich in an unstuffy atmosphere at the venerable **Brighton Coffee Shop**, a '30s-era BevHills anomaly that's been thumbing its nose at Rodeo Drive, one block over, for generations.

After lunch, acquaint yourself better with your opulent surroundings on a **Beverly Hills Trolley Tour**, which covers some great historic landmarks. Or, book ahead and take a private *one-hour salsa lesson* at **3rd Street Dance**, one of L.A.'s most reliable places to learn the moves—and a great way to prepare for an evening at the Conga Room. For something completely different, couples can get cooking together (literally) at the 20-year-old **Epicurean School of Culinary Arts** with its scrumptious one-day workshops, including one called "The Art of the Tart."

Evening: On to a night of *music under the stars* at the legendary **Hollywood Bowl**, official home of the Hollywood Bowl Orchestra and a summer lineup of top musicians and entertainers. In the off-season, head to West Hollywood's most renowned rock concert hall, the **Troubadour**. Or check out the big names playing over at **The Wiltern**, a stunning Art Deco landmark with a new lease on life. Broadway musical fans can head to the beautifully restored **Pantages Theatre**, shining like new on Hollywood Blvd.

Eat like a king or queen—or at least like a best-supporting actor, at **Morton's**. On any given weekend night, there may be enough *Hollywood heavyweights* at this time-honored Cal-Continental restaurant to throw an impromptu Oscar party. Occasionally there *is* an Oscar party. Or, get your name on the list at **Le Dome**, a swanky Sunset bistro that's been drawing in the celebrities for the last quarter-century. For a fanciful evening of Italian home-cooking under the stars, **Il Cielo** is consistently ranked among L.A.'s most *romantic dining* scenes.

You could take the easy way and cap off your evening with a drink at **The Bar at Hotel Bel-Air**. Better yet, put your salsa moves to the test at **The Conga Room**, L.A.'s hottest *latin stage and ballroom*. (Dining at La Boca del Conga Room, the venue's swank Nuevo Latino restaurant, is another dinner option. You can soak up enough mojitos here to lose your inhibitions when the music starts.)

Day 3

Morning: There are Sunday brunches and there are *Sunday brunches*. And then there's a little event known as brunch at the **Hotel Bel-Air Restaurant**. Sit out on the terrace with champagne and a warm, homemade brioche in hand, In the foreground, a symphony of flowers, in the background, a glassy pond with fluffy white swans. Choose—if you can—between the ricotta soufflé pancakes or the lobster and patty pan squash.

For more casual brunching (and exploring) head down to the **Farmers Market**, a vaunted *hive of food counters*, fruit stalls, butchers, bakers, key chain vendors, incognito celebrities, and octogenarians staring into space. For the *hottest stack of pancakes* in the city, have a seat at **Du-Pars**. For a sanitized browse, check out The Grove, a new outdoor shopping and entertainment center right next door.

Or escape the glitz altogether and spend some time exploring Classic Hollywood's wilder exteriors. Have room service prepare a picnic lunch (okay, so you can bring some glitz with you). Then head west to **Will Rogers State Historic Park**, the former family ranch and estate of the legendary cowboy humorist. The first thing you'll notice here before heading off on one of the property's lovely hiking trails are the famous *polo grounds* and Will's farmhouse-mansion. For a real ersatz Old West experience, visit **Paramount Ranch**, a more remote outpost in the Santa Monica Mountains that was once the busiest *Western film site* in the biz. There's still an old ghost town here, and well-maintained hiking trails with wonderful views.

Afternoon: Head back to Hollywood and see a Sunday matinee at the **Silent Movie Theatre**, where actions have been speaking louder than words for more than 60 years. *Pre-talkie classics* here hark back to the days of mega-talents like Charlie Chaplin, Buster Keaton, and Laurel & Hardy.

For something a little more contemporary after the movie, unwind with a treatment at **Spa Mystique**, L.A.'s new ultimate spa facility in the Century Plaza Hotel. Or opt for *high tea* back at the **Beverly Hills Hotel**, a tradition that's actually older than silent movies. Gather 'round the Steinway in the elegant Sunset Lounge to sip premium teas, nibble fresh scones with Devon cream, and request "As Time Goes By."

Evening: A fantastic dining option is **Campanile**, which specializes in rustic Cal-Med cuisine in a dramatic historic setting. *Celebrated restaurants* come and go in L.A., but this one never leaves the A-list. Or you may prefer to make a whole night of it at the famous **Polo Lounge**. Stars and movie moguls have been schmoozing here since the whole Hollywood thing got going. Reserve a large, dark booth (hopefully dark enough to overlook the $140 price tag on the Beluga caviar) and order the flawless herb-crusted rack of lamb, the scrumptious sautéed whitefish, the marvelous penne with oolong tea–smoked free-range chicken ... Whatever. You're in the Polo Lounge. Clearly, you're a somebody. (No autographs please.) Linger over liqueurs and baked Alaska.

Classic Hollywood: The Hotels

Beverly Hills Hotel & Bungalows

9641 Sunset Blvd., Beverly Hills, 310-276-2251 / 800-283-8885
www.beverlyhillshotel.com

Chances are, at least a few of the stars immortalized on the Hollywood Walk of Fame showered in your room before cutting a deal in the Polo Lounge or the pool. Built in 1912 (and purchased, 75 years later, by the Sultan of Brunei for a cool $185 million) on 12 acres of prime real estate covered in palms and hibiscus, the "Pink Palace" has been an institution for Hollywood's rich and famous from the get-go. Two hundred and three rooms and suites (including the 21 legendary bungalows) are all accented in the hotel's signature palette of pinks, greens, apricots, and yellows. Custom furnishings include English-style sofas, canopied beds, '40s-style oval desks, and plush marble bathrooms. Most rooms also have fireplaces and balconies or patios. Recreation facilities include a full fitness center, an Olympic-size swimming pool, and tennis courts. $$$$

Chateau Marmont

8221 W. Sunset Blvd., West Hollywood, 323-656-1010 / 800-242-8328
www.chateaumarmont.com

Since 1927, L.A.'s homage to some castle in Amboise, France has been hiding above a curve at the top of the Sunset Strip—well, "hiding" the way that stars "hide" from the public. (Lots of Garbo- and De Niro–caliber guests have engaged in that very activity here.) With its lovely garden cafe, a funky attic exercise room, and a secluded, brick-decked pool court, this elegant yet quirky spot offers as much peace, privacy, and European-style charm as one could expect from a celebrity-studded chateau on the most frenzied stretch of Sunset Boulevard. If small doesn't charm you, avoid the standard rooms and opt for one of the suites with balconies and Shangri-la views of the Hollywood Hills. Or splurge on a Spanish-style garden cottage or a famous poolside bungalow. Renting bungalow #3 lets you stand in the very kitchenette where in 1940 Robert Mitchum fried bacon (much better than Bungalow #2, where John Belushi checked in and permanently checked out). Each of the Chateau's 63 rooms are uniquely decorated, ranging from Gothic and Arts and Crafts to Fabulous '50s. $$$

Hollywood Roosevelt Hotel

7000 Hollywood Blvd., Hollywood, 323-466-7000 / 800-950-7667
www.hollywoodroosevelt.com

The first Academy Awards were held in the Blossom Room here in 1929, and it took a merciful 15 minutes for the host, Douglas Fairbanks, to do the honors. An ambitious $15 million reno of this Spanish Colonial–style hotel firms up its reputation as Hollywood's best blast from the past. (Plans of boosting itself to a four-star establishment will see room rates bumped accordingly.) Some guests swear that Suite 1200 is haunted by Marilyn Monroe, and rumor also has it that Montgomery Clift is still learning his lines on the ninth floor. The hotel's 305 rooms include two dozen suites and 68 cabana rooms overlooking the pool. For impressive city views, opt for a room on one of the upper floors in the main 12-story building. There's also a complete fitness center and a new-and-improved Cinegrill supper club on the ground floor. $$

Hotel Bel-Air

701 Stone Canyon Rd., Bel-Air, 310-472-1211 / 800-648-4097
www.hotelbelair.com

Set on 12 acres of gorgeous grounds in L.A.'s most exclusive neighborhood, the Hotel Bel-Air's quiet reputation as the loveliest, most romantic hideaway in the city hasn't much budged in the last 50 years. Back in the day, folks like Cary Grant, Grace Kelly, and Jackie Gleason checked in here for some "me" time. Today's bigwigs are just as drawn to this dreamy Mission-style property with its cobbled paths, bubbling fountains, swan lake, and floral overload. Privacy is guaranteed in 91 uniquely-designed rooms and suites, all with private entrances from the garden or courtyard. Exquisite furnishings include romance enhancers like canopy beds, wood-burning fireplaces, and French doors opening onto intimate tiled patios. The oval-shaped pool and surrounding terrace with its spry attendants proffering premium waters, fresh fruits, and pink swan towels is an oasis within an oasis. The nearby fitness center, housed in a former cottage frequently checked into by Marilyn Monroe and Joe DiMaggio, is now filled with top-of-the-line cardio and muscle-toning equipment (open 24 hours). A destination unto itself, the hotel's bougainvillea-engulfed restaurant terrace will be forever considered one of L.A.'s most romantic spots for any meal. $$$$

Maison 140

140 S. Lasky Dr. Beverly Hills, 310-281-4000 / 800-342-5444

Silent movie star Lillian Gish would no doubt approve of the intimate and stylishly offbeat B&B that her old Beverly Hills residence has been transformed into (at least that's what the management—the same visionaries who reworked the nearby Avalon and Santa Monica's Viceroy—assures you). Lots of opposites attract at this warm pied-a-terre, a few doors down from the frosty Creative Artists Agency building and a quick zig-zag from Barneys and Saks. Unassuming on the outside, its ornate interior is a bold blend of French chandeliers, Far Eastern red-white-and-black, and breezy California touches—all for the right price, by Beverly Hills standards. Forty-four comfy individually-designed rooms include overstuffed French Bergère chairs, Frette Egyptian cotton linens, Philosophy toiletries, plus cordless phones, data ports, and media centers that somehow manage to gel nicely with the antiques. $$

Regent Beverly Wilshire Hotel

9500 Wilshire Blvd., Beverly Hills, 310-275-5200 / 800-427-4354
www.regenthotels.com

Elvis once called Suite #850 home. Warren Beatty crashed here for more than a decade. And on it goes. For 75 years, a celestial roster of celebs, dignitaries, and Hollywood location scouts have naturally gravitated to this icon of Beverly Hills opulence—now in Four Seasons hands—on the extortionate corner of Wilshire and Rodeo. Having received more face-lifts than most of its guests, the Beverly Wilshire is everything you've seen in *Pretty Woman* or *Beverly Hills Cop*, right down to the Italian tile bathrooms, sumptuous terry robes, silk hangers, and a new 5,000-square-foot, three-bedroom penthouse suite (a bargain $7,500 a night). This is the way Beverly Hills will always want to be seen. Three hundred ninety-five large and lavish rooms (120 of them suites) are divided between the hotel's Classical-style Wilshire Wing and the more contemporary Beverly Wing. Impeccable facilities include a full-service health spa, an Italian villa–style pool, and world-class dining. $$$$

Classic Hollywood: The Restaurants

Brighton Coffee Shop

9600 Brighton Wy., Beverly Hills, 310-276-7732

All-day breakfast, killer meatloaf, and good honest cups-a-joe. We're talkin' real food served on real honest-to-god Formica, and not an iota of attitude. Sometimes it just don't get no better in them glitzy Beverly Hills. *Open Mon.–Sat. 7 a.m.–5 p.m., Sun. 7 a.m.–3 p.m.* $

Campanile

624 S. La Brea Ave., Los Angeles, 323-938-1447

Long before chef-duo Mark Peel and Nancy Silverton turned this dramatic building into a James Beard Outstanding Restaurant, Charlie Chaplin scouted it as an office. Simply arriving at this heavenly setting with its towering ceilings, cloistered patio, and signature bell tower feeds you even before you sit down. So does the rustic Cal-Med menu, which changes daily, and the inspired wine list. *Open for lunch Mon.–Fri. 11:30 a.m.–2:30 p.m; dinner Mon.–Thurs. 6–10 p.m., Fri.–Sat. 5:30–11:00 p.m.* $$

Dan Tana's

9071 Santa Monica Blvd., West Hollywood, 310-275-9444

The Maitre d's name is Jimmy. The pricey menu's got a 16 oz. slab of meat named after Dabney Coleman. Jerry Seinfeld celebrated his 45th birthday here. So... you know, the place is first rate. The chicken parmigiana and lasagna are too, but what this West Hollywood fixture has always been known for is its steaks and its red leather booths crammed with bloodthirsty locals and Beverly Hills Goodfellas. There's just one kind of cow on the menu, Bub—the New York Strip. Just decide whether it'll be the twelve- or sixteen-ounce. *Open daily 5 p.m.–1 a.m.* $$

Du-Pars

Du-Pars, Farmers Market, 6333 W. Third St., 323-933-8446

The menu is unnecessarily long at this beloved restaurant/bakery at the gates of the Farmers Market. A piping stack of pancakes and a bottomless cup of joe is the only thing you really need to know. Homemade pies are a close second. Their other location in Studio City (see p. 48) is open much later. *Open Mon.–Fri. 6 a.m.–10:30 p.m., Sat.–Sun. 6 a.m.–11 p.m.* $

Hotel Bel-Air Restaurant

701 Stone Canyon Rd., Bel-Air, 310-472-1211

This Cal-French beauty wins the blue ribbon for romantic dining. Seasonal tasting menus change every Friday and are in the hands of executive chef Douglas Dodd, who spent years at Aspen's Little Nell before becoming something of a California purist—using only fresh indigenous herbs and produce in his exceptional dishes. There's a formal dining room inside but the casual terrace gets you closer to Bel-Air's version of the great outdoors, where a profusion of flowers fills the foreground and a pretty little pond with swans (not on the menu) the background. Sunday brunch ($48 per person) is a weekly highlight, featuring a page of exquisite appetizers and main courses. *Open daily for breakfast 7–9:30 a.m.; lunch noon–2 p.m.; dinner 6:30–9:30 p.m. Sun. brunch 11 a.m.–2 p.m.* $$$

Il Cielo

9018 Burton Way, Beverly Hills, 310-276-9990

If there's a greater aphrodisiac than rose crème brûlée with candied rose petals on a bed of white chocolate and raspberry sauce, we don't know about it. That's just the coup de grace at this ultra-romantic Italian charmer tucked away in a low-hype section of Beverly Hills. Ceiling frescoes, private nooks, and a fireplace in the cozy main dining room are upstaged by the alfresco settings—a pair of vine-shrouded patios in the front and back. Thankfully, the food is just as heart warming as the ambience. Bestsellers include fresh Maine lobster with hand-rolled fusili from Calabria, and a whole grilled branzino filleted at tableside. *Open for lunch Mon.–Sat. 11 a.m.–3 p.m.; dinner 6–11 p.m.* $$$

La Scala

434 N. Canon Dr., Beverly Hills, 310-275-0579

Twenty or thirty years ago, this time-honored Italian-lite restaurant was arguably the snooty power lunch spot in Beverly Hills. Age and a recent move (just a few doors up the street) has softened the place into a friendly local hangout for regulars who no longer bother lying about their age. The bread is warm, the pastas are tasty, but the place is still most famous for its chopped salads. *Open Mon.–Sat. 11:30 a.m.–10:00 p.m.* $$

Le Dome

8720 W. Sunset Blvd., West Hollywood, 310-659-6919

The Strip's most significant celebrity bistro celebrated its 25th anniversary with a complete $2-million overhaul. The new decor still includes those

great views in the back, and the menu sticks with the same coq au vin–type cuisine that has drawn everyone-who's-anyone here in the past.
Open Mon.–Sat. lunch 11 a.m.–2:30 p.m.; dinner 6–10 p.m. $$$

Miceli's

1646 N. Las Palmas St., Hollywood, 323-466-3438

Red-and-white checkered tablecloths, waiters bursting into song, autographed Chianti bottles everywhere, and a friendly bar where you can just be yourself. Now take that dream scene and locate it on a relaxed side-street half a block south of Hollywood Blvd. and—there you have it. Thankfully, not much has changed at Miceli's since 1949. The spaghetti and meatballs won't be just like Mama's, but it's easy to pretend they are at this homey joint.
Open Mon.–Thurs. 11:30 a.m.–11 p.m., Fri. 11:30 a.m.–midnight, Sat. 4 p.m.–midnight, Sun. 4–11 p.m. $

Morton's

8764 Melrose Ave., West Hollywood, 310-276-5205

One of the city's great power-grills, this classy, skylit room and veteran Cal-Continental hotspot run by Arnie (of the steakhouse chain) Morton's kin, Pam and Peter, is a reliable place to see stars and an even better place to dine like one. Service and food are just plain flawless, from Caesar salad to chocolate truffle cake. What's in between? Lots more good stuff, like sesame-crusted ahi with shiitake mushrooms, basmati rice, bok choy, and ponzu sauce, free-range lime-grilled chicken with shoestring potatoes, and a New York steak that would make Dad proud. *Open for lunch Mon.–Fri. noon–2:30 p.m.; dinner Mon.–Sat. 6–10 p.m.* $$$

Musso & Frank Grill

6667 Hollywood Blvd., Hollywood, 323-467-7788

Hollywood's oldest restaurant (est. 1919), with its cavernous booths, red-jacketed waiters, swivel-chair barstools, and dusty lamb chops will hopefully outlive us all. The hallowed dual dining rooms have hosted the guzzling of regulars like Faulkner, Fitzgerald, and Nathanael West, and the restaurant has watched its peers (like the Brown Derby and Mocambo) come and go. Musso's tough old flannel cakes are a popular breakfast item (served until 3 p.m.), and a couple of Bloody Marys makes for a nice lunch, thank you. Don't be surprised if you're drawn back for martinis and steak at sundown.
Open Tues.–Sat. 11 a.m.–11 p.m. $$

Pig 'n Whistle

6714 Hollywood Blvd., Hollywood, 323-463-0000

Clark Gable, Judy Garland, Shirley Temple, Loretta Young, and others held court here after their movie premieres next door at the Egyptian. Shuttered for years, a full restoration has granted this establishment its old Art Deco good-looks. There's a full Continental menu (but it still steers the eye toward a cheeseburger and pint of Bass) and a late-night bar scene. *Open daily 11:30 a.m.–10:30 p.m.; bar open until 2 a.m. most nights.* $

Polo Lounge

9641 Sunset Blvd., Beverly Hills, 310-276-2251

Even if you're not staying at the Beverly Hills Hotel, you can simply pretend that you are at this definitive leisure room for schmoozers and dealmakers. Savor divine Continental cuisine, sip premium cocktails, and—don't look now, but guess who's sitting over there. In this world-famous lounge, you're always in good—and usually recognizable—company. For an even steeper tab, visit the hotel's opulent newcomer, the Polo Grill. *Open daily 7 a.m.–11 p.m., appetizers until 1:30 a.m.; Sun. brunch 11 a.m.–3 p.m.* $$$

Smoke House

4420 Lakeside Dr., Burbank, 818-845-3731

Across the road from Warner Brothers Studios, this classic steakhouse is way older than anyone you know. It's said that both Gable and Bogart, on occasion, liked to order the liver here. Good food on a fairly-priced traditional American menu still makes this an off-Hollywood nerve center in the most nostalgic sense. Go easy on the garlic bread. *Open daily 11:30 a.m.–10:30 p.m.* $$

Yamashiro

1999 N. Sycamore Ave., Hollywood, 323-466-5125

People come to this Japanese perch in the Hollywood Hills for drinks and great views either before or after eating somewhere better. Originally built to house a private Asian art collection, this 90-year-old hilltop mansion remains one of Classic Hollywood's most storied properties, doing time as an exclusive club for silent movie idols like Lilian Gish and Roman Navarro. Today it's all about pricey courtyard dining beside koi ponds and—most of all—gulping down those sunset views from the lounge. No table reserv-ations. To ensure a window berth, be here for first seating, just after 5 p.m. *Open nightly 5 p.m.–2 a.m.* $$

Classic Hollywood: The Nightlife

The Bar at Hotel Bel-Air

701 Stone Canyon Rd., Bel-Air, 310-472-1211

You might half-expect one of Nancy Reagan's neighbors to ask to see your membership card at L.A.'s most refined hotel bar. In fact, this genial drinking den in the heart of Bel-Air is open to anyone who can behave themselves in polite, snifter-sipping society among visiting British gentry and others who look pretty in tweed. You'll get the whole leather armchair–peaty-scotch-by-the-fire–humidor-on-the-premises–suave-gent-tickling-the-ivories deal here. But don't bother to bring your bathing trunks unless you're checking in as a guest—a smashing idea, what? *Open Sun.–Thurs. 11 a.m.–12:30 a.m., Fri.–Sat. 11 a.m.–1:30 a.m*

The Conga Room

5364 Wilshire Blvd., Los Angeles, 323-938-1696

Tito Puente, Celia Cruz, and Chucho Valdez are some of the salsa legends who've graced the stage at The Conga Room, a caliente Latin club/scene that opened with a sizzle in 1998 and hasn't cooled down since. Star-fueled by co-owner Jimmy Smits, the two level club (dining downstairs, dancing upstairs) attracts a dressy crowd that isn't shy about strutting its stuff on the ballroom's large wooden floor. If you need to learn some salsa steps fast, show up at 8 p.m. for a one-hour lesson. It's free with admission. *Open Wed.–Sat. 7:30 p.m.–2 a.m.* $

Egyptian Theatre

6712 Hollywood Blvd., Hollywood, 323-466-3456

The Egyptian Theatre got a badly needed $14-million surgery in 1998, and now the place looks at least as good as it did when Sid Grauman was hosting screenings here of *Robin Hood* (the one starring Douglas Fairbanks Sr.). Predating Grauman's better-known Chinese Theatre (just down the block) by five years, this equally themey and ornate movie palace started into a tailspin right after premiering Barbra Streisand's *Funny Girl* (—coincidence?). Mothballed for years, the new home of the American Cinematheque screens a wide range of generally non-Hollywood films. For the full experience, book a guided afternoon tour of the theatre. An hour-long house documentary, *Forever Hollywood*, plays on Saturdays and Sundays at 2 and 3:30 p.m. $

Formosa Café

7156 Santa Monica Blvd., West Hollywood, 323-850-9050

Humphrey Bogart had a special place in his liver for the Formosa, as did Jack Benny and many other stars now stuck on the wall. Nearly torn down a decade ago, this 1929 converted railcar-that-could was saved by Hollywood preservationists who felt that its strong drinks, red banquette booths, and dog-eared wallpaper of 8x10 glossies were all worth fighting fiercely for. To show its appreciation, the perfunctory Chinese menu here has improved and a smoking patio has been added. Good for another hundred years. *Open daily 4 p.m.–2 a.m.* $

Grauman's Chinese Theatre

6925 Hollywood Blvd., Hollywood, 323-464-8111

Host to countless Hollywood premieres, the Oscars (briefly, in the '40s), and a celebrity-fossilized forecourt that needs no introduction, the Chinese is as impressive as most of the movies it now plays are not. To see this shrine in all of its fake-Orient glory, take the half-hour tour, which covers the main lobby, auditorium, VIP balcony, and backstage area. *Four tours daily between 10 a.m. and 3 p.m. Several screenings daily.* $

Hollywood Bowl

2301 N. Highland Ave., Hollywood, 323-850-2000

Former boxholders at this world-famous amphitheater include Mr. And Mrs. Cecil B. DeMille, Sid Grauman, and Charlie Chaplin. Vladimir Horowitz played here. Sinatra sang here. Fred Astaire danced here. Abbott and Costello and Monty Python did their shticks here. The Bowl is now home to its own resident orchestra and a stacked summer concert calendar. Come with a bottle of wine (and a seat cushion). Or, for the whole shebang, reserve box seats and have a gourmet meal delivered straight to you by the doting staff. *Open July–September.* $–$$$$

Pantages Theatre

6233 Hollywood Blvd., Hollywood, 323-468-1700

A $10 million restoration has revived this stunning Art Deco structure—home to the Academy Awards throughout the '50s—turning it into a top venue for Broadway musicals. Recent productions include *The Lion King* and *The Producers. Showtimes vary.* $$$$

Troubadour

9081 Santa Monica Blvd., West Hollywood, 310-276-6168

Some very famous bands and musicians have strummed, pounded, and screamed inside this wood-paneled rock 'n' roll shrine over the last five decades. But so have some very unfamous bands and musicians (for example, at the free Monday shows). No multimillion-dollar renovations here. The Troub is essentially what it's always been—a loud no-frills forum for local talent, flavor-of-the-month groups, and every now and then, a few legendary drop-ins. Blasting mainly alt-rock these days, the scene is friendly, and music fans of all ages are welcome. *Open nightly 8 p.m.–2 a.m.* $

The Wiltern

3790 Wilshire Blvd., Los Angeles, 213-388-1400

Built in 1931 and recently renovated, this classic Art Deco performance hall was actually on the chopping block not too long ago. Awful, considering that it's really the only good thing that has happened or ever will happen to the otherwise drab midtown intersection it graces. In a given month, performers as varied as Widespread Panic, Hall & Oates, Pat Benatar, Eddie Izzard, and Bela Fleck might be jamming under this 2,300-seat auditorium's sunburst ceiling (sadly, not all together). Bob Dylan, the Rolling Stones, Los Lobos, Bonnie Raitt, and Penn & Teller aren't strangers here either. *Box office open noon–6 p.m.* $$$

Classic Hollywood: The Attractions

Beverly Hills Trolley Tours

Rodeo Dr. and Dayton Wy., Beverly Hills, 310-285-2438

Meet your docent at the trolley stop on the northwest corner of Dayton and Rodeo for one of two educational spins through Beverly Hills. The 40-minute Sites and Scenes Trolley Tour features the city's most prominent attractions including Rodeo Drive. The 50-minute Art and Architecture Trolley Tour includes the Gagosian Gallery, the Beverly Hills City Hall, CAA, and the the Museum of Television & Radio. *Sites and Scenes, Sat. only on the hour from noon–4 p.m. during the spring and fall; Tues.–Sat. noon–5 p.m. on the hour during the summer. Art and Architecture, Sat. 11 a.m. from May–December.* $

Book City

6627 Hollywood Blvd., Hollywood, 323-466-2525

What looks like another dirty old bookshop along the Walk of Fame houses the city's best arsenal of Hollywood scripts and memorabilia. Need to look at an old *Will and Grace* or two before writing that spec script? Looking for something by Billy Wilder or the final draft of *My Cousin Vinny*? You're at the right place. It's also got a huge stock of autographed pictures, movie press kits, and lots of other industry junk. If you want to buy an actual book, it carries many of those too. *Open Mon.–Sat. 10 a.m.–10 p.m., Sun. 11 a.m.–8 p.m.*

Epicurean School of Culinary Arts

8759 Melrose Ave., West Hollywood, 310-659-5990

The CIA grads (that's Culinary Institute of America) who started this delicious school nearly 20 years ago believe that food, not music, is the "food of love." Fall back in love by taking a class with your partner here. Beginners and aspiring chefs alike come here for intensive programs that can run several weeks, but many one-day workshops are also offered that focus on just about anything you and your beloved haven't yet made together—Punjab-style chicken curry, spicy tuna rolls, or chocolate soufflé with crème anglaise—whatever tickles your taste buds. Classes are usually three hours long and, of course, some kind of a meal is always included. *Call for class times.* $$$$

Farmers Market
6333 W. Third St., Los Angeles, 323-933-9211

The apples aren't cheap and the east side of the market could often be mistaken for an outdoor geriatric ward. That said, this is one of the few places in Los Angeles upon which tourist buses and devout locals (who hate tourist buses) descend with equal enthusiasm. Just how time-honored a hangout is this casual maze of fruitmongers, open-air restaurants, and souvenir stalls? Walt Disney allegedly sat at a table here working on a design for Disneyland. For a sanitized browse, check out The Grove, a new outdoor shopping and entertainment center right next door. *Open Mon.–Fri. 9 a.m.–9 p.m., Sat. 9 a.m.–8 p.m., Sun. 10 a.m.–7 p.m.*

Frederick's of Hollywood Lingerie Museum
6608 Hollywood Blvd., Hollywood, 323-466-8506

Tucked in the back of Frederick Mellinger's flagship panty shop—a tradition since 1946—is this salute to the stars and their undergarments. Highlights include Mae West's nightgown, Ava Gardner's petticoat, an authentic Cyd Charisse leotard, and bras worn by Madonna, Cybill Shepherd, Shirley MacLaine, and Tony Curtis. *Open daily 10 a.m.–9 p.m.*

Greystone Park & Mansion
905 Loma Vista Dr., Beverly Hills, 310-550-4796

Believe it or not, you can actually pull into the driveway of the largest home ever built in Beverly Hills and not draw a squad of security cars. Sitting gray, empty, and most likely haunted on 16 acres of public grounds, the 55-room Greystone Mansion was built by oil baron Edward L. Doheny as a housewarming gift to his son, who lived here for all of six months before dying in a bizarre murder-suicide in 1929. The house (which has starred in many movies) is closed to the public, but the grounds are wide open, with nice hilltop views, plenty of grassy picnic space, and a labyrinth of old stairways, stone walkways, and secluded courtyards. Admission is free and parking is available within the gates. *Open daily 10 a.m.–5 p.m.*

Hollywood Entertainment Museum
7021 Hollywood Blvd., Hollywood, 323-465-7900

A museum on Hollywood Boulevard about movies and TV? Go figure. It's also the only one on this street to be taken more than half-seriously, going so far as to call its subject matter "the entertaining arts." About a century of film, television, and radio art is showcased here, including a number of memorabilia exhibits, multiscreen video presentations, and interactive displays demonstrating various facets of production, and a Foley Room where you can create your own sound effects. A reconstruction of a studio lot in the back includes famous sets from *Star Trek: The Next Generation* and *Cheers*. Visit the museum gift shop for old stage props and clothes worn by the stars. *Open 11 a.m.–6 p.m., closed Wednesdays during the winter.* $

Hollywood Forever Cemetery

6000 Santa Monica Blvd., Hollywood, 323-469-1181

Where are they now? Some of Tinseltown's biggest ex-living legends are resting in these peaceful old grounds in full view of the Hollywood Sign. Want some names? Rudolph Valentino, Douglas Fairbanks, Peter Lorre, Clifton Webb, Jesse Lasky, Janet Gaynor, and Darla & Alfalfa from *The Little Rascals. Open Mon.–Fri. 7 a.m.–7 p.m., Sat.–Sun. 7 a.m.–5 p.m.*

Hollywood Walk of Fame

Hollywood Blvd. and Vine St., Hollywood

Part publicity stunt, part tribute to great entertainers like Bob Hope and Big Bird, and part sorry-but-no-cigar to rejected applicants like Suzanne Somers—Hollywood's most famous roll of credits stretches along the sidewalks of Hollywood Blvd. between La Brea and Gower, and along Vine St. between Sunset and Yucca. More than 2,100 illustrious names in film, television, radio, recording, and live theatre are emblazoned on these bronze-and-marble stars, and it's amazing how many do not ring a bell. This year's new arrivals include Anthony Hopkins, Britney Spears, and Journey.

Hollywood & Highland

6801 Hollywood Blvd., Hollywood, 323-960-2331

Hollywood is back! At least this $700-million, 1.3 million-square-foot, five-story entertainment complex, modeled after D.W. Griffith's *Intolerance* set, with its 60-plus shops and restaurants, 640-room hotel, and gala Kodak Theatre (new home to the Academy Awards) would have you think so. Spoilsports may call it a glorified mall. But as far as Hollywood's latest renaissance goes, this may be as good as it gets.

Kodak Theatre

6801 Hollywood Blvd., Hollywood & Highland, Hollywood, 323-308-6300

The Oscars have had many homes over the years, but its grandest venue yet promises to be permanent. If you're not nominated for anything this year, you can still get inside for a variety of other shows ranging from Barry Manilow, Prince, and Harry Connick Jr. concerts to *Sesame Street Live* and American

Ballet Theatre performances of the *Nutcracker*. The best way to snoop around is on a guided tour, which includes a visit to the exclusive George Eastman VIP room (where those postshow Oscar parties are held) and an introduction to an Oscar statuette, presented to the Eastman Kodak Company in 1991. *Tours run daily every half-hour from 10:30 a.m.–2:30 p.m.* $

Paramount Pictures
5555 Melrose Ave., Hollywood, 323-956-5000

Unfortunately, public tours here were suspended after 9/11. For a quick fix, drive past the very recognizable Bronson or Melrose gates. For a longer one, attend a television taping. It'll get tedious once the novelty wears off, but at least you'll be standing inside the last major studio in Hollywood. Reservations can be made up to 30 days ahead by calling guest relations at 323-956-1777. *Shows usually start around 5 p.m. and run for 3–4 hours.*

Paramount Ranch
Paramount Ranch Rd., Agoura Hills 818-597-9192

In the 1920s, Paramount Pictures purchased this set piece of mountains, canyons, and creeks in the Santa Monica Mountains and turned it into a bustling Western movie factory—home of *Gunsmoke, Gunfight at the OK Corral,* and *The Adventures of Tom Sawyer.* Walk through the property's old Western Town façade and follow the chaparral-covered Coyote Canyon Trail to a quiet picnic ground with nice vistas. *Open daily 8 a.m.–sunset.*

Red Line Tours
6773 Hollywood Blvd., Hollywood, 323-402-1074

A small fry on the Hollywood tour circuit, Red Line leads one of the most personalized and informative walks through historic Hollywood. The standard tour includes inside access to Grauman's Egyptian Theatre, Disney's El Capitan Theatre, the Roosevelt Hotel, and Hollywood's last remaining speakeasy, hiding in a place you'd otherwise never find. Guides point out archeological highlights, spout local trivia, and provide good updates on Hollywood's billion-dollar resuscitation effort. Customized walks and tours of Downtown are also available. *Four Historic Hollywood tours daily between 10 a.m. and 4 p.m.* $

Rustic Canyon Golf Course

15100 Happy Camp Canyon Rd., Moorpark, 805-530-0221

Savvy golfers are happy to make the hike out to this top new public course, *Golf Digest*'s pick for Best New Affordable Course in the country and a recent host of Southern California's Amateur Championship. About 50 miles northwest of downtown Los Angeles, the 6,906 yard, par 72 is a testament to low-impact design, blending seamlessly into its broad 350-acre canyon and offering purists plenty of opportunities to outwit nature on the golf course. Don't be deceived by the 70-yard-wide fairway on the first tee and the relatively flat front nine. That all changes on the hilly back nine and 16th fairway alley. Tee times can (and should) be booked up to a week in advance. *Open daily, sunrise to sunset.* $$$

Silent Movie Theatre

611 N. Fairfax Ave., Hollywood, 323-655-2120

Hollywood's first generation of movie stars gets its due at this little gem that hails itself as "the last fully operational silent cinema in America." Sit back, give the live organist a warm welcome, enjoy some *Felix the Cat* cartoon openers, and gain an appreciation for pre-talkie legends like Rudolph Valentino, Mary Pickford, and Buster Keaton. *Open Tues.–Sat. at 8 p.m.; Sun. matinees at 1 p.m.* $

Spa Mystique

2025 Avenue of the Stars, Century City, 310-551-3251

The crown jewel of the Century Plaza Hotel's recent $70-million renovation is this 35,000-square-foot spa, stocked with more than 30 private treatment rooms and the Westside's largest menu of Asian-style health, relaxation, and beauty services. A feng shui expert was on call during the design of this elegant two-story building, which includes a pair of Japanese furo pools, a meditation garden, a salon and cafe, a state-of-the-art fitness center, and alarmingly relaxed guests milling around in kimonos. Nonguests, use the valet service at the side entrance on Constellation Blvd. *Open daily 8 a.m.–9 p.m.; last treatment is at 7 p.m.*

3rd Street Dance

8558 W. 3rd St., Los Angeles, 310-275-4683

Even if you're not getting hitched in two weeks, you need to know a few dance steps, just to be civilized. Steps of all kinds are taught at this top-notch dance school, which offers basic and advanced classes in salsa, swing, tango, ballroom, and other popular styles (if Viennese waltzes are your thing, the staff can usually accommodate special requests). Group classes usually run for several weeks, so book a private lesson and one of the school's five professional dance studios plus an instructor is all yours for an hour. Cedars Sinai Hospital is right across the street if you twist something. *Classes run Mon.–Thurs. 10 a.m.–10 p.m., Fri. 10 a.m.–6 p.m., 10:30 a.m.–5 p.m.* $$$$

Warner Brothers Studios
4000 Warner Blvd., Burbank, 818-954-1744 / 818-972-8687

Long before it belonged to AOL, this 110-acre dream factory in Burbank was churning out *Casablanca, Rebel without a Cause, Bonnie & Clyde, Dirty Harry, Chariots of Fire*, and countless other movies and TV productions. And the show at this busy lot goes on. Get behind the scenes on a two-hour VIP tour, which offers a candid look at life on the lot without the aid of a theme park ride. Warner's Deluxe Tour (Wednesdays only, at the moment) is twice as long and includes lunch. *Tours depart weekdays on the half hour, 9 a.m.–3 p.m.*

Will Rogers State Historic Park
1501 Will Rogers State Park Rd., Pacific Palisades, 310-454-8212

This former home of the famous cowboy humorist Will Rogers is now the only state park in the Santa Monica Mountains featuring a 31-room mansion and polo grounds. Back in the day, Rogers and buddies like Walt Disney, David Niven, and Gary Cooper mounted their ponies and gallivanted around the 186-acre estate's regulation-size polo field before retreating to the Beverly Hills Hotel's Polo Lounge for grub—which is allegedly how the place got its name. Players and spectators still gather here for Saturday games, but the real prize is a rejuvenating mile hike up to Inspiration Point, with its wide-angle views of the Westside and the Pacific Coast. Picnic grounds are down the hill by the parking lot. Don't forget to pay respects at the old Rogers ranch house (closed for renovation until late 2004). *Open daily 8 a.m.–sunset.* $

New Hollywood

Hollywood isn't a place—it's a myth, a symbol, a state of mind, an imaginary red carpet that's rolled out, soiled, and replaced every few years. Okay, so Hollywood actually is a place. You can read its sign, check out its theaters (dodge the junkies), drink in its bars, eat at Musso's, and have a copy of *Dianetics* forced into your hands. Then you can forget all that and enter the New Hollywood, which is harder to define geographically. It's a Never Never Land of West Hollywood velvet ropes, Burbank sound stages, Beverly Hills salons, Robertson Boulevard shops, and all those beautiful names you've heard or dreamt about: Spago, Skybar, The Ivy, and—admit it, Universal Studios. Who doesn't want to make inroads into this other Hollywood, the glamorous alter-ego to the rest of the world? Here's the latest road map.

New Hollywood: The Itinerary

Three Great Days and Nights

Day 1

Your Hotel: **The Peninsula Beverly Hills**

Morning: Start at the very top—on the Peninsula hotel's manicured *roof garden*, that is, where a dream world hovers above the city, including a 60-foot lap pool, a Jacuzzi, and a patio restaurant serving herbal tonics, teas, and nutritionist-certified spa cuisine. Grab a robe and slippers and savor the amenities, in whatever order you see fit.

Stroll into downtown Beverly Hills, and go straight for New Hollywood's jugular—*Rodeo Drive*. Lined with shops from the world's highest-end designers, this three-block Walk of Fashion Fame is great for people-watching (and for finding out just how much a pair of Italian gym shorts can cost). Prices drop, in theory, on neighboring Camden, Bedford, and Beverly Drives, where chichi shops, boutiques, and salons keep right on coming.

When dizziness sets in, caffeinate yourself at **Le Pain Quotidien**, a favorite European-style pastry and *latte stop* for models and just-botoxed BevHills soccer moms. For a classic 90210 coif, take your head over to the famous **Cristophe Salon**. Yep, that would be the same Cristophe who gave Bill Clinton his notorious $200 (or was it $300?) haircut. Now you can get one too, just not on Air Force One.

Afternoon: *Doing lunch* is one of the most important pastimes of the denizens of New Hollywood. Do yours at **Spago**, one of the all-time hottest of industry hot spots (try to get seated on the patio, but then act nonchalant about it). Or, for the über-power-lunch setting, book a table at **The Grill on the Alley**, the classic Beverly Hills schmooze site; be sure you've worked up a hearty appetite for chops and strawberry shortcake. A more casual option in the power-lunch bracket is **Barney Greengrass**, the top floor deli at Barney's department store.

After dining with the movers and shakers, take a closer look at their work. The **Museum of Television & Radio** is a *media library* like no other, stocked with more than 100,000 programs spanning eight decades of magic-making. Step into a private console where you can tune in to almost anything you'd like, from an old *Tonight* show interview to that one elusive *Gilligan's Island* episode you missed.

Evening: After you've repaired to you hotel to freshen up, have a drink, and don your evening duds, join the Hollywood dining cognoscenti at one of the "of the moment" restaurants spread among Beverly Hills, West Hollywood, and Third Street. **Dolce** and **Ago** are a slick pair of *celebrity-owned restaurants* known for their famous regulars as well as for their carefully-prepared Italian food. High-end Vietnamese cravings are best satisfied at **Crustacean**, a happening dining destination in downtown Beverly Hills where celebs have a separate entrance and their own commoner-free dining rooms upstairs. Or you can share small delicate portions of French-Mediterranean cuisine and explore a superb wine bar at **A.O.C.**, Third Street's hottest newcomer.

After dinner, for *every imaginable sort of martini* and a laid-back scene, drop by **Lola's**. For DJs, dancing, and—yes—chocolate fondue with a stylin' Westside crowd, head over to **Joya** in downtown Beverly Hills. Cap off the evening with a nightcap back at your hotel in the Peninsula's handsome **Club Bar**, abuzz with after-hours showbiz glitterati.

Day 2

Morning: Enjoy the bounty of room service, and then, since this is New Hollywood, you need *"me" time* each and every day. Take full advantage of the Peninsula's diverse menu of decadent spa treatments, from Hot Rock or Crystal therapy to Rosemary Body Micro Dermabrasion.

Then, it's time to get in touch with nature (yes, that's possible in Hollywood). There aren't any fairways in Beverly Hills (at least without tall hedges and private gates), but tidy **Rancho Park Golf Course** across from the 20th Century Fox lot is in close range. If you don't golf and aren't about to start, make like the celebs and go for a hike—or, well, a *hike lite*. For a pleasant morning ramble and possible run-ins with stars and their canine companions, head over to Hollywood's **Runyon Canyon Park**.

Afternoon: Start with lunch and—do you dare? Yes—***a martini on the front porch at*** **The Ivy**. This is where Danny DeVito ordered off the menu and then left before the food arrived in the movie *Get Shorty*. It's also where real-life stars come when they're craving chopped salads, crab cakes, and extra exposure. A more casual and equally popular choice is directly across the street at the **Newsroom Café**, where stars, players, vegans, and mere mortals can sip smoothies and order from a fun, health-conscious menu.

Head over the hill to **NBC Studios** for a ***70-minute walking tour*** that aims to educate, entertain, and—most of all—to make Must-See-TV-watchers of us all. Return to the *Tonight* show auditorium, this time as an audience member, for a taping with host Jay Leno and special guests (a word to the wise: reserving well in advance is better than lining up at dawn).

For the more culturally inclined, explore one of L.A.'s most stunning artistic achievements, **The Getty Center**. There are enough masterpieces inside these stone edifices to exhaust several visits. Check your type-A personality at the door and take time to savor the ***art and architecture*** and the divine gardens with excellent views.

If you're looking for an elevated experience at sundown, head to Van Nuys airport and hook up with **Heli USA** for a privileged trip around town in a ***chartered helicopter***. For once, you can gaze down at all those little people fenced in Bel-Air estates and soar above the Hollywood Sign and Universal Studios.

Evening: Make a fashionably late dinner reservation at the white-hot **White Lotus**, one of Hollywood's latest ***see-and-be-seen restaurants*** and clubs. The fusion menu lets you go from dim sum to duck-leg confit and back again, and the convenient club scene means you can settle in for the evening. Or, take a tropical turn with your evening and dine on Cuban delicacies at the equally trendy **Paladar** before moving the party to the swinging club next door, **Nacional**. It wouldn't be right not to mention at least a few very happening picks from Beverly Blvd.'s emerging restaurant row. For New American haute cuisine, book a banquette at **Grace**. For classic American comfort food, park your appetite at **EM Bistro**.

How to finish off your evening? Different strokes for different folks. If you're still needing a *nightclub fix* and are craving a monolithic DJ scene, enter the futuristic world of **Ivar**. If, on the other hand, you're more in the mood to watch burlesque with a well-heeled Hollywood "in" crowd, reserve well ahead at **Forty Deuce**. For a more no-nonsense skin experience, dive right in to **Deep**, Hollywood's hottest go-go scene. Late diners can grab a booth at **Kate Mantilini**, a power-agent's version of a diner, serving cocktails and a huge variety of American comfort food until 2 a.m. on weekends.

Day 3

Morning: Grab an *outdoor table* at **Clafoutis**, over at the Sunset Plaza, where breakfasting is best done in your shades and on your cell. Then, wouldn't you know it, one of L.A.'s hottest spas and skincare specialists is right around the back. A trip to **Ole Henriksen Face/Body** clinic gets you exfoliated to within an inch of your life in a soothing, zen-like setting. It will start you thinking about your skin the way movie stars do, which you'll need to do if you want to be mistaken for one.

The *Sunset Strip*, it ain't what it used to be. And who knows what it will be years from now? But you can always count on this ever-changing roster of bars, clubs, roadhouses, boutiques, cafes, comedy stages, exclusive pool decks, hot restaurants, tattoo parlors, sex shops, bookstores, photo studios, pancake houses, doggie daycare centers, psychic hucksters, wellness spas, and personal-trainer billboards to dominate L.A. lore. Spend some time getting acquainted with the city's most attention-grabbing thoroughfare, between Laurel Canyon and Doheny Drive.

Settle down with the industry crowd for lunch at **Fenix at The Argyle**, where culinary-fusion magic is performed on the historic *hotel patio*, which also offers great city views. (If you end up here in the evening instead, dining privileges include entrance into the hotel's popular lounge.)

Afternoon: Onward to one of the most important hubs of New Hollywood, **Universal Studios Hollywood**. Get the most pampered close-up of the world's largest movie studio with a VIP Experience Pass, which provides two hours of access. Then breeze over to the latest *movie-inspired rides* and shows in the theme park (your VIP Pass lets you bypass the lines). After that? Decompress, sort of, next door at Universal Citywalk, a surreally bright-and-shiny-L.A.–themed happy trail of restaurants, clubs, theaters, and stores. For one comfortably numb moment, you may start to think L.A. is a squeaky clean small world after all. (If you want more time at Universal Studios, shave down the morning's itinerary and come for a full day. The hours do fly by.)

Evening: Fix yourself up and hustle yourself down to the sleek, chic Mondrian hotel's *hot Latin-Asian* fusion restaurant **Asia de Cuba**. Between the mojitos and the endless eye candy, it won't matter whether you've managed to wrangle a table on the famous patio or are seated in the sleek, narrow dining room. After dinner, linger over a few pricey cocktails at the hotel's exclusive *poolside scene*, **Skybar**, and drink out of plastic cups with beautiful, plastic people (separate reservations are required; alternately, you can stake out a space on the pool deck before 8 p.m., when the velvet rope comes out). Other dining options? Look right across the street. The city's hottest new sushi and robata restaurant, **Katana** is opposite the Mondrian. If reservations fail here, **Koi** is another happening scene where you can sample sake cocktails and creative Japanese cuisine. For New Hollywood's sublime take on a romantic evening, try the courtyard at the luscious **Little Door**, featuring Mediterranean cuisine served with a heavy French accent.

You've eaten. You're thirsty and you're restless. And you've forgotten where you parked. You're ready to grease many a doorman's palm to fully experience the Sunset Strip's premium bar scene. For the ultimate in velvet-rope cachet and pea-soup-thick attitude, smooth-talk your way into **Barfly**. For less hype and more possible *rock-star sightings*, squeeze onto the late-night guest list at the **Whiskey Bar**. For a suaver setting, great martinis and more star power, hit **Bar Marmont**. If you still can't remember where you parked, who cares?

New Hollywood: The Hotels

The Argyle

8358 W. Sunset Blvd., West Hollywood, 323-654-7100 / 800-225-2637
www.argylehotel.com

The fact that this 1929 Art Deco masterpiece was actually on the chopping block 25 years ago says something about the Sunset Strip in the late '70s. Fortunately, it was spared and has been revitalized into one of the city's most sophisticated properties, with 64 stunning rooms, suites, split-level townhouses, and an eye-popping pair of penthouses all far nicer even than the pleasure pads Errol Flynn, John Wayne, and Howard Hughes used to crash in when the place was called the Sunset Tower. Deco Guest Rooms include a queen bed, a marble bath, and unbeatable floor-to-ceiling window views. Up it a notch and get a Deco Suite, which comes with a full living room and separate master bedroom with a king bed. Deco Grand Suites throw in a formal dining room and, in most cases, an extra guest bath with a steam shower. With its hip fusion restaurant, Fenix, downstairs and an exclusive pool with great cityscapes on its rooftop, it's clear that this edifice's hard times are far behind it. $$$

Four Seasons Hotel Los Angeles at Beverly Hills

300 South Doheny Dr., Beverly Hills, 310-273-2222 / 800-332-3442
www.fourseasons.com

As 90210 as any hotel in Beverly Hills, the five-diamond Four Seasons exists in its own quiet residential pocket, providing easy access to but also relief from Rodeo Drive and the nearby Beverly Center. The lobby's outstanding floral displays and 24-hour concierge service is pure Four Seasons. Furnished in tasteful pastels, the 285 well-appointed guest rooms and suites provide extra-stuffed Sealy mattresses, Heavenly linens, marble bathrooms, and French doors opening out to balconies that, in the lavish upper suites, wrap around for full panoramic views. Guests converge on the fourth floor terrace with its always-80-degree lap pool, a Jacuzzi, a fully-equipped fitness center, and a poolside grill specializing in lite spa cuisine. A 4,000-square-foot spa is a recent addition, stocked with eight treatment rooms and a range of sybaritic options, from the signature Punta Mita Massage and Margarita Salt Scrub to one of the most raved-about 75-minute facials in town. Gardens restaurant serves award-winning Cal-Med cuisine in a tranquil indoor/outdoor setting. Windows lounge is known for its martinis and its schmoozing industry regulars. $$$$

Luxe Hotel Rodeo Drive

360 N. Rodeo Dr., Beverly Hills, 310-273-0300 / 800-468-3541
www.luxehotels.com

Just how Rodeo Drive is this boutique hotel smack in the Golden Triangle? How does a pair of Valentino boutiques—his and hers—right inside the building grab you? If you're looking for an oversized room and lots of great on-site facilities, truth be told, this compact little gem from the Luxe gang doesn't fit the bill. But for the novelty of living right above one of the world's most famous fashion districts in a classy, somewhat European-style setting, it can't be beat. Eighty-eight charming guest rooms and suites feature Frette linens, DSL, CD players, a small desk, and well-appointed bathrooms with signature robes. Deluxe rooms have either balconies or Rodeo Drive views. Café Rodeo, the hotel's small restaurant, serves fresh Cal-cuisine in an intimate setting from morning to night. $$$

Mondrian

8440 W. Sunset Blvd., West Hollywood, 323-650-8999 / 800-525-8029
www.mondrianhotel.com

Some 12-story apartment buildings have all the luck. If not for its location smack in the middle of the Sunset Strip, this once-drab bit of '50s architecture probably wouldn't have won the attention of über-hotelier Ian Schrager and designer Philippe Starck about a decade ago. As it stands, a total makeover turned it into a chic magnet for celebrities, industry power players, and the people who love being near them. Enter the Mondrian's lobby with its diaphanous curtains and almost ridiculously attractive and radiant clerks, and you can practically smell Hugh Grant's cologne. The 240 guest rooms are spare—or perhaps you'd say minimalist, depending on how you view your half-glasses. The white, beige, and gray color scheme and a sparcity of furnishings are just part of the design team's "uncomplicated sophistication" approach, which is as deliciously pretentious as it sounds. But with oversized bathrooms, kitchenettes (in the suites), and floor-to-ceiling glass walls offering excellent views, who's complaining? Two of L.A.'s hottest destinations, Skybar and Asia de Cuba, are right here—and if you're a privileged hotel guest, you're as good as in. $$$

The Peninsula Beverly Hills

9882 S. Santa Monica Blvd., Beverly Hills, 310-551-2888 / 800-462-7899
www.peninsula.com

A spectacular French Renaissance–style property hiding on the edge of the Golden Triangle, The Peninsula by most accounts is tied with the Hotel Bel-Air (see p. 75) for the title of top hotel. Never mind the courtesy Rolls Royce service—a quick zigzag on foot leads you straight to Rodeo Drive for that emergency trip to Tiffany's or Louis Vuitton. Best of all, the hotel's secluded grounds are near all the glitz yet feel far removed. Lose a day up at the rooftop pool and spa; luxuriate over afternoon tea and superb Cal-cuisine at the Belvedere Restaurant; and revel in the fact that all those Hollywood agents infesting the Club Bar will have to go home at some point. One hundred ninety-six lavish guest rooms (36 suites and 16 private villas) include custom and antique furnishings, marble bathrooms with oversized tubs, Italian linens, and French doors looking out on lovely gardens. A 24-hour check in/check out policy means there's really no such thing as arriving late here. $$$$

Raffles L'Ermitage Beverly Hills

9291 Burton Way., Beverly Hills, 310-278-3344 / 800-323-7500
www.lermitagehotel.com

Just before residential Burton Way curves into Little Santa Monica Blvd. and downtown Beverly Hills, there it is—a five-star, five-diamond 90210 boutique hotel that you can drive right past every day and somehow never notice. That's just how the entertainment and recording industry fat cats who hole up in this gorgeous eight-story sanctuary would like it to stay: kind of hidden, yet just around the corner from everything. Tasteful contemporary Euro-Asian decor meets state-of-the-art technology in the 124 double-size guest rooms, which include large separate living and work spaces, plus a vanity area stocked with Aveda products and your choice of terry or plain cotton robes. French doors open onto private balconies with mountain or city views. Rooms come with 40-inch TVs, CD/DVD players with Bose speakers, DSL, five phone lines, a cell phone for use during your stay, and a panel of bedside controls that has everything but a steering wheel. Outstanding facilities include a full-service spa, a state-of-the-art fitness center, a rooftop pool with private cabanas, and a French-Indochine restaurant, Jaan. $$$$

New Hollywood: The Restaurants

A.O.C.

8022 W. 3rd St., Los Angeles, 323-653-6359

Occasionally, Third Street's restless roster of "hot new restaurants" produces one with enough style and substance to make it through one year and draw an even hungrier crowd the next. Enter A.O.C., the latest A-list hangout on this mini restaurant row. There's enough style sitting at the wine bar and enough substance in the cheese menu alone to beat the odds. Delicate small-plate creations on the revolving menu—a French take on tapas—are meant to be savored and shared. The menu starts with a robust list of cheese and charcuterie selections, followed by fish, meat, and wood-burning–oven dishes that might include seared albacore with shell beans and bottarga, lamb skewers with carrot purée and cumin yogurt, or steamed fingerlings with crème fraiche. More than 50 wines are available by the bottle, carafe, glass, or even half-glass. The main scene is at the bar and in the sleek main dining room; for a more intimate setting, request a table upstairs on the back patio (where the no-smoking rule still applies). *Open Mon.–Fri. 6–11 p.m., Sat. 5:30–11 p.m., Sun. 5:30–10 p.m.* $$

Ago

8478 Melrose Ave., West Hollywood, 323-655-6333

This trendy trattoria in West Hollywood has enjoyed a constant buzz ever since word somehow got out (on day one, seven years ago) that Robert De Niro and a handful of other movie types had a piece of the place. Thankfully, Ago isn't resting on these laurels alone. Power-lunchers (and-dinner-ers) don't mind paying a little extra to savor perfectly done pastas, risottos, grilled fish, and chef Agostino Sciandri's signature bistecca alla Fiorentina (a 22-ounce Angus T-bone steak prepared in the wood-burning oven). If you pick the right evening, you'll be dining with the in-crowd and usually some guest stars. On weekend nights (which seems to include Wednesdays and Thursdays here) don't think of walking into this discreet-from-the-outside/happening-on-the-inside, split-level dining room without a reservation. Alfresco fans can ask/beg for a table on the leafy patio. *Open for lunch Mon.–Fri. noon–2:30 p.m.; dinner Mon.–Sat. 6–11:30 p.m., Sun. 6–10:30 p.m.* $$

Asia de Cuba

8440 W. Sunset Blvd., West Hollywood, 323-848-6000

The Hollywood scene at this Asian-Latin eatery is everything you'd expect from a dining room in the trendy Mondrian. For starters (besides all that eye candy, the tasty mojitos, and the great views) try the calamari salad or the restaurant's signature oxtail spring rolls. Favorite entrees (like hacked lime-and-garlic chicken and Hunan-wok crispy whole fish stuffed with crab escabeche) arrive in let's-share portions, as do some very decadent desserts. Food is served either in the chic narrow dining room or out on the hotel's famous patio area. Contrary to what you might hope, dining here does not get you into the Mondrian's ultrachic poolside bar, Skybar. *Open for breakfast daily 7–11 a.m.; lunch 11:30 a.m.–3:30 p.m.; dinner Mon.–Thurs. 5:30–11:30 p.m., Fri.–Sat. 5:30–p.m.–1 a.m., Sun. 5:30–10:30 p.m.* $$

Barney Greengrass

9570 Wilshire Blvd., 5th Floor, Beverly Hills, 310-777-5877

This fancy-ish deli on the top floor of Barneys in downtown Beverly Hills is your best shot at noshing on chicken matzo ball soup, pickled herring or, for that matter, $165 Beluga caviar beside someone sort-of-famous. The biggest hit here is the smoked fish—sturgeon, Nova Scotia salmon, sable, whitefish, house-cured gravlox—all flown in from the Big Apple and served a la carte or beside a mess of eggs any style. Top deli sandwiches include the smoked fish club (Nova Scotia Salmon, sturgeon, cream cheese, sprouts, and avocado) and the straight-out-of-New-York pastrami sandwich piled high on a rustic roll with slaw on the side. Top non-deli desserts include German chocolate cake and Apple Strudel. If you're looking for the traditional brown naugahyde deli with waitresses who call you "honey," Nate 'n Al's is just up the street (310-274-0101). *Open Mon.–Wed. 8:30 a.m.–6 p.m., Thurs.–Fri. 8:30 a.m.–7 p.m., Sat. 9 a.m.–7 p.m., Sun. 9 a.m.–6 p.m.* $

Clafoutis

8630 W. Sunset Blvd., West Hollywood, 310-659-5233

What could be better than lounging in shades at a sidewalk table on the swankier end of Sunset with a plate of eggs or a salade Niçoise seated beside a bunch of Europeans yapping on their cells? Experience it for yourself at this popular recently reopened Cal-French bistro at the Sunset Plaza. The tireless menu runs all the way from a Paris ham and Swiss cheese omelet with a fresh croissant to a grilled filet mignon with garlic spinach and herbed potatoes topped with a brandy peppercorn sauce. Marvelous people watching is also served all day. *Open daily 11:30 a.m.–11 p.m.* $

Crustacean

9646 Little Santa Monica Blvd., Beverly Hills., 310-205-8990

Sure, there's an epidemic of hot fusion restaurants in L.A. But only one has a long koi-filled aquarium walkway leading into its main dining room and a famously secret kitchen where prized family recipes from the old country (French Colonial Vietnam) are heavily guarded. Euro-Asian Crustacean is a phenomenon even by Beverly Hills standards. Try the signature roasted Dungeness crab in garlic sauce and you'll understand why the recipe is padlocked. Major celebrities flock to the side entrance and eat amongst themselves upstairs. Let them. The garlic noodles, lobster in tamarind sauce, and that amazing crab are just as ambrosial down below. *Open for lunch Mon.–Fri. 11:30 a.m.–2:30 p.m.; dinner Mon.–Thurs. 5:30–10:30 p.m., Fri.–Sat. 5:30–11:30 p.m.* $$$

Dolce

8284 Melrose Ave., West Hollywood, 323-852-7174

Not even constant press or a flaming backlit bar can fully guarantee a trendy restaurant's future. But this chic young Italian eatery co-owned by Hollywood stallion Ashton Kutcher is the place to dine among stars like Ashton, his girlfriend-du-jour Demi Moore, and their cohorts. Heavy on the leather and marble, the main dining room is lined with spacious booths built for VIPs and a candlelit patio that feels more like a room with no ceiling. The classic Italian menu may be secondary to the scene, but it holds up admirably. Diners on a budget or a diet can opt for smaller bites by requesting the separate Enoteca tasting menu. Thursdays through Saturdays, DJs arrive after the plates are cleared, so stay a while and soirée with the stars. *Open nightly 6 p.m.-2 a.m.* $$

EM Bistro

8256 Beverly Blvd., Los Angeles, 323-658-6004

Craving some classic and classy American comfort food? This of-the-moment white-linen dining room hits the spot with its succinct but substantial menu of hearty meat and seafood dishes. Best-sellers include port-raised beef short ribs served with soft polenta and broccolini, horseradish-crusted salmon with couscous and roasted root vegetables, grilled lake superior whitefish with roasted shiitake and corn succotash, and a good ol' bistro burger covered with bacon and Gruyère. Save room for an indulgent black & tan (that's chocolate and butterscotch) pudding swirl spiked with whipped cream and English toffee or an apple brown butter tart with blackberry sauce and crème fraiche. *Open Mon.–Thurs. 6–10 p.m., Fri.-Sat. 6–11 p.m.* $$

Fenix at The Argyle
8358 W. Sunset Blvd., West Hollywood. 323-848-6677

If the stylish industry crowd in the Argyle's Deco dining room doesn't arouse you, surely the Tuna Three Ways, the Heavenly Soup with Lemongrass, or the "Rock" of Lamb Baked in Terra Cotta (the clay is broken at tableside) will. Here's one more sexy young fusion kitchen in L.A. to put on your short list. Privileges of dining here include entrance into the Argyle's popular lounge with views from the poolside patio. *Open daily 7 a.m.–10 p.m.* $$

Grace
7360 Beverly Blvd., Los Angeles, 323-934-4400

A warm and inviting place bathed in earth tones and furnished with comfy banquettes, Grace leads Beverly Blvd.'s latest dining renaissance with a creative New American menu from renowned local chef Neal Fraser. The menu at this hit newcomer changes regularly, but keep an eye out for the Dungeness crab salad appetizer, halibut wrapped in Swiss chard, grilled Hawaiian ono, braised New Zealand lamb shank, and tenderloin of wild boar. *Open Tues.–Thurs. 5:30–11 p.m., Fri.–Sat. 5:30 p.m.–midnight, Sun. 5:30–10 p.m.* $$

The Grill on the Alley
9560 Dayton Way (Wilshire Blvd.), Beverly Hills, 310-276-0615

There's a time and a place to drink martinis, eat chicken pot pie, and order strawberry shortcake, seated next to a table full of showbiz gods and monsters. That time is around midday. That place is at this power-lunch capital of Beverly Hills. If you just got bumped from the next open table, it's probably because David Geffen or his equivalent just walked through the door. Dinner (seven days a week) is also a scene in this dignified and clubby dining den. Reservations are always recommended. *Open Mon.–Thurs. 11:30 a.m.–11 p.m., Fri.–Sat. 11:30 a.m.–midnight, Sun. 5–9 p.m.* $$$

The Ivy
113 N. Robertson Blvd., Beverly Hills, 310-274-8303

It would be hard to invent a more contrived movie set than the raised front porch at The Ivy, with its white picket fence, chintz-covered chairs, conspicuous cars by the curb, and celebrity guests stopping by to make an entrance and pay big money for crab cakes or a chopped salad. However you play it on this tasty New American stage, it's a jolly good show. *Open Mon.–Fri. 11:30 a.m.–10 p.m., Sat.–Sun. 10:30 a.m.–10 p.m.* $$$

Katana

8439 W. Sunset Blvd., West Hollywood, 323-650-8585

A high concept in all regards, this instant hit from the Sushi Roku gang manages to rise above the Sunset Strip while remaining firmly rooted in it. Walk up the stone steps to the lovely Piazza del Sol building, into this brilliantly done Japanese eatery on the first floor. Into the late hours, you'll find a crowd of industry types and in-the-know yuppies plowing through tasty skewers of robatayaki (traditional open-flame cooking) and realizing just how much tastier a spear of filet mignon wrapped in fois gras and asparagus is than a slab of raw fish—which is also widely consumed here too. For a show with dinner, sit at the robata bar, where a crew of busy chefs always find time to yell cheerful greetings and farewells to guests. Drinks and sushi selections are $5 during weekday happy hours (5:30–7 p.m.) *Open Sun.–Mon. 6–11 p.m., Tues.–Wed. 6–11:30 p.m., Thurs.–Sat. 6 p.m.–12:30 a.m.* $$

Kate Mantilini

9101 Wilshire Blvd., Beverly Hills, 310-278-3699

Before Beverly Hills gets out of bed and long after it lies back down, this stylish neighborhood diner is wide awake, serving reliably tasty upscale breakfasts, salads, pastas, and sandwiches to the town's movers and shakers. The famous calves' brains have recently been pulled from the menu, either in honor of regular lunch guest Billy Wilder's passing or because he was the only one who ordered them. Highlights include seared ahi medallions, a perfect chicken breast sandwich with basil and aioli, and the turkey Cobb. *Open Mon. 7:30 a.m.–midnight, Tues.–Thurs. 7:30 a.m.–1 a.m., Fri. 7:30 a.m.–2 a.m., Sat. 11 a.m.–2 a.m., Sun. 10 a.m.–midnight.* $

Koi

730 N. La Cienega Blvd., Los Angeles, 310-659-9449

Sushi snobs might not be as taken with this stylin' Japanese joint as are the trend-conscious bunch who flock here to sip sake martinis on the firelit patio, but don't knock it 'til you try it. Catering perfectly to its young Hollywoodish audience and feng shui'd just so, Koi is a seriously hip place to linger over sea urchin, shiitake tempura, and an assortment of Cal-inflected signature entreés to further tempt the taste buds. Hot dishes include black cod bronzed with miso, jumbo soft shell crab with ponzu sauce, and Alaskan king crab legs with garlic butter. Make weekend reservations fashionably late (not before 9 p.m.), at least a few days in advance. *Open for lunch Mon.–Fri. 11:30 a.m.–2:30 p.m.; dinner Mon.–Thurs. 6:30–11 p.m., Fri.–Sat. 6:30 p.m.–midnight, Sun. 6:30–10 p.m.* $

Le Pain Quotidien

9630 Little Santa Monica Blvd., Beverly Hills, 310-859-1100

A vital niche has been filled by this imported boulangerie chain, with its quaint atmosphere and great crusty loaves. For a split second, you've stepped out of Beverly Hills and into Brussels or Paris. Then you're back just as fast, clearly breaking bread (or, more likely, homemade pastries) with the local facelifted gentry. Hearty country-style breakfasts are served along with a wide variety of salads, soups, and gourmet sandwiches. *Open Mon.–Fri. 7 a.m.–7 p.m., Sat.–Sun. 7:30 a.m.–7:00 p.m.* (Two additional locations are in Brentwood at 11702 Barrington Ct. and West Hollywood at 8607 Melrose Ave., different opening hours.) $

The Little Door

8164 W. 3rd St., West Los Angeles, 323-951-1210

The door may be little, but it's what's behind it (and the buff attendant blocking the way) that counts. Reservations are a must at this white-hot French-Mediterranean charmer that doesn't deign to hang a sign out front. If you're on the list, the door opens onto a fabulous canopied patio where young, beautiful people smoke and laugh and drink and propose to each other between mouthfuls of mussels. Hustling French waiters are as charming as can be, right up to the presentation of the sobering bill. Beyond the patio is a tighter crunch of indoor tables strewn with rose petals. Unless you like eavesdropping, request a patio berth up front. *Open Sun.–Thurs. 6–10 p.m., Fri.–Sat. 6–11:00 p.m.; Sun. brunch 11 a.m.– 3 p.m.* $$$

Newsroom Café

120 N. Robertson Blvd., West Hollywood, 310-652-4444

While folks across the street at The Ivy invest in their fancy-pants salads and bisque, you can read a magazine, open a laptop, and take a seat at this tasty and healthy lunch scene featuring Indonesian gado gado, grilled vegetable chop-chop, smoked tofu with mixed organic field greens and—our personal favorite—homemade soup in a big ol' multigrain bread bowl. While the menu takes its health consciousness seriously enough to include several vegan items and a message right at the top to "stop poisoning your body with bad food," it's not all about organic oatmeal, wheatgrass, and basmati rice pudding here. The Newsroom's smart menu includes lots of "fun" stuff for people without yoga mats too—think grilled ahi burger, house-smoked chicken quesadilla, spicy noodles diablo, and a chocolate espresso brownie served with cappuccino crunch ice cream. It would be wrong not to mention the fire-grilled artichoke appetizer, which is simple and great. Lunch can be a wait, and midday reservations aren't taken, so prepare to put your name on the list and browse the restaurant's in-house magazine rack for awhile. *Open Mon. 8 a.m.–9 p.m., Tues.–Thurs. 8 a.m.–9:30 p.m., Fri. 8 a.m. –10 p.m., Sat. 9 a.m.–10 p.m., Sun. 9 a.m.– 9:30 p.m.* $

Paladar

1651 Wilcox Ave., Hollywood, 323-465-7500

Unless some Hollywood up-and-comer has booked all 60-or-so table settings for a private Old Havana–style soiree, you too can sqeeeze into this tight, steel grill–partitioned room wallpapered with glossy tobacco leaves. Come here expecting inspired rum drinks, meaty Cuban fare, and a very happening scene. After dinner, should you line up next door at the equally hot Cuban nightclub Nacional? You bet your yucca mash. *Open Mon.–Fri. 11:30 a.m. –11 p.m., Sat.–Sun. 5:30–11:30 p.m.* $

Spago

176 N. Cañon Dr., Beverly Hills, 310-385-0880

Everyone knows the word Spago, at least as a synonym for the Hollywood high life. It's also the epicenter of Wolfgang Puck and wife Barbara Lazaroff's culinary empire, and the same hallowed spot that half of L.A.'s glitterati will be fighting over for patio reservations come dinnertime. Go for the tasting menu or choose from a broad selection of American, Asian, and European entreés. Outdoor courtyard seating is the most coveted, but for action-packed views into the open kitchen, head to the back tables inside. *Open for Lunch Mon.–Fri. 11:30 a.m.–2:15 p.m., Sat. noon–2:15 p.m.; dinner Sun.–Thurs. 5:30–10 p.m., Fri.–Sat. 5:30–11 p.m.* $$$

White Lotus

1743 Cahuenga Blvd., Hollywood, 323-463-0060

Times really are changing in Hollywood. The makers of the Sunset Room and Pig 'N Whistle have feng-shuied a former dance dungeon (Crush Bar) into one of the hottest "it" dining and clubbing scenes on either side of La Brea Ave. The restaurant includes a full sushi bar and a canopy-tented patio serving fancy Euro-Asian grub that covers all the bases—dim sum, deep-fried red snapper, duck leg confit, a New York steak, etc. Once the meal is over, a separate club area draws the same well-heeled eye candy, and you're invited because dinner gets you into the club. People eat fashionably late here, so book a table for 10 p.m., unless you like eating alone and wondering what all the fuss is about. *Open for dinner Tues.–Sat. 6 p.m.–12:30 a.m.; club open Thurs.–Sat. 9 p.m.–4 a.m.* $$

New Hollywood: The Nightlife

Barfly

8730 W. Sunset Blvd., West Hollywood, 310-360-9490

So what if the attitude at this dark, velvety nightclub is as thick as cheese, from the aloof doorman to the dressy parade of posers, pretenders, and the odd star hiding back in the VIP area. Isn't that why you came here? Take Barfly for what it is (i.e., a place not to take yourself or anyone else too seriously) and the apple martinis, tight dance floor, groovy music, emergency sushi, and borrowed Parisian ambience all add up to something that's so totally L.A. Try not to be over thirty-five. Arrive with a dinner reservation to leave the doorman in the dust. *Open Mon.–Sat. 7:30 p.m.–2 a.m.* $

Bar Marmont

8171 W. Sunset Blvd., West Hollywood, 323-650-0575

Chateau Marmont's stylish neighbor is now a famous destination in its own right for its dark, cozy lounge, popular patio, butterfly-painted ceilings, and specially-prepared drinks priced to attract young celebrities and whispering fans. Seeing as you'll be forking over close to ten bucks for the privilege of drinking a beer here, you might as well go large and get the highly-recommended Marmont Cosmo or the #9 Mint Martini. By the by, one of the city's best filet mignon cheeseburgers in town is served here into the late hours. *Open Mon.–Sat. 6 p.m.–2 a.m., Sun. 7 p.m.–2 a.m.*

Club Bar at The Peninsula Beverly Hills

9882 S. Santa Monica Blvd., Beverly Hills, 310-551-2888

Peaty scotch just tastes better at this classy, birch-paneled drinking den housed in what is commonly called the city's finest hotel. If the Peninsula's Club Bar took memberships as the name suggests, Hollywood agents would buy them out. As it stands, you're welcome to sink into a red leather chair, order a Millionaire Margarita (double reserve Cuervo tequila, 150-year-old Grand Marnier, Cointreau, and fresh lime juice) and listen to this congregation of schmoozers have at it. Better yet, sit by the fire where there's less of a chill in the air. *Open Mon.–Sat. 1 p.m.–1 a.m., Sun. 1 p.m.–midnight.*

Deep
1707 N. Vine St., Hollywood, 323-462-1144

Change is good on the fabled crossroads of Hollywood & Vine, or at least frequent. The latest development where The Brown Derby and Jack's Sugar Shack once stood is a naughty-but-nice-enough go-go scene serving fondue and oysters and providing every opportunity to stare at people without them seeing you. Beyond the front bar, enter a pleasure maze that includes a pounding glass-cubed dance floor, lots of one-way-mirrors, and a set of former walk-in refrigerators that are now private VIP boxes (some furnished with poles). Beat the steep weekend cover by reserving a table. *Open Tues.–Sat. 7 p.m.–2 a.m.* $

Forty Deuce
5574 Melrose Ave., Los Angeles, 323-465-4242

This themey retro-lounge reinvention by nightclub entrepreneur Ivan Kane (of Deep) is famous for its *Moulin Rouge*–style burlesque shows attended by Nicole Kidman and fifty of her closest friends. Frequent capacity crowds mean that just showing up out of the blue will get you about as far as a polite conversation with the tuxedoed guy at the entrance. Avoid all that by reserving a table in advance. Keep a close eye on your martini—the low-level bar is also a striptease runway. *Open Wed.–Sat. 9 p.m.–2 a.m.* $$

Ivar
6356 Hollywood Blvd., Hollywood, 323-465-4827

Inside these tall frosty doors is the new Cadillac of nightclubs in Hollywood—a stark futuristic landscape with four bars, several VIP pods, a roster of top DJs, and a large pulsing dance floor. Despite its 14,000-square-foot size, it can still be pretty hard to get into, so dress to impress. *Open Wed.–Sat. 9:30 p.m.–2 a.m.* $

Joya
242 N. Beverly Dr., Beverly Hills, 310-274-4440

There aren't many places to shake it late at night in Beverly Hills, and even fewer to do it over some fondue. When you're a block from Rodeo Drive with such cravings, this stylish split-level night club lets you have your hip hop, dance, house, groove, or whatever else DJ Richie Rich is spinning tonight and still have a bowl of melted Swiss, too. Dress to impress, reserve in advance for the four-course fondue dinner, or come fashionably late to drink with well-heeled Westsiders who may not be on the real A-list, but definitely know how to look and act the part. *Open Tues.–Sun. 5 p.m.-2 a.m.*

Lola's

945 N. Fairfax Ave., Los Angeles, 213-736-5652

Anyone coming to this unassuming block of Fairfax above Melrose is either dropping off a broken VCR or, hopefully, checking into Lola's—a cottagey bar/restaurant with an aspiring sitcom-cast crowd, an antique pool table, a leopard-skin sofa, and a menu of 50-or-so martinis. It all hangs together well after a few candied cups of gin or vodka. *Open nightly 5:30 p.m.–1:30 a.m.*

Nacional

1645 Wilcox Ave., Hollywood, 323-962-7712

Old Havana sells in Hollywood as long as it's done just right, boasts a long guest list of somebodies, and draws a cast of young, beautiful patrons to pay through the teeth for sugary rum drinks. This slick, upscale nightclub has it all down, especially that last part. Done up in marble, wrought-iron, and Cuba-inspired frescoes, the two-level lounge has a DJ booth, two full bars, a wood-burning fireplace, L.A.'s most flirtatious balcony, and about 350 people. Dress to dazzle, then get in line. *Open Tues.–Sat. 10 p.m.–2 a.m.*

Skybar

8440 W. Sunset Blvd., West Hollywood, 323-848-6025

Every night the attractive pool deck of the hotel Mondrian becomes its even sleeker self, an exclusive see-and-be-seen scene. But you already knew that. The "A-list" crowd here now includes co-stars from the WB Network who are doing an ace job holding the place up. The best way to get in if you're not a guest of the hotel or a former star of *Saved by the Bell* is to get here before 8 p.m. when the doorman reports for duty. *Open daily 11 a.m.–2 a.m.*

Whiskey Bar

1200 Alta Loma Rd., West Hollywood, 310-657-0611

At most hotels, this would just be the bar beside the lobby. At the Sunset Marquis, known for its famous musical guests, it's the place where Bruce, Bono, and the Black Crowes might be having a drink or six. This cozy rocker's lounge has a decidedly cool, exclusive vibe but can't nearly fit all the people who want to be part of it. Your best bet is either being a beautiful woman, knowing someone, or getting here before 10 p.m. *Open nightly 5 p.m.–2 a.m.*

White Lotus

1743 Cahuenga Blvd., Hollywood, 323-463-0060

See New Hollywood p. 105 for listing.
Open Thurs.–Sat. 9 p.m.–4 a.m. $$

New Hollywood: The Attractions

Cristophe Salon

348 North Beverly Dr., Beverly Hills, 310-274-0851

Haircuts start at $100 at this vintage Beverly Hills salon—and that's a bargain compared to what clients like Goldie Hawn, Nicole Kidman, Stephen Spielberg, and a certain former U.S. President have personally paid the great Cristophe to do the do himself. Hair, skin, nail, and cosmetic treatments are provided by a doting staff. *Open Tues.–Sat. 8:15 a.m.–7 p.m., Thurs. until 9 p.m.*

The Getty Center

1200 Getty Center Dr., Los Angeles, 310-440-7300

Only a portion of the vast J. Paul Getty collection fits into its new dream home and Foundation headquarters. Rumor has it that there was no budget set for this modern architectural wonder, designed by Richard Meier and perched like an urban San Simeon in the Santa Monica Mountains. Construction took just under 15 years and the final cost was...well, it's only money. A short tram-ride from the parking structure leads to five pavilions full of paintings, decorative arts, photographs, manuscripts, drawings, and other masterpieces that require at least a few visits, especially if you take time to enjoy the gardens and views. Admission is free, but it's five dollars to park your car. Parking is first-come, first-served and busiest at midday. A free shuttle operates from the overflow lot two miles south of the museum on the northwest corner of Sepulveda Blvd. and Constitution Ave. *Open Tues.–Thurs. & Sun. 10 a.m.–6 p.m., Fri.–Sat. 10 a.m.–9 p.m.*

Heli USA

16303 Waterman Dr., Van Nuys, 818-994-1445

Most helicopters in L.A. are chasing white Broncos or scouting highway traffic, but a few are available to the common man. For a leisurely ride in the skies, Heli USA's half-hour Hollywood/Skyscraper flight packs in great views of famous movie locations, Bel-Air mansions, The Getty Center, Universal Studios, Beverly Hills, the Hollywood sign, and Downtown's batch of high-rises. For an extra hundred bucks the City of Angeles Flight will soar down the beach with you at sunset. $$$$

Museum of Television & Radio

465 N. Beverly Dr., Beverly Hills, 310-786-1000

Like its sister facility in New York, the name's a tad misleading. You won't be finding any examples of old transistors or '50s-era Zenith user's manuals at this stark Richard Meier-designed building in the heart of Beverly Hills. In fact, except for a few art exhibits, the joint appears pretty empty until you get your paws on a library database of more than 100,000 radio and television programs spanning 80-odd years. After enough time with a headset in a private console, you'll forget where you are and what year it is—which is what good TV has always been about. Stuff from the collection is also screened in the facility's two main theaters. *Open Wed.–Sun. noon–5 p.m.*

NBC Studios

3000 W Alameda Ave., Burbank, 818-840-3537

Sadly, there's no suggestion box here for Jay Leno's joke writers, but otherwise NBC is, as it proudly claims to be, "the only network that opens its doors to you!" How wide that door opens is beside the point. You do get some "behind-the-scenes" perspective when you take the studio's walking tour. Just over an hour long, it pokes inside the wardrobe, makeup, set construction, and other departments, which nicely deflates the myth that working in Hollywood is the least bit exciting. Your chipper guide will also lead you through a soundstage and an FX room or two and very likely the set of the *Tonight* show. For free tickets to the Tonight show with Jay Leno, be at the NBC ticket counter well before 8 a.m. or request in advance by mail (NBC Tickets/3000 W. Alameda Ave. Burbank, CA 91523). *Tours depart regularly 9 a.m.–3 p.m. weekdays, plus weekends during the summer.* $

Ole Henriksen Face/Body

8622-A W. Sunset Blvd., West Hollywood, 310-854-7700

Whip your epidermis into shape at this full-service spa run by one of the great authorities on skin care (he's served as a Ms. Universe judge and he's been on Oprah). The soothing environs of this 4,000-square-foot Japanese-style spa include several zen-like treatment rooms with glowing candles and shoji doors. If there's a signature treatment on the aptly-named menu of "tranquility packages," it's the Six-Step Body Treatment—a rapturous 90 minutes that includes the famous sea mineral scrub. Don't leave Ole's without one. *Open Mon. 8:30 a.m–5 p.m., Tues.–Sat. 8 a.m.–8 p.m., Sun. 9:30 a.m.–4:30 p.m.*

Rancho Park Golf Course

10460 W. Pico Blvd., Los Angeles, 310-838-7373

The good news if you're staying anywhere near Beverly Hills or Westwood is that one of the city's nicest public golf courses is just down the street. The bad news is that you're not the only one in on this little secret. Traffic is heavy at this hilly 6,681-yard, par 71, with an additional 9-hole par 3. Good facilities include a two-tiered driving range, an executive course, plus an onsite restaurant and bar. To reserve a time, you'll have to first obtain a City Parks golf card (213-473-7055). *Open daily until sundown. $$*

Runyon Canyon Park

2000 N. Fuller Ave., Hollywood, 213-485-5111

There may be much nicer trails farther afield in the Santa Monica Mountains, but for sheer convenience and star power it's hard to beat this one-mile ramble up to the top of Hollywood. On a clear day, views stretch to Catalina Island. On a not so clear day, views will make you want to write a sympathy card to your lungs. For a quieter trailhead (one that starts at the top), use the Mulholland entrance. *Open until sundown.*

Universal Studios Hollywood

100 Universal City Plaza, Universal City, 818-508-9600

Somewhere on this huge lot, the world's biggest blockbusters are being produced. Of course, the spotlight at Universal Studios is reserved for movies that return home as theme park attractions—including old favorites like Back to the Future and Jurassic Park and a roster of newcomers including The Mummy Returns: Chamber of Doom and Shrek 4-D. The standard offering is the 45-minute Studio Tour which whisks past sets and soundstages with enough fun surprises to keep the experience feeling very ridelike. To better appreciate what's going on back there, a VIP Tour provides two hours of far less rehearsed access, plus six hours in the theme park with front-of-the-line privileges. At nearly three times the price of general admission it's an investment, but it's likely the best one you can make in the Valley on a crowded summer day. Reserve at least a week in advance (818-622-5120). *Summer park hours Mon.–Fri. 9 a.m.–8 p.m., Sat.–Sun. 9 a.m.–9 p.m. VIP Tours depart daily 9 a.m. and noon, usually on the hour.* $$$$

Hipster L.A.

It takes commitment to be an L.A. hipster. All that attitude, and all those clothes! Not to mention all the time you have to devote to finding the latest hotspot and insinuating yourself into it. Lucky you—for three fun-filled days and nights you can pretend you're the real deal, and then you can go home. What's in store? The most shagadelic hotel rooms, the blackest coffee and the bluest pool decks, the strongest margaritas and mojitos, the tastiest gospel brunch, the latest late-night comfort food, the least restricted golf courses, the coolest art scenes, and the most happening restaurants and bars. Come and get it.

Hipster L.A.: The Itinerary

Three Great Days and Nights

Your Hotel: **The Standard Hollywood**

Morning: Have breakfast with the in-crowd over a steaming bowl of *espresso-strength coffee* at **King's Road Cafe**. Or try **Toast**, the latest breakfast/lunch "it" spot on Third Street. If both places are mobbed, check out the pleasantly grungy patio at **Highland Grounds** for an artsier atmosphere and a helluva tasty breakfast burrito.

Walk it off with an entertaining jaunt along the *Melrose Strip* between Fairfax and La Brea. Never mind all the blue-haired teens—this congested stretch of urban-wear stores, fake Rolex dealers, sunglass brokers, and aggressive shoe salesmen is still one of L.A.'s most active and lively retail clearinghouses, fortified with enough weird and eccentric little shops to keep things interestingly offbeat. When you've had enough (or if you're just in the mood for something completely different), the country's most impressive *vehicles of the past*, present, and future await you at the **Petersen Automotive Museum**.

If you can handle two wheels and an engine, you could instead join L.A.'s *weekend chrome convention* by renting a Harley Davidson at EagleRider (11860 S. La Cienega Blvd., 310-320-3456) or Route 66 Riders (4161 Lincoln Blvd. Marina del Rey, 310-578-0112) and blasting off into V-twin nirvana along the coast of Malibu and the **Mulholland Highway**. You'll pass few cars and many, many motorcycles on this winding ride through the Santa Monica Mountains. For lunch (and lots of company in leather pants), pull over at the Rock Store (30354 Mulholland Hwy, 818-889-1311), a *friendly burger shack* overrun with cruisers and sportbikes.

Afternoon: Have lunch **Vert**, a smart new brasserie that's opened under the Wolfgang Puck company banner. Or, hang back at your hotel in the **24/7 Restaurant at The Standard** and soak up the scene in and around the open lobby. The revolving cast of Standard guests and drop-ins could make a really fine reality TV show. There are inflatable dinghies that are larger than the hotel's pool out back, but sprawling out on the sunny blue deck with its decent views and *studiously cool crowd* has to be done at some point, so why not now? If you're so inclined, you can also take a seat at Rudy's Barbershop—right in the hotel—for a quick weekend makeover haircut. (Dropping in to put your name on the list before breakfast will save a wait).

You may have noticed that your hotel is smack dab in the middle of the Sunset Strip. Take some time to explore your famous surroundings and appreciate their timeless beauty—er, well, their ultraslick celebration of commercial excess, maybe? Stroll west to Tower Records, Sunset Plaza, Hustler Hollywood, Tattoo Mania—whatever turns you on. You can burn some calories before dinner just by watching people sweat it out at **Crunch Fitness**, one of L.A.'s *trendiest gyms* (guests at The Standard get in for half price).

Evening: In a city filled with stages, small and large, the **Actors' Gang Theater** is a reliable choice for an evening of *quality drama* in the heart of Hollywood. This award-winning theatre houses one of L.A.'s most honored cutting-edge ensembles, stacked with recognizable names including artistic director and celebrity activist Tim Robbins. You'll also get your share of political statements, though probably lighter and wackier ones, at the **Acme Comedy Theatre**, a good bet if you're looking for biting sketch comedy.

Dine fashionably late at **Linq**, one of the newer see-and-be-seen spots, featuring top California cuisine and a sexy bar scene. Or head over to **Cha Cha Cha** (one of the funkier local chains) in West Hollywood for Caribbean food and some of the best rum concoctions in town. If all else fails, check into a leather booth at **Jones Hollywood** where *well-heeled thirtysomethings* are rubbing hips at the bar on any given night. Dinner is served here until 1:30 a.m.

Then, get your introduction to the *Hollywood lush life* at **The Burgundy Room**, **Beauty Bar**, **Daddy's**, or any of the other classic, cool, or just plain kitschy venues on and around the Cahuenga Corridor. For live music, **Sixteen-Fifty** is one of the top venues in the neighborhood. Take a breather down the street at **The Well**, a dark, laid-back lounge tucked inconspicuously into the side of an office building. When you've gotten your second wind, knock down a few pins at **Lucky Strike Lanes**, a groovy booze-and-bowl scene in the Hollywood & Highland complex.

Got the munchies? Head east on Hollywood Blvd. to **Sanamluang Cafe**, a local favorite in Thai town that serves *heaping plates of tasty noodles* until deep into the night.

Day 2

Morning: Wake yourself up in a breakfast booth souped-up like the back of an old Chevy at **Fred 62**. It's your first stop on a day-trip through the *artsy enclaves* of Los Feliz, Silver Lake, and Echo Park. For a little less decor with your hangover, have your triple espresso at the nearby **Hollywood Hills Restaurant**.

Explore the gentrifying backbone of Los Feliz along Vermont Street between Hollywood Blvd. and Franklin Ave., with its excellent bookstore, a handful of wacky shops, and a Starbucks if you must. Continue east along Sunset into the cafe- and theatre-dotted neighborhood of Silver Lake. Then, your next stop is Echo Park, where the latest *underground art scene* is hiding from the Westside. To check it out, make your way to the cluster of galleries a few blocks above Sunset on Echo Park Ave.

Afternoon: Have lunch at **Madame Matisse**, a colorful *Euro-style cafe* that serves wholesome sandwiches and designer omelets to a very local crowd. Plunked in that bland-looking strip mall next door is **Alegria on Sunset**, lauded by *carne asada* aficionados as one of the city's best Mexican kitchens.

After lunch, take a look at the bigger picture. For ***city panoramas*** (and a visual smog report), drive up to the Griffith Park Observatory and have a good look around—um, if you can. Or get out of the sun and compare ***cowboy and Indian histories***. See one side of the story at the **Autry Museum of Western Heritage** and the other at the much underappreciated **Southwest Museum**.

Evening: For tonight's dinner, savor a ***cool atmosphere*** and excellent Cal-French cuisine at **Vermont**, a most welcome recent addition to Los Feliz's scrunched restaurant row. Or go old-school a few doors down at **The Dresden Room**, a classic supper club whose popularity was rekindled by the movie *Swingers*.

After dinner, you could fight your way through all the commuters from Hollywood, Glendale, and Westwood to take a ***swing lesson*** at **The Derby** and order Singapore Slings at **Good Luck Bar**. But for more of-the-moment drinking holes right here in the area, try **4100 Bar** in Silver Lake or **The Roost** and **The Bigfoot Lodge** in neighboring Atwater Village. For some aural stimulation, **Spaceland** ranks among L.A.'s top alternative music venues.

Day 3

Morning: If you think L.A.'s vast Griffith Park seems too large not to have a regulation-size course hiding on it somewhere, you're actually doubly right. A pair of ***historic par 72s*** hugs the eastern rim of this park, the largest municipal park and urban wilderness in the U.S. **Wilson/Harding Golf Courses** come well equipped with a 50-tee double-decked driving range, four practice putting greens, two pitching and chipping greens, anda well-appointed clubhouse. You can golf a round here for about 25 bucks (make sure to reserve a time in advance, especially on the weekend) and grab a bite at the course's restaurant as early as 6 a.m. Looking for something easier to work with that hangover—say, nine holes? The somewhat puny and flat **Los Feliz Municipal Golf Course** nearby is a great place to pretend to be a much better golfer than you actually are this hazy morning.

If you're not into swinging clubs today, grab a mornin' cup-a-joe, then swing over to West Hollywood's **Burke Williams Day Spa** instead for a rejuvenating 90-minute deep-tissue massage to fully *recharge your weekend battery*. Allow time before or after your appointment to make the most of the excellent facilities—wet steam, sauna, whirlpool, rinse, repeat—at this premier full-service spa.

Hallelujah! It's time to head over to the **House of Blues** for its most happening weekly ritual, the *Sunday Gospel Brunch*. On a Sunday morning, it really just doesn't get any better than this: stuff your face, hear great live music, and be completely justified in starting your day with cajun meatloaf and crawfish cheesecake. The all-you-can-eat Southern spread runs the gamut from cornbread muffins, homemade waffles, and custom omelets to shrimp jambalya, fried chicken, and cheddar grits. Lively local gospel bands fuel this feast with soulful tunes during two sessions, with seatings at 10 a.m. and 1 p.m.

Afternoon: You've sated your stomach (and your soul), now feast your eyes on L.A.'s *bountiful art scene*. **The Museum of Contemporary Art** (MOCA) is one of the country's finest collections of modern American and European works. Admission to MOCA also includes entrance to its cool off-site property, **The Geffen Contemporary**, just five minutes away in Little Tokyo. The smaller and lesser known **Museum of Neon Art** (MONA) is another *illuminating art* stop in the area.

Evening: Dine at **Lucques**, a sophisticated *Cal-French hotspot* set in a unique converted carriage-house. (And you can go as late as you like: their bar menu is served until midnight on weekends.) For a livelier atmosphere and great Spanish tapas, squeeze yourself into **Cobras & Matadors**, a spirited new restaurant on Beverly Blvd.'s reemerging dining circuit.

To top off your trip, stop in for a *tequila shot* at **El Carmen**, or have a margarita with the effect of several shots at **El Coyote**. After a few shots or several margaritas, people have been known to want to eat again. Don't worry—it's never too late to nosh with other inebriated folks at nearby **Canter's** delicatessen. Finsh up back on Sunset with a chill-out nightcap at the **Lobby Lounge at The Standard**.

Hipster L.A.: The Hotels

Avalon Hotel

9400 W. Olympic Blvd., Beverly Hills, 310-277-5221 / 800-535-4715
www.avalonbeverlyhills.com

A full-on makeover earned this once ailing '50s apartment complex the 2000 Westside Historic Preservation prize. It also saved the place from resting too heavily on its laurels as former home to Marilyn Monroe and a handful of *I Love Lucy* episodes. The savvy media types who check in here now don't much care about all that stuff, but they do appreciate the modern-retro kidney-shaped pool, the cabanas, and the hip indoor/outdoor dining area called "Blue on Blue," serving lobster-and-pumpkin ravioli and a drink called "A Walk in Space." There's a state-of-the-art fitness center and a nifty house-call spa service that does shiatsus, facials, manicures and pedicures, seaweed marine wraps, and so on in the comfort of your own room. Style and practicality coexist in the 88 guest rooms, which flaunt Noguchi tables, Eames chairs, and bubble lamps and don't skimp on the basics: Frette linens, internet access, fax machines, and Philosophy toiletries. Tucked away in a residential pocket of lower Beverly Hills, this chic boutique hotel will be cool for at least another 50 years. $$

The Standard Hollywood

8300 W. Sunset Blvd., West Hollywood, 323-650-9090
www.standardhotel.com

Don't worry, you haven't had that much to drink, the hotel sign is upside down. Maybe this converted retirement home will one day return to its roots and house a bunch of drooling old Gen-Xers remembering the days when they read *Details* and William Burroughs books sitting on beanbag chairs in hotel lobbies. Until then, it's a motel-ish pleasure playground right on the Strip, devoted entirely to virtual youth. Everything about this place is calculatingly cool, retro, and over-the-top image conscious, from the bubble swings and human vitrine in the lobby to the blue AstroTurf pool deck. If you can deal with a first-floor "Sunset View" (as in Blvd.), rooms start as low as $99—a steal if you don't plan on sleeping anyway. All the 139 guest rooms include balconies, cordless phones, CD players, VCRs, and spare motel-style furnishings that are so much cooler than anything "nice." If you'd rather stay near your banking buddies, check into the Standard's new downtown location (550 S. Flower St.). $$

Sunset Marquis Hotel & Villas

1200 N. Alta Loma Rd., West Hollywood, 310-657-1333 / 800-858-9758
www.sunsetmarquishotel.com

Sequestered below Sunset on a leafy cul-de-sac, the Sunset Marquis is about as far as you can get from the Strip in half a block. Secure; beautifully laid-out grounds offer the sort of cool gentility that reels in famous country singers, aging rock stars, and a steady roster of special guests—musical or otherwise—who no doubt appreciate the onsite recording studio and the fact that the hotel's velvety Whiskey Bar is puny enough to keep out most of the groupie riffraff. The main draw is the Mediterranean-inspired setting with its lush gardens, cobblestone walkways, lovely pools, and homey living quarters. One hundred and two one-bedroom or junior suites occupy the main building, and a dozen self-contained villas are planted out in the garden. King beds, marble bathrooms, empty fridges (and separate minibars), balconies, high-speed internet connections, twice-daily maid service, and tasteful modern furnishings are standard. If you check into a villa, you also get a butler. The poolside Patio Cafe provides light bites and the hotel's elegant Room restaurant serves Cal-Pacific cuisine. $$$$

W Los Angeles Westwood

930 Hilgard Ave., Westwood, 310-208-8765 / 888-625-4988
www.whotels.com

While Westwood isn't exactly breaking the hip meters these days, this cyber-age makeover of the old Westwood Marquis is one very chic exception. Hiding behind frosted glass doors on a leafy residential street, the L.A. chapter of Starwood's successful boutique hotel chain is what those pimply UCLA undergrads guzzling microbrews down the road may aspire to when they land their first expense accounts. Blurring the line between work and play, the W's stylish, modern lobby is also its living room, filled with funky chairs, cozy couches, stocked bookshelves, and W-brand board games. On weekends, this open area becomes a nerve center for the stylin' crowd over at the bar and the suave Latin restaurant, Mojo. Two hundred fifty-eight large one- and two-bedroom suites are fitted with cozy sofas, custom-designed African wood furnishings, and Westin Heavenly beds. They also come wired for high-speed internet and offer a full entertainment system with 24-hour access to the hotel's extensive CD/video library. If you need a printer, scanner, fax machine, Dodger tickets, or anything else, W's Whatever/Whenever desk is at the ready. Add two outdoor pools, a fitness center, and the full-service AWAY Spa—and suddenly this corner of Westwood is where it's at. $$$

Hipster L.A.: The Restaurants

Alegria on Sunset

3510 W. Sunset Blvd., Silver Lake, 323-913-1422

Far better than its strip mall location would indicate, this family kitchen is the place to go for wonderful Mexican food that brings back your childhood—if you grew up in Oaxaca. The single nod to the aging boho Silver Lake crowd that flocks here is a vegetarian burrito—which comes with chicken or steak if you want to bend the rules. Otherwise, go for the best-sellers: tacos *a la crema,* tacos *de pescado,* or a *carne asada* burrito stuffed with lemon-marinated grilled skirt steak, rice, cilantro, and refried beans. When owner/chef Nadine Trujillo's *mole* sauce is bubbling in the back, you should at the very least order some on the side. *Open Mon.–Thurs. 10 a.m. –10 p.m., Fri.–Sat. 10 a.m.–11 p.m.* $

Canter's

419 N. Fairfax Ave., Hollywood, 323-651-2030

Like any deli worth its sodium, this famous landmark hasn't changed in decades, and whether you park yourself in a booth at 4 a.m. or 4 p.m., they won't treat you any better or worse, even if you happen to be Matt Damon behind those shades. Star sightings are common here at any hour of the day or night, which just proves that matzo balls and salty meats served on rye are some of the world's great equalizers. *Open daily 24 hours.* $

Cha Cha Cha

7953 Santa Monica Blvd., West Hollywood, 323-848-7700

This Cuban sleeper in West Hollywood recently joined the ranks of this eccentric chainlet (other members are a colorful bungalow in lower Silver Lake and a location down in Long Beach). Mojitos were a bar specialty here long before the whole fad started—lovingly made with real limes squashed with a pestle. A long starter list of spicy Nuevo Latino tapas could serve as a menu on its own. Some of these items, like the sweet-peppery *camarones negros,* come in generous entrée portions too. Steer clear of the jerkyish jerk pork and opt instead for the succulent *chuleta al limon.* Or go whole hog with the seafood. *Open daily for lunch 11:30 a.m.–3:30 p.m.; dinner 5:30–11 p.m.* $

Cobras & Matadors

7615 W. Beverly Blvd., Los Angeles, 323-932-6178

Before this smart addition to Beverly Blvd.'s rekindled restaurant row came along, anyone craving Spanish tapas around here usually had to settle for linguine primavera or a ticket to Barcelona. You'll want to make advance reservations at this lively little hive because, as it turns out, lots of people like the idea of drinking Malvasia and nibbling on mini-plates of grilled octopus and *patatas fritas* in a charming little cafe with a wood-burning oven. Start by sampling some of the 25-or-so tasty tapas selections and move on to the bigger plates—e.g. Catalan-style Cornish game hen or skirt steak. Save room for *crema caramela.* A handful of outdoor tables are first-come-first-served—but someone's usually come first. *Open Sun.–Thurs. 6–11 p.m., Fri.–Sat. 6 p.m.–midnight.* $

Fred 62

1850 N. Vermont Ave., Los Feliz, 323-667-0062

Depending on which side of Hollywood they happen to be on, L.A.'s proverbial crowds of struggling actors, writers, drummers, and anyone else looking for a better agent or band can be found eating (or serving) upscale Denny's fare at either Swingers (8020 Beverly Blvd./323-653-5858) or at this 24-hour scene in Los Feliz. The food is adequate. More important, ham on rye is called a "Charles Bukowski," poptarts are homemade, eggs can be scrambled with tofu, the noodles are soba, and the retro-green ambience includes a toaster at every table and a pachinko machine in the restroom. Meat loaf and Raisin Bran never tasted so L.A. *Open daily 24 hours.* $

Highland Grounds

742 N. Highland Ave., Hollywood, 323-466-1507

For years, one of Hollywood's best least-known breakfast and lunch patios has been hiding behind a brick wall like concealed evidence that even folks with tattoos on their necks enjoy a nice brunch. The big new sign out front may draw in a few more faces, but the low-profile location (think donut shop and gas station) should still keep weekend lines at bay. A hearty mishmash of earthy-ish and south-of-the-border fare includes chipotle or tofu scramble, Cuban panini, sour cream pancakes, the famous Phil's black bean burger, and a soothing yogi tea cappuccino. Evening entertainment here features the sort of fringe L.A. music and comedy shows you've been warned about. Wednesday open mic nights can be particularly lethal. *Open Tues.–Sat. 9 a.m.–11:30 p.m., Mon. 9 a.m.–5 p.m., Sun. 9 a.m.–3:30 p.m.* $

Hollywood Hills Restaurant

1745 N. Vermont Ave., Los Feliz, 323-661-3319

Jon Favreau and Vince Vaughn (of *Swingers*), the scribes behind *Everybody Loves Raymond*, and no doubt many actors and screenwriters we'll never hear about all found inspiration and sustenance at this no-frills diner back when it was in a Hollywood Best Western down the road. The new location a few miles east in Los Feliz serves the same all-day breakfasts and "cowboy chili" to a similar clientele. *Open daily 9:30 a.m.–midnight.* $

House of Blues

8430 W. Sunset Blvd., West Hollywood, 323-848-5100

Downstairs, it's the best concert hall on the Strip. Upstairs, it's a nice place (by concert hall standards) to eat Delta-inspired grub before or during the show. Catfish Nuggets, Voodoo Shrimp with a Dixie Beer reduction, a fine blackened chicken burger called "The Elwood," and other themey menu items that aren't much closer to Mississippi than Disneyland are served in the main dining room above the stage or out on the back "porch." If you're coming for dinner and a show, you get first dibs in the concert hall before the show. The most anticipated weekly event is the Sunday Gospel Brunch, featuring live gospel performances and a huge Southern-style, all-u-can-eat spread that let's you nourish your soul and stuff your face. *Open nightly 5–11 p.m., concert hours vary; Sunday Gospel Brunch seatings are at 10 a.m. and 1 p.m.* $$

Jones Hollywood

7205 Santa Monica Blvd., Hollywood, 323-850-1727

The main event at this industry hangout near the Warner Hollywood lot is the young-ish crowd flirting at the bar and ordering cocktails named after rock stars (like Sid Vicious) who'd probably never drink here—but you never really know at a place like this. Usually seated at secluded booths in the surrounding dining room is a more eclectic crowd that, on one night, included a couple of local TV news anchors, the late film director Ted Demme, and Vegas's Siegfried Fischbacher. Thin-crust pizzas, vegetarian spring rolls, ahi sandwiches, wasabi mashed potatoes, and other smart comfort foods are served until 1:30 a.m. *Open for lunch Mon.–Fri. noon–4:30 p.m.; cocktails nightly 4:30–7 p.m.; dinner nightly 7 p.m.–1:30 a.m.* $

King's Road Cafe

8361 Beverly Blvd., Los Angeles, 323-655-9044

A super-strong bowl of coffee perked with espresso beans is the most popular item on the menu, best digested with an omelet, pancakes, or breakfast risotto in the a.m., or with an assortment of salads and gourmet sandwiches in the p.m. The best time to be at this always-trendy corner cafe is during packed weekend brunch hours when at least a few sunny sidewalk tables are occupied by TV or movie personalities whose faces you recognize. *Open daily 7:30 a.m.–10 p.m.* $

Linq

8338 W. Third St., Los Angeles, 323-655-4555

Candles, fireplaces, chic white walls, black marble finishes, a floor-to-ceiling waterfall, and one of L.A.'s sexiest bar scenes, raised like a proscenium in front. Is there a restaurant in this picture? Those who make it past cocktails at Linq will savor one of L.A.'s more exciting Asian fusion newcomers. The sleek restaurant section is set up in a chain of intimate-sized dining spaces which shrugs off certain practical matters like having enough light to read a wine list by. Fortunately, there's enough delicious substance to justify the style. Fish dishes are especially good, the Soy-Mirin Glazed Chilean Seabass in a Lemongrass Cilantro Sauce taking top honors. For dessert, try the apple tart or hot chocolate cake with a molten fudge center. *Open nightly 6:30 p.m. –1 a.m.* $$

Lucques

8474 Melrose Ave., West Hollywood, 323-655-6277

Gaining even greater buzz with their latest hit restaurant, A.O.C., celebrated local chef Suzanne Goin and business partner Carolyne Styne warmed up for nearly five years at this unique Cal-French hotspot in West Hollywood, which continues to draw a stylish crowd craving something more inspired after a movie than another ahi burger. It starts with the setting itself—an old brick and wood-beam room with a fireplace and adjoining patio that was once the carriage house for the Harold Lloyd estate. The innovative seasonal menu might begin with a salad of apples, Asian pears, radicchio, and mint in a buttermilk dressing or a medley of reed avocado, beets, and Dungeness crab with chili, lime, and crème fraiche. Ambitious entrees sometimes sound better on paper but most often hit the mark. They include a grilled pancetta-wrapped trout with sorrel, fennel, verjus, and crushed grapes, and a very successful plate of braised beef shortribs with sautéed greens, pearl onions, and horseradish cream. One of the neighborhood's best late-dining spots on the weekend, Lucques keeps its bar menu going until midnight on Fridays and Saturdays. *Open for lunch Tues.–Sat. noon–2:30 p.m.; dinner Mon.–Sat. 6–11 p.m., Sun. 5:30–10 p.m.* $$

Madame Matisse

3536 W. Sunset Blvd., Silver Lake, 323-662-4862

Paris meets Silver Lake at this sweet ten-table sidewalk cafe run by a classically-trained French chef. Fresh-squeezed juices and custom-made omelets satisfy a local clientele accustomed to eating their first meal at around 3 p.m. The lunch menu includes a variety of salads, pastas, and sandwiches. On weekend evenings, out comes the coq au vin and steak au poivre and the place moonlights as a charming French bistro. *Open daily 7:15 a.m.–3:15 p.m.; dinner Thurs.–Sat. 5–9:30 p.m.* $

Sanamluang Café

5176 Hollywood Blvd., Hollywood, 323-660-8006

This late-night Thai stop has been adopted by just about everyone in this East Hollywood neighborhood. Sanamluang is a bright decorless place but they will feed you steaming noodle dishes and savory curries well after the bars in Hollywood and Silverlake have squeezed out all their guests. Start with a big plastic cup full of sweet Thai iced tea and make it easy on yourself: just say "General's Noodles, please." *Open daily 10 a.m.–4 a.m.* $

Toast

8221 W. Third St., Los Angeles, 323-655-5018

For some reason, this perfectly good corner on busy Third St. has housed a few failed cafe attempts in the last several years. Along comes Toast—-the neighborhood's latest breakfast and lunch hotspot—with the winning combination. Is it the cool name? Are the coffees, pastries, waffles, eggs, granola, soups, salads, wraps, melts, quesadillas, and burgers really that much better this time around? Whatever the reason, brunch herds now come in droves. *Open daily 7:30 a.m.–5:30 p.m.* $

24/7 Restaurant at The Standard

8300 W. Sunset Blvd., West Hollywood, 323-650-9090

Standard guests and non-guests (it's often hard to tell the difference at this place) converge at the hotel's groovy all-hours staple eatery, featuring separate breakfast, lunch, dinner, weekend brunch, and "overnight" (midnight–6 a.m.) menus. An eclectic array of midday favorites include yellowtail carpaccio, Japanese sweet potato soup, and oysters-on-the-half-shell appetizers, a free-range chicken club, "Moroccan" pizza with carmelized onions, merguez, and goat cheese, and an organic omelet. *Open daily 24 hours.* $

Vermont

1714 N. Vermont Ave., Los Feliz, 323-661-6163

Here's some tasty proof that Los Feliz is no longer monopolized by hip overpriced diners and aging supper clubs. A pair of talented first-time restaurant owners are behind this sophisticated New American favorite. Poached salmon, tender short ribs, roasted chicken, a mountain of fresh mussels, and filet mignon with blue cheese potato gratin are a few staples on the revolving menu. The flourless chocolate cake and old-style vanilla custard with caramel sauce are equally lauded. Tasteful modern decor is embellished with white columns, vaulted ceilings, and a lovely picture window looking out onto the restaurant's namesake street. Adding to the atmosphere is a slick lounge next door. *Open for lunch Mon.–Fri. 11:30 a.m.–3 p.m.; dinner Sun.–Thurs. 5:30–10:30 p.m., Fri.–Sat. 5:30–11:30 p.m.* $

Vert

6801 Hollywood Blvd., 4th Floor, Hollywood, 323-491-1300

The smart menu at this sleek, Italian-accented brasserie high up in the Hollywood & Highland complex includes snails, onion soup, and a croque monsieur (where else in L.A. can you get this?), but since this is another Wolfgang Puck production, there's definitely something for everyone. Choose from French and Italian comfort food (pastas, steak frites), some playful salads, and more wood-fired-oven pizza creations. *Open Mon.–Fri. 11:30 a.m. –10 p.m., Sat.–Sun. noon–10 p.m.* $

Hipster L.A.
The Nightlife

Acme Comedy Theatre

135 N. La Brea Ave., Los Angeles, 323-525-0202

In L.A.'s ragtag world of sketch comedy, this perfectly nice 99-seat theatre is the equivalent of Carnegie Hall. The highly-acclaimed Acme Players and an emerging school of talented improv performers strut their twisted stuff on this inventive and always funny stage. One night's demented fare included a sketch centered on the ramblings of a fingerless shop teacher facing his first sex education class. *Shows Fri.–Sat. at 8 p.m. and 10:30 p.m., Sun. 7:30 p.m.* $

Actors' Gang Theater

6209 Santa Monica Blvd., Hollywood, 323-465-0566

One of the city's longest-running theatre ensembles has collected more than 100 awards for its daring interpretations of classic plays and equally bold, politically-charged new material—from a co-production of Eric Bogosian's *Suburbia* to the recent in-house hit, *Bat Boy: The Musical*. Board members include actors Giancarlo Esposito and founding member and artistic director Tim Robbins. $

Beauty Bar

1638 Cahuenga Ave., Hollywood, 323-464-7676

Where else in Hollywood can you drink Amstel Lite under an old-fashioned hood-style hair dryer? Drawing on the success of its precursor in New York, Beauty Bar seems even better suited to the vainer and kitschier L.A. Part hip Hollywood bar, part low-rent '60s-style salon with a dash of John Waters, this place saves you the bother of making an extra trip to get your nails or henna tattoos done before heading out to meet the frisky Hollywood drinking crowd. During the early hours on Friday and Saturday evenings, order a glass of Prell (vodka, pineapple, and Midori) or some other ten-dollar concoction and your manicure is on the house. *Open Sun.–Wed. 9 p.m. –2 a.m., Thurs.–Sat. 6 p.m.–2 a.m.*

The Bigfoot Lodge

3172 Los Feliz Blvd., Atwater Village, 323-662-9227

"Rough it" in the Eastside's themeiest drinking scene. Order a Toasted Marshmallow (Stoli vanilla, butterscotch liqueur, Frangelico, half & half, and an ignited Bacardi-dipped marshmallow) or a Girl Scout Cookie (crème de menthe, Irish Cream, half & half) in this fake-log barn of a bar favored by the wallet-chain crowd and decorated with stuffed rodents and forest fire messages. Camping was never this fun. *Open nightly 8 p.m.–2 a.m.*

Burgundy Room

1621 1/2 Cahuenga Blvd., Hollywood, 323-465-7530

As the address implies, this classic shotgun shack could be just a tad wider on those capacity nights when drinking here is not unlike being pinned in a long, dark hallway with Joe Strummer screaming at you. It's one of Hollywood's genuinely cool bars—a friendlier smoosh of scenesters than it looks, without all the Beauty Bar or Star Shoes gimmickry. After 10 p.m., the excellent jukebox retires and an equally good DJ usually cranks up old-school punk. *Open nightly 8 p.m.–2 a.m.*

Daddy's

1610 N. Vine St., Hollywood, 323-463-7777

Maybe because it used to be a stylish supper club, this converted Hollywood hipster bar maintains a dark, sexy vibe that the drinking closets and kitsch-shops one block over on the Cahuenga corridor can't quite match. A 20- and 30-something crowd of viable partners rubs against the bar. Cozy ottomans and low-tabled booths hug the opposite wall, providing places for closer conversations and gentle groping. When you reach the "quieter drink" stage (or age), head to The Well (see p. 130), an equally sleek but toned-down version of Daddy's, run by the same owners. *Open Mon.–Sat. 8 p.m.–2 a.m., Sun. 9 p.m.–2 a.m.*

The Derby

4500 Los Feliz Blvd., Los Feliz, 323-663-8979

The swingin' happy ending of the movie *Swingers* happened right on the dance floor of this '40s-era supper club, launching the '90s fad that's come and gone. If you miss those lindy-hop days, The Derby's beautiful brass-railed bar, curtained wood booths, and smooth live bands haven't lost their luster. Nor have the folks on the compact dance floor, who don't need those free swing lessons. If you do, be here at 8 p.m. The club's Italian-ish menu is from Louise's Trattoria next door. *Open daily 4 p.m.– 2 a.m.* $

The Dresden Room

1760 N. Vermont Ave., Los Feliz, 323-665-4294

The last stop on the *Swingers* film location tour is most importantly the home of the inimitable husband-and-wife duo, Marty and Elayne, who've been crooning in this time warp of a lounge six nights a week for the last 23 years. Like a living-and-breathing museum set with its gorgeous bar, tuxedoed drink mixers, Bob Hope Road movie–era photos, and creamy white banquettes in the dining area, the Dresden at first seems above the flighty crowd it draws. That thought goes out the window when the Munster-ish house band opens their next set with "Rudolph the Red-Nosed Reindeer" even though it's late May. *Open daily 10 a.m.–2 a.m.*

El Carmen

8138 W. 3rd St., Los Angeles, 323-852-1556

This stylishly campy cantina with its odd mix of imported Mexican wrestling posters and Asian mushroom lamps is another winning invention from L.A.'s Midas of late-night life, Sean McPherson (Swingers, Jones, Good Luck, Bar Marmont). On weekends (which include Thursdays here), the boxy room is stuffed with a young, attractive crowd of tequila swillers who appreciate the humongous selection of rare brands, until its time to figure out how the hell to get home. Tacos, guacamole, and other quick Mexican snacks take the edge off. *Open Sun.–Thurs. 5 p.m.–2 a.m., Fri.–Sat. 7 p.m.–2 a.m.*

El Coyote

7312 Beverly Blvd., Los Angeles, 323-939-2255

Some L.A. traditions shouldn't be questioned. One of them is parking yourself at this '30s-era dive, gulping down stiff, cheap margaritas, and delaying the aftershock with plates of lard cleverly disguised as rice, refried beans, and mystery meat rolled in a tortilla and topped with a warm blanket of Day-Glo cheese. If you start seeing Christmas lights and large, frowning waitresses in gaudy folk dresses, you're actually not hallucinating. *Open Sun.–Thurs. 11 a.m.–10 p.m., Fri.–Sat. 11 a.m.–11 p.m.*

4100 Bar

4100 W. Sunset Blvd., Silver Lake, 323-666-4460

Garnished with flying dragons and a phat candlelit Buddha at the back, the Eastside's hippest new lounge proves that opium-den designs are tough to resist even in this gimmick-cautious part of town. An eclectic bunch of

Silver Lakers, straight and gay, come here and leave that other, better-known Far East–themed hotspot (the Good Luck Bar) to trendoids and tourists. *Open nightly 8 p.m.–2 a.m.*

Good Luck Bar

1514 Hillhurst Ave., Los Feliz, 323-666-3524

This trend-setting singles lounge next to a vacuum store in Los Feliz takes the Far East theme about as far as it can go. You'll find just about every clichéd piece of decor here: Paper lanterns—check; bamboo stools and dragons on the ceiling—check-check; opium-den–style lounge in the back—check; plus some nifty extras like a last-call gong. After a few Singapore Slings it all somehow works. The house special is The Good Luck—Amaretto, Midori, juice, and milk, served by women with chopsticks in their hair—check. *Open nightly 7 p.m.–2 a.m.*

Lobby Lounge at The Standard

8300 W. Sunset Blvd., West Hollywood, 323-650-9090

Looking the part helps, but all you really have to be to join the party in the Standard's open-concept, retro-ish lobby lounge is over 21 years of age. Then just go ahead and commingle—with the cool crowd in the beanbag chairs, the coquette sitting in a glass box, the coteries on the blue pool deck, and the caucus of junior producers hunched at a sprinkle of tables that the staff likes to call the Cactus Lounge. Don't forget to order a cosmopolitan. *Open daily until 1:30 a.m.*

Lucky Strike Lanes

6801 Hollywood Blvd., Hollywood, 323-467-7776

Bowling in Hollywood has always been a great way to fit in a few more cheap brews before breakfast. Now even this seedy practice is undergoing a Hollywood renaissance at Lucky Strike Lanes, a fancy new ten-pin lounge in the Hollywood & Highland complex. A dozen state-of-the-art lanes with automatic scoring and retractable video screens won't much remind you of your last experience chucking gutter balls down well-worn lanes. There's a nice long bar here, a menu of catered finger foods, and a hot DJ to help you throw strikes. If someone in your party is important enough, there are also four VIP lanes. *Open daily 11 a.m.–2 a.m.* $

The Roost

3100 Los Feliz Blvd., Atwater Village, 323-664-7272

Silver Lake's trendy bar scene has sent some of its most talented young boozers sailing to find a divier safe harbor in neighboring Atwater Village. If the tacky "Big TV" sign outside doesn't send the caramel-apple-martini crowd running, the fake-wood paneling, the old dartboard, the jukebox full of Eagles and Johnny Cash, and the empties strewn everywhere will finish the job. If this sounds good to you, however, don your best Goodwill hipster garb and—welcome home. *Open daily 10 a.m.–2 a.m.*

Sixteen-Fifty

1650 Schrader Ave., Hollywood, 323-465-7449

While this quality stage can't seem to settle on a name for itself (formerly Vynyl and Hollywood Moguls), it consistently books some of the highest-caliber funk, fusion, and jazz-rock bands passing through town. Ample floor space with good sound and sightlines makes this a favorite venue for groupies who'll be following these performers back to Athens, Georgia or the High Sierra Music Festival. Several dance clubs are hosted here throughout the week. *Open nightly 6 p.m.–2 a.m.* $

Spaceland

1717 Silver Lake Blvd., Silver Lake, 323-661-4380

This funky concert space continues to be L.A.'s top alternative music venue, showcasing artists—famous and fringe—in a loud, intimate setting that's as laid-back and purely music-oriented as all those moneyed halls aren't. Covers are cheap when local bands rock the house. Spaceland productions are also held at Hollywood's Henry Fonda Theatre (6126 Hollywood Blvd.) and at The Echo (1822 Sunset Blvd.). *Open nightly 8 p.m.–2 a.m.* $

The Well

6255 W. Sunset Blvd., Hollywood, 323-467-9355

Most Hollywood lounges are as loud and frantic as any other old bar. This new lounge is a lounge, right down to its sedate entrance on the side of a office building. If it's late, you're tired, and you suddenly find yourself to be older than 25, dropping into this dark, sleek room with its smooth centerpiece bar, comfy nooks, unchallenging jukebox (James Brown, Bob Marley), and good vibes is like sneaking into business class. Being in the right company is important here, as you'll actually be able to carry on a conversation. *Open Mon.–Fri. 6 p.m.–2 a.m., Sat. 8 p.m.–2 a.m., Sun. 9 p.m.–2 a.m.*

Hipster L.A.: The Attractions

Autry Museum of Western Heritage

4700 Western Heritage Way, Griffith Park, 323-667-2000

So just how was the West won? This enormous collection of artifacts, artwork, historical documuments, film footage, and—let's not forget—firearms tackles that question largely from the perspective of the white male winners. Founded by "Singing Cowboy" Gene Autry, the expanded museum now includes seven permanent galleries and two revolving exhibition areas which explore historical and contemporary topics relating to the development of the American West. *Open Tues.–Sun. 10 a.m.–5 p.m. (Thurs. until 8 p.m.)* $

Burke Williams Day Spa

8000 W. Sunset Blvd., West Hollywood, 323-822-9007

One of the original sites of the fast-growing Burke Williams chain will at some point beckon your knotted muscles into its cavern of steam rooms, saunas, whirlpools, cold plunges, and treatment chambers. All clichés aside, you will be a new person—or at least feel like one—after that hour-long massage, facial, wrap, herbal bath, whatever signature treatment your body needed and got here. Separate men's and women's facilities open an hour before the first treatment slot at 9 a.m. *Open daily 8 a.m.-10 p.m.* $$$

Crunch Fitness

8000 W. Sunset Blvd., West Hollywood, 323-654-4550

Fitness is about as hip, high-tech, and hyper-social as it gets in this two-level, 28,000-square-foot gym. You may need a buff trainer to navigate your way through the curriculum here, which includes tai boxing boot-camp classes, ballet pilates, yoga, and an ice-breaker called "cardio striptease." Hammer Strength and Icarian machines are state-of-the-art. Multitaskers will enjoy the stationary bikes with Web access. *Open Mon. –Thurs. 5 a.m. –11 p.m., Fri. 5 a.m.–9 p.m., Sat. 7 a.m.–8 p.m., Sun. 8 a.m.–8 p.m.* $

The Geffen Contemporary

152 N. Central Ave., Downtown, 213-621-2766

MOCA's satellite art hall in Little Tokyo, Helped by a $5 million donation from David Geffen) lives on as the institution's coolest, funkiest wing. Larger exhibits and interactive installations that need their space are housed in this former LAPD garage retooled by Frank Gehry, who kept its essential warehouse feel intact. Popular displays include works by Rauschenberg, Warhol, and Oldenburg. Tickets issued at either MOCA or the Geffen include entrance. *Open Tues.–Sun. 11 a.m.–8 p.m., Thurs. until 8 p.m.* $

Los Feliz Municipal Golf Course

3207 Los Feliz Blvd., Los Feliz, 323-663-7758

Cheap and easy in every way, Griffith Park's little-league course (1,065 yards, flat as a pancake) would be a great place to impress a six-year-old step-kid if only you had one. This nine-hole, all-par-three playground is frequented by 20-somethings who are cash tight and feeling better about their game than they should. There's a coffee shop, and rental clubs are available. No tee times or jackets required. *Open daily 7 a.m.– 4:30 p.m.* $

Mulholland Highway

Not to be confused with Mulholland Drive, this even longer and windier road through the Santa Monica Mountains is a beautiful escape valve for stressed-out Angelinos, running between Malibu and Woodland Hills in the west San Fernando Valley. On weekends, you'll see (and hear) far more motorcycles than cars buzzing around this network of cliffs, canyons, and country roads. From Los Angeles, Mulholland Highway can be reached by taking the Pacific Coast Highway (Hwy. 1) west for about 30 miles. Stop in at the Rock Store (30354 Mulholland Hwy., 818-889-1311) for a cheeseburger, beer, and chrome convention on a Sunday afternoon.

Museum of Contemporary Art (MOCA)

250 S. Grand Ave., Downtown, 213-626-6222

L.A.'s main modern art hub houses permanent and revolving exhibits from 1940 to the present in an arresting East-meets-West building from architect Arata Isozaki. More than 5,000 largely American and European works include abstract masterpieces as well as more recent additions from emerging names. Gallery tours (free) run on the hour between noon and 2 p.m. Celebrity chef Joachim Splichal is behind the menu at Patinette, MOCA's Mediterranean cafe. Entrance includes admission to the Geffen. *Open Tues. –Sun. 11 a.m.–5 p.m., Thurs. until 8 p.m.* $ (Free Thursdays.)

Museum of Neon Art (MONA)

501 W. Olympic Blvd., Downtown, 213-489-9918

Los Angeles was filling tubes with argon gas and hanging them all over town before the rest of the country caught on to this novel advertising—and, yes, art—form. The neon tradition is honored in this small gallery's revolving collection of electric media. To get a taste of what's still out there, book a Neon Tour on MONA's open-air, double-decker bus for an evening's exploration of L.A.'s coolest, brightest, gaudiest signs (tours run between April and October). *Open Wed.–Sat. 11 a.m.–5 p.m.* $

Petersen Automotive Museum

6060 Wilshire Blvd., Los Angeles, 323-930-2277

Unlike LACMA across the street, dragging yourself to this monolith on Wilshire Blvd.'s "Museum Row" doesn't require a rainy day. Founded by publishing mogul Robert Petersen, it's a most appropriate homage to a city that evolved around wheels and engines. Four floors of permanent, revolving, and interactive exhibits include more than 150 rare and classic cars, trucks, and motorcycles spanning a century. All the cool hot rods and celebrity vehicles are one flight up. *Open Tues.–Sun. 10 a.m.– 6 p.m.* $

Southwest Museum

234 Museum Dr., Los Angeles, 323-221-2163

Slightly off the radar in Mt. Washington, L.A.'s oldest museum dedicates itself to the people who were already here when the Europeans arrived to wreak havoc and build museums. The lovely 90-year-old hilltop hacienda contains one of the best collections of American Indian art and artifacts in the U.S. Four main exhibit halls focus on the Southwest, California, the Great Plains, and the Northwest Coast. Highlights include a Chumash rock-art site replica and an 18-foot Cheyenne summer tipi. Loads of pre-Columbian pottery, textiles, baskets, paintings, and other relics cover Native groups from Alaska to South America. *Open Tues.–Sun. 10 a.m.–5 p.m.* $

Wilson/Harding Golf Courses

4730 Crystal Springs Dr., Griffith Park, 323-664-2255

Golfers of all levels have been populating Griffith Park's two regulation-size courses almost from the time Wilson and Harding were in office. Well-staffed and maintained, they share all facilities including a pro shop, lockers, a cart and club rental, a snack bar, and a driving range that's open until 10 p.m. Which course is more challenging? The jury's been out on that for the last 70 or 80 years. Wilson (par 72, 6,947 yards) is longer and has more trees. Harding (par 72, 6,536 yards) has tighter fairways. Walk-ons are easier during the week. On weekends especially, be sure to get a reservation card from the pro shop or by calling the City of Los Angeles Golf and Tennis Reservation Office (213-473-7055). *Open sunrise to sunset.* $$

Coastal L.A.

Don't tell anyone east of the 405, but L.A. is right on the water. More than 75 sunny miles of coastline between Malibu and Long Beach are dotted with beaches, boardwalks, volleyball nets, tide pools, the biggest manmade pleasure boat harbor in the world, the largest working port in the nation, and (because you really ought to know these things) the first-ever solar-powered Ferris wheel. There's no visible border dividing coastal L.A. from the rest of the city. It's just in the air, which gets cooler and cleaner and free-and-easier somewhere along the drive west from Hollywood, Downtown—or Delaware. Breathe in enough of it and a pleasant narcosis sets in. You won't feel the need to turn back. In fact, you could roll up and down this edge of the world quite contentedly forever, with or without rollerblades. Here's a push.

Coastal L.A.: The Itinerary

Three Great Days and Nights

Your Hotel: **Shutters on the Beach**

Morning: Have a light breakfast with front-row ocean views at **Pedals**, the informal but elegant downstairs dining room at Shutters. Or, start your day right with a *malt waffle* slathered in rum butter at **Blueberry**, one of the hottest new breakfast/lunch spots in downtown Santa Monica.

Take the rest of the morning to explore the revitalized heart of Santa Monica, starting with the **Third Street Promenade**. Bounded by a pair of topiary dinosaurs, these three blocks of restaurants, cafes, shops, boutiques, and theatres have blossomed into the city's most popular pedestrian zone, and remain one of the few places people actually walk in L.A. Hardcore shoppers will find an even *ritzier Westside shopping* and latte-sipping mecca on **Montana Avenue**, where nearly a dozen tree-lined blocks full of top designers' boutiques, trendy shops, galleries, home-furnishing stores, cafes, and yoga studios stretch from Seventh St. to Seventeenth St.

Afternoon: Enjoy a *leisurely lunch* with your toes in the sand at **Back on the Beach**. If the tables at this front-row burger dive were much closer to the waves you'd feel the spray. Upcoast in neighboring Pacific Palisades, **Patrick's Roadhouse** serves a mean plate of fish & chips (with malt vinegar of course) in an old Irish-themed building brimming with character. For a more upscale midday meal by the sea, grab a patio seat at **Ivy at the Shore**—Santa Monica's slightly more relaxed version of The Ivy, the original *celebrity haunt* that is a home away from home for stars and their publicity hounds in the Beverly Hills area.

Everyone's heard something about Venice Beach, Santa Monica's crazy next-door neighbor. Whatever you've heard, there's no resisting its magnetic pull once you're this close. The nicest route is along the **South Bay Bicycle Trail**, which continues all the way down to L.A.'s lower beach communities. Walk or roll to Venice's new-and-improved strand, **Ocean Front Walk**, where a pageant of tourists, skaters, bladers, vendors, weight-lifters, sculptors, circle drummers, and various freaks and bums all gather. When you've had your fill, you can always retreat to the actual beach at Venice which is large and curiously vacant. Or head a few blocks in the other direction to trendy Main Street, where Starbucks, Patagonia, The Gap, and several blocks of other mainstream staples provide an easy gentrified retreat from all the zaniness by the water. If that's a little too status quo, lose some of the crowds farther north on Venice's *artsy corridor*, Abbot Kinney Blvd., where a row of unique galleries mixes with a mellowed out crowd of hip bohemian types.

All this lazing along the coast is pretty darn stressful. *Loosen up* with a massage at Shutters. Or haul your knotted muscles over to the steaming pools of **Aqua Day Spa**, Santa Monica's favorite place to "take the waters," and indulge in one of several pampering scrubs, rubs, wraps, masks, or peels—whatever your body craves.

Evening: There's a profusion of excellent restaurants in Santa Monica and Venice, but **The Lobster** is the only place you need to know about that's *right on Santa Monica Pier*. Savor front-row ocean views and outstanding seafood on the outdoor deck of this recently reopened and re-invented hotspot. Three more top reservations almost as close to the water are **Capo** in Santa Monica, **One Pico** at Shutters, and **Jer-ne** at the Ritz Carlton in Marina del Rey.

Santa Monica's late-night scene has been steadily improving over the last few years. One of the hotter new clubs of note in the neighborhood is **Zanzibar**, a velvety *Moroccan-themed* space that hosts a roster of top DJs. Vying to be voted the Westside's answer to Skybar is **Cameo Bar** at the chic Viceroy Hotel, with its *studiously beautiful crowd*, its hip lobby lounge, and its see-and-be-seen–scene pooldeck. Nearby **Chez Jay** is the other end of the spectrum—a friendly old dive serving frosty brews to a colorful local crowd.

Day 2

Morning: Start today's journey through the South Bay on the patio at **Uncle Bill's Pancake House**, where *huge breakfasts* accompany some sweet views of Manhattan Beach and the ocean. Walk it off on the strand running south to Hermosa Beach, arguably the prettiest and definitely the blondest boardwalk in L.A. Just to your right, folks, is SoCal's best barely-dressed weekend beach *volleyball scene*, but we guess you'll figure that out for yourself. Have a seat and watch the action or—if you've got the *cojones*—kick off your shoes and join in.

Afternoon: See all that water out there? It's not just some decorative backdrop—it's an afternoon's adventure waiting to happen. There are too many options to choose from, so start by *getting your feet wet* with one of these top sellers: Surfers, both experienced and novice, can take a private lesson with some of California's best wave-riding tutors at **Pure Surfing Experience** in Manhattan. Halibut-lovers (and whale-watchers in season) can pop a Dramamine and comb Santa Monica Bay for big fish and bigger mammals with **Marina del Rey Sportfishing**. Sailors and yachters can *rent a variety of vessels* for a half-day with **Marina Sailing**, or even hitch a ride on a luxury 42-foot Catalina Sailing Yacht with **Paradise Bound Yacht Charters**.

Landlubbers can enjoy their beautiful day at **Manhattan Beach** and neighboring Hermosa Beach. For lunch in the area, have a bite at Good Stuff (310-545-4775), Hennessey's (310-372-5759), Fat Face Fenner's Fishack (310-379-5550), or at one of numerous other *casual eateries* scattered all along the strand.

Evening: Santa Monica and Venice increase their gravitational pull at dinnertime. On restaurant-stuffed Main Street, it's hard to go wrong at Wolfgang Puck's raucous **Chinois on Main**, at the stylish Cal-Asian **Chaya Venice**, or at the artful Cal-Continental favorite **Röckenwagner**. For a more romantic evening, escape to the cozy *cottage-and-fireside setting* of **Chez Mimi**, one of Santa Monica's finest French restaurants that boasts a wonderfully rustic ambience. The South Bay isn't famous for its haute cuisine, but if you're still down there, some favorite evening venues are **Mangiamo** for martinis and Italian cuisine, **Fonz's** for steaks and seafood, and the **Side Door**—a *jazzy little lounge* that's good for a few drinks with the local elite (i.e., surfers and financiers).

Stroll along Santa Monica's **Third Street Promenade**, a nightly hive of clubs, theatres, shops, and street performers. For *a late set of blues*, head up a block to historic **Harvelle's**. Slightly off the beaten path, the landmark **McCabe's Guitar Shop** hosts one of the city's most eclectic evening concert lineups in its back guitar room.

Day 3

Morning: After a leisurely room-service breakfast, head up to the hidden stables at **Escape on Horseback** for a *guided horseback tour* through Topanga State Park and the Santa Monica Conservancy, L.A.'s lofty and lovely backcountry. Hikers can strike out on some beautiful mountain trails at **Point Mugu State Park** in Malibu. Or, for a shorter commute and the same great views of the coast, take a morning ramble at **Temescal Gateway Park** in nearby Pacific Palisades.

Golfers: L.A.'s coast is more than just one big sand trap. Spend your morning over nine or *eighteen scenic holes* at the **Malibu Country Club**. Nestled in a mountain valley above the coast, these public fairways have a nice private feel to them.

All that work builds up an appetite. Enjoy lunch with *million-dollar views* out on the famous terrace at **Geoffrey's**, one of L.A.'s best Pacific dining perches. Or have a seat on the creekside terrace at **Inn of the Seventh Ray**, an ultra-serene and romantic setting deep in Topanga Canyon that features a concience-boosting all-organic menu that includes a cow-free burger and the popular Buddha Salad.

Afternoon: Little-known fact (at least to visitors): only a small patch of Malibu's long sandy shoreline is set aside for those private Colony people.

The rest is all yours. *Swim, surf*, beachcomb, boogie-board, frolic, or just slowly roast yourself. Or park your towel at **Zuma Beach**, a popular spot with excellent facilities. You can also head farther north to **Leo Carillo State Beach**, where a quality strip of sand borders a 3,000-acre state park. Art lovers can return to Santa Monica and gallery-hop through one of L.A.'s most *eclectic art scenes*, **Bergamot Station**, a former industrial site that now showcases the works of painters, sculptures, jewelry designers, photographers, and other local artists in more than 30 galleries.

Evening: Come early to get an *oceanfront patio table* at **Duke's Malibu** for cocktails at sunset. Follow up with dinner at **Granita**, Malibu's version of Spago. For Japanese cuisine, head to **Nobu Malibu**, Malibu's version of Matsuhisa. If you'd rather eat your sushi in Santa Monica with Westside hipsters, head to **Sushi Roku**.

For live music, the ever-cool **Temple Bar** draws Westside trendoids with its fiery *Latin, hip hop, and jazz* grooves in a dark, Buddha-inspired setting. A Far East color palette continues over at **Circle Bar**, one of the neighborhood's coolest and liveliest meet markets.

Cap the evening off with liqueurs in a perfect setting at **The Veranda at Casa del Mar**, a *grand lobby bar* in Santa Monica's most historic oceanfront hotel.

Coastal L.A.: The Hotels

Beach House at Hermosa

1300 The Strand, Hermosa Beach, 310-374-3001 / 888-895-4559
www.beach-house.com

Off the beaten path by Santa Monica standards, this deluxe property in the South Bay is a well-kept four-star secret. Savvy couples and corporate execs who like to jog along the ocean before meetings get a real deal down here compared to the ransom rates they could be paying up at Shutters or Casa del Mar. Just steps from one of the city's loveliest and liveliest beaches, more than 100 identical studio suites are tastefully assembled with large king beds, down comforters, and generous work spaces with high-speed internet access in loft-style bedrooms. There's a mini-kitchen with a microwave, small stove, and fridge. Spacious bathrooms have deep soaking tubs and come stocked with Aveda products. Sunken living rooms are dressed with plush couches, wood-burning fireplaces, stereo systems, and walk-onto balconies with ocean views. A complimentary continental breakfast is included, and room service is provided by two nearby restaurants. The hotel's holistic spa service offers private yoga sessions on the beach and in-room massage treatments. $$$

Casa del Mar

1910 Ocean Way, Santa Monica, 310-581-5533 / 800-898-6999
www.hotelcasadelmar.com

A new heyday has dawned at this posh seaside landmark, which was the toast of Santa Monica's private beach club scene back in the '20s. Stunningly restored in Renaissance revival style and reopened in 1999, Casa del Mar joins its neighboring sister property Shutters as the most celebrated L.A. digs on the coast. The immense lobby lounge is the first show stopper, with its lavish wood- and ironwork, huge stone hearth, plush velvet sofas, club chairs, and a gorgeous bar overlooking the Pacific. To your left, the elegant Oceanfront dining room serves innovative New American cuisine accompanied by the same postcard views. All of this tasteful opulence continues throughout 129 guest rooms and suites, dressed in fruitwood furnishings, handpainted armoires, Matisse-inspired art, and gauzy white curtains with thick wood Venetian blinds. Stereos, DVDs, VCRs, and high-speed internet access are all standard, as are large Italian marble bathrooms with glass-enclosed showers and computer-controlled whirlpool tubs. A full fitness area boasts state-of-the-art Cybex cardio equipment and individual workout stations with headphones and TVs. A range of spa treatments can be enjoyed in private cabanas on the lovely fifth-floor pool deck above Santa Monica Bay. $$$$

Inn at Playa del Rey

435 Culver Blvd., Playa del Rey, 310-574-1920
www.innatplayadelrey.com

You'd expect the beach-going masses to have found Playa del Rey by now. The fact that they're still bypassing this sleepy community tucked between LAX, Marina del Rey, and 300 acres of wetlands lends even more charm and romance to this grand B&B, an unlikely piece of Cape Cod perfection just three blocks from the Pacific. Sitting in the sunny yellow breakfast area, out in the rose garden hot tub, on the back deck facing a channel of passing sailboats, or in the cozy living room stocked with books about birds, it seems impossible that one of the world's biggest international airports is just down the road. Especially in vast L.A., it's always a nice surprise when great escapes like this New England–style beach house are so close. Twenty-one guest rooms and suites are individually designed for couples, corporate travelers, and families. Romantic Suites include a king canopy bed, a fire-place, and marvelous views from two-person Jacuzzis. View Rooms provide balconies overlooking the Marina or the wetlands. Standard rooms might feature not-so-standard accoutrements like pine sleigh beds and handmade Amish quilts. All come with a full hot breakfast, afternoon tea, evening wine and hors d'ouevres, and peaceful sunsets in a transporting setting. A small exercise room is on the property, and bicycles are available for an even quicker commute to the beach. $$

Malibu Beach Inn

22878 Pacific Coast Highway, Malibu, 310-456-6444 / 800-462-5428
www.malibubeachinn.com

Malibu's stretch of premium coast offers very little in the way of accommodations, which is just the way those private Colony folks like it. The next best thing to crashing at Johnny Carson's place is a few nights at the Malibu Beach Inn, which accurately enough calls itself the neighborhood's only luxury beachfront hotel. With its assortment of "Beachcomber" and "Surfrider" rooms and suites done up in soft pinks and greens, the relaxed vibe here is more about a quick weekend escape with front-row ocean views than five-star luxury. Mexican-tiled bathrooms, casual wicker furnishings, and private balconies are standard, and most suites have gas fireplaces and Soft Tub Jacuzzis right above the surf. For a small extra charge, the "romantic-getaway" package includes champagne, Godiva chocolates, rose petal turndown service, and breakfast in bed. Complimentary Continental breakfasts are otherwise served out on the patio; room-service is 24 hours; and stairs lead right down to the beach. If you can't live in Malibu, this charming fixture right on PCH provides a sweet taste. $$$

Shutters on the Beach

1 Pico Blvd., Santa Monica, 310-458-0030 / 800-334-9000
www.shuttersonthebeach.com

If you haven't seen a celebrity yet and you want to, have a seat in Shutters' two-fireplace lobby lounge and wait. Honored time and again as L.A.'s finest luxury hotel right on the sand, Shutters hasn't much competition in this category save for Casa del Mar next door, which boasts the same cosmic room rates without the balconies (something about tampering with a historic landmark). But Shutters has balconies, three per room sometimes, and they're all close enough to the surf to hear the waves, smell the salt, and spot bobbing sea lions (or are those empty oil drums?) with the handy binoculars provided in some of the upper suites. Shutters has a pair of destination restaurants, One Pico (formal, upstairs) and Pedals (casual, downstairs), serving top contemporary American cuisine with front-row ocean views. In your room you can close the pretty clapboard shutter doors, crank the A/C, and pretend you're wintering in the Hamptons. Then, you can open them to reveal that you are (in case we failed to mention this) right on the sand in Santa Monica. One hundred eighty-six guest rooms are outfitted with warm wood furnishings, upholstered beds, oversized Jacuzzis in spacious marble bathrooms, and soft aqua color schemes. A dozen suites provide generous extra living space. If you want a fireplace and those three balconies, check into a Presidential suite (just $2,500/night). All guests can enjoy the small but pretty pool deck and a fully-equipped fitness room where spa treatments may be arranged. $$$$

Viceroy

1819 Ocean Ave., Santa Monica, 310-260-7500 / 800-622-8711
www.viceroysantamonica.com

Full of retro-whimsy and suave British-y decor, this hip $15-million reinvention of the Pacific Shore Hotel is just the sort of place where Austin Powers and James Bond might fight each other for a penthouse suite. Scene-questers who want an ocean view with their chic boutique digs will find the vibe at the Viceroy and its slick Cameo Bar to be Santa Monica's closest relation to a city place like the Mondrian—but still a distant cousin. In fact, the rooms here are nicer and more interesting, the attitude isn't in the same league, and the hotel's sophisticated Cal-French restaurant, Whist, won't care as much if you aren't impossibly young and beautiful and dressed in black. Furnished in the Viceory's signature palette of soft whites, parrot greens, and driftwood grays, with lots of chrome and glassy accents, 163 boldly designed guestrooms and suites offer balconies (most with ocean views), Frette linens and bathrobes, custom beds with down comforters and pillows, and marble baths with seated vanities and deep soaking tubs, as well as flat-screen TVs, CD-DVD players, and high-speed internet access. A pair of outdoor pools is also on the property along with a fully-equipped fitness center and massage and in-room spa service by Fred Segal Beauty. Santa Monica's Third Street Promenade, Main Street, and the beach are all just steps away. $$$

Coastal L.A.: The Restaurants

Back on the Beach

445 Pacific Coast Highway, Santa Monica, 310-393-8282

All walks of life line up at this shack right on Santa Monica Beach to eat eggs, burgers, and chicken piccata with their toes in the sand. Like the decor (plastic tables surrounded by a knee-high lattice fence) the food is unremarkable, but it tastes better without shoes on. Two-hour validation is offered if you park in the pricey public lot in the back. *Open 8 a.m.–9 p.m. (summer), 8 a.m.–5 p.m. (winter).* $

Blueberry

510 Santa Monica Blvd., Santa Monica, 310-394-7766

As "adorable" breakfast-and-lunch cafes go, Blueberry ranks high with Santa Monica locals for its friendly atmosphere, paisley cushions, open kitchen, upstairs dining loft with a white-picket fence, and jars of preserves lining the front wall. Large windows and high ceilings lessen the claustrophobia, but this small place can get packed on weekends when cravings for everything blueberry (pancakes, muffins, syrup) are especially high. Other top items include a fluffy malt waffle rimmed with fresh strawberries, powdered sugar, and rum butter, and a variety of omelets, sandwiches, and salads. *Open daily 8 a.m.–3 p.m.* $

Capo

1810 Ocean Ave., Santa Monica, 310-394-5550

Homemade pastas, heirloom tomato salads, and fire-grilled chops don't come cheap at this exclusive spot which hides its 16 candlelit tables behind a thick velvet curtain in a little gabled building with no sign. The message is clear. Nobody's going to be just walking in off the street (especially since weekend reservations can require a week's notice). This modern Italian mecca bursting with Cal creativity is the latest endeavor of chef/owner Bruce Marder, whose culinary range (from the late West Coast Cafe to Rebecca's to Broadway Deli) has made an indelible mark over the last few decades. His most haute effort yet is housed in the sort of rustic-yet-refined wood-beamed room you'd sooner expect to find in Vail than a block from the beach. The regular clientele is as affluent and the service as flawless as the menu demands. Highlights include the burrata and heirloom tomato appetizers, a perfectly grilled Dover sole, and steaks cooked right over the dining room fireplace. A 900-bottle wine list assures finding just the right vintage with your *verdure. Open Tues.–Thurs. 6–10:30 p.m., Fri.–Sat. 6–11:30 p.m.* $$$$

Chaya Venice

110 Navy St., Venice, 310-396-1179

Japanese art on the ceilings, French posters on the walls, floating rice-paper sea sculptures, white linen tablecloths, an open kitchen, and *Venice Magazine* by the door. It's just what you'd expect from a trendy Pan-Asian restaurant that's just a tad too boho to be in Santa Monica but draws in droves of artsy types (with full wallets) one block over to Venice. The sushi is excellent if you can tear yourself from the main menu, which includes lobster enchiladas topped with cilantro cream sauce, sesame-crusted bluefin tuna with wasabi mashed potatoes, and sea scallops wrapped in New York steak. If you like bananas, the warm banana tart with banana ice cream and a frozen chocolate-covered banana wants you to save room for dessert. *Sushi "happy hour" is from 5–7 p.m. every day. Open Mon.–Fri. 11:30 a.m. –midnight, Sat. 5 p.m.–midnight, Sun. 5–10 p.m.* $$

Chez Mimi

246 26th St., Santa Monica, 310-393-0558

Quebecois chef/owner Micheline Hebert ("Mimi") presides over this utterly romantic French restaurant set up in three cottagey dining rooms that are really more like living rooms, with fireplaces, tasteful furnishings and bric-a-brac, and charming imported waiters. There isn't a hint of "nouvelle" in Mimi's classic French cuisine, which sticks with the sort of classic recipes that charter members of the Julia Child Fan Club will appreciate. Signature dishes include bouillabaisse, cassoulet, escargots, a simple roasted leg of lamb with rosemary and lemon, and a handful of specialties from the old country (Montreal) including a sinfully sweet cake called *chomeur.* On warmer Santa Monica evenings, reserve a table on the lovely outdoor patio. *Open for lunch Tues.–Sat. 11:30 a.m.–3 p.m.; dinner Tues.–Sun. 5:30 –9:30 p.m., Fri.–Sat. 5:30–10 p.m.* $$

Chinois on Main

2709 Main St., Santa Monica, 310-392-9025

Once you've got Spago under your belt, this action-packed production, brought to you by Wolfgang Puck and his designer wife Barbara Lazaroff, is your next stop. After more than two decades, this compact dining room is still drawing in the stars, kept abuzz by its neon lights, modern art, bursts of bright flowers, and an open-kitchen that doesn't help in keeping the noise down. The menu, a melange of bold Cal-French-Asian creations (with an eight-dollar plate of brown fried rice thrown in just to make a point) is pure Puck. Dishes change, as do the chefs, but some classic items have gained a religious following, namely the Shanghai lobster with spicy ginger curry sauce and crispy spinach, the sizzling catfish stuffed with ginger and ponzu sauce, and the grilled Mongolian lamb chops with cilantro vinaigrette and wok-fried vegetables. *Open for lunch Wed.–Fri. 11:30 a.m.–2 p.m.; for dinner Mon.–Sat. 6–10:30 p.m., Sun. 5:30–10 p.m.* $$$

Duke's Malibu

21150 Pacific Coast Hwy., Malibu, 310-317-0777

Surfing memorabilia and Polynesian thatching decorates this busy ocean-front satellite of a popular Hawaiian restaurant chain. The fish is fresh (if best suited to tacos), the mai tais at the Barefoot Bar are rum-soaked (and cheap on Fridays), and the servers are chipper surfer dudes and babes. But the best thing here is the location. The views through 300 feet of picture windows are some of the most beautiful on the Malibu coast. The patio is a dream at sunset and gets sprayed at high tide. And the parking lot, of course, is full. *Open Mon.–Thurs. 11:30 a.m.–10 p.m., Fri.–Sat. 11:30 a.m. –10:30 p.m., Sun. 10 a.m.–10 p.m.* $

Fonz's

1017 Manhattan Ave., Manhattan Beach, 310-376-1536

Happy hour is generally a bigger deal than haute cuisine in this neighbor-hood, but Manhattan Beach does have a few restaurants worth knowing about. One of them is Fonz's, a relaxed surf-and-turf spot co-owned by Olympian Mike Dodd (who got the silver in 1996 for—what else—beach vol-leyball). Read the framed congratulatory note from Bill Clinton posted inside the door. Then join a friendly fair-haired crowd in the comfortable dual dining room or out on the front patio. The fun-loving menu divides its fare into "land" (prime rib, filet mignon, baked Canadian pork tenderloin) and "sea" (blackened swordfish, grilled albacore, balsamic basted grilled salmon) with some wild cards like wild mushroom risotto, herb roasted chicken, and "yesterday's soup." The wine pairings suggested with every dish might be seen as a belittling gesture in some snottier parts of town. In these parts, it's just plain considerate. *Open daily 5:30–10 p.m., Sun. brunch 9 a.m.–2 a.m.* $$

Geoffrey's

27400 Pacific Coast Hwy., Malibu, 310-457-1519

More than a decade after that power-lunch scene from *The Player* was shot here, Geoffrey's is still the place to eat outdoors in Malibu. You'll pay a little more for only decent seafood, chicken, or chops, but a big part of that investment is the location—an unbeatable perch right above the ocean. Lunches, brunches, and cocktails at sunset are very popular. The most romantic time to be here, though, is at night when the midday schmoozers are gone, the waves are crashing, and the heaters are glowing. Request a table by the outer rail for the best views. *Open Mon.–Fri. noon–9:30 p.m., Sat. 11 a.m.–10:30 p.m., Sun. 10:30 a.m.–10 p.m.* $$

Granita

23725 W. Malibu Rd., Malibu, 310-456-0488

Some of L.A.'s best restaurants are in strip malls. No surprise then that one of them is wedged in Malibu Colony Plaza, steps from all of those heavily guarded celebrity homes on the beach. A neighborhood restaurant at heart, Granita just happens to serve neighbors that are also guests and former hosts of the *Tonight* show. It's another smart move by celeb chef Wolfgang Puck. He's parked one of his traditional wood-fired ovens here to turn out designer pizzas and pastas (along with an inventive Cal-Mediterranean menu overseen by protégé Jennifer Naylor). While a fanciful underwater motif borders on upscale kitsch, the food compensates with wonderful fish selections—a peppery bouillabaisse stuffed with Gulf prawns, sea bass, mussels, and clams—and a crisp Cantonese duck that regulars swear by. *Open Tues.-Fri. 6–10:30 p.m., Sat.–Sun. 5:30–10:30 p.m.; Sat.–Sun. brunch 11 a.m.–2:30 p.m.* $$

Inn of the Seventh Ray

128 Old Topanga Canyon Rd., Topanga, 310-455-1311

Over the last century, this one-of-a-kind spot tucked into the hills of Topanga Canyon has done time as a church, a garage, a gas station, and a junkyard before blooming into one of the city's most stunning natural dining spots. In keeping with the earthy neighborhood, there's an unmistakable New Agey vibe going. Organic entrees are listed "in order of esoteric vibration," and an assortment of goddessy statues adorns a spectacular terrace surrounded by trees, flowering vines, and a bubbling brook. Wholesome lunch selections include the Buddha Salad (naturally raised chicken, Chinese snow peas, roasted red bell peppers, julienne vegetables, sesame seeds, and water chestnuts in ginger dressing) and the I-can't-believe-it's-seitan Seventh Ray Burger. For dinner, there's vegan "duck," smoked tofu, rack of naturally raised lamb, and two five-course tasting menus (one of them vegetarian). *Open for lunch Mon.–Fri. 11:30 a.m.–3 p.m., Sat. 10 a.m.–3 p.m.; dinner nightly 5:30–10 p.m.; Sun. brunch 9:30 a.m.–3 p.m.* $$

Ivy at the Shore

1541 Ocean Ave., Santa Monica, 310-393-3113

If you don't need to eat your chopped salad or crab cakes with celebrities and paparazzi, this laid-back spinoff of the original Ivy in Beverly Hills (see p. 102) features the same impeccable service and reliable but pricey New American menu. For the best oceanfront dining, request a table on the terrace. *Open Mon.–Tues 11:30 a.m.–10:30 p.m., Wed. 11:30 a.m.–10:45 p.m., Thurs. 11:30 a.m.–11 p.m., Fri.–Sat. 11:30 a.m.–11:30 p.m., Sun. 10:30 a.m. –10:30 p.m.* $$

Jer-ne

4375 Admiralty Way, Marina del Rey, 310-574-4333

A few years ago, the Ritz-Carlton at Marina del Rey rethought its traditional dining room and entered the 21st century with Jer-ne (pronounced "journey"), a forward-thinking New World reinvention that's gotten local buzz for its artfully prepared bento boxes and five-course tasting menus. Head chef Troy Thompson's precise approach to blending international cuisines makes this spot more than just another pretty new fusion place. Though pretty it is, with French windows, hardwood floors, a classic wood-and-glass bar in the two-level dining room, and an outdoor patio overlooking the Marina. For a real show, watch your seared fish, vegetables, or duck breast sizzle right at your table on a steaming-hot river rock. *Open for breakfast/lunch 6:30 a.m.–2:30 p.m.; dinner 5:30–10 p.m.* $$$

The Lobster

1602 Ocean Ave., Santa Monica, 310-458-9294

Shuttered for years, this former shack on Santa Monica Pier now reels in both A-list crowds and schools of tourists with its seafood, some of the finest on the coast. Great oceanfront views are capitalized on in an all-glass building that thankfully isn't just about scoring a window or patio table for cocktails and calamari at sunset. The real show-stealers are the Maine lobsters, sold by the pound and either steamed, herb roasted, or—a house specialty—pan roasted with Jim Beam bourbon sauce. Top toque Allyson Thurber (formerly of L.A.'s Water Grill and Philadelphia's Striped Bass) is behind a menu of superb fish dishes, like pepper-crusted rare yellowfin with shrimp, asparagus, and a hearts of palm salad. Save room for the chocolate bread pudding with Tahitian vanilla ice cream. Reservations are advised. *Open Sun.–Thurs. 11:30 a.m.–10 p.m., Fri.–Sat. 11:30 a.m.–11 p.m.* $$$

Mangiamo

128 Manhattan Beach Blvd., Manhattan Beach, 310-318-3434

Just steps from the pier, this top South Bay restaurant is one of Manhattan Beach's toughest tickets on the weekend, when the front bar is crammed with yuppies clinking martini glasses. Neatly dressed with white linen table cloths and framed photos of the Cinque Terre on the wall, the straightforward but elegant Italian dining room sets a stage for a menu that revolves mainly around excellent seafood dishes. Bestsellers include a peppercorned swordfish poached in champagne and fresh grilled scallops in saffron sauce with spinach and angel hair. For pasta, try the king crab linguine in a spicy marinara sauce or the blackened chicken penne tossed with bell peppers and portobello mushrooms. The hidden nook of tables back in the wine cellar area is a great local secret for intimate dining, if you can snag a seat. *Open Sun.–Thurs. 5:30–10:30 p.m., Fri.–Sat. 5–11 p.m.* $$

Nobu Malibu

3835 Crosscreek Rd., Malibu, 310-317-9140

Japanese fusion master Nobu Matsuhisa is best known for his Beverly Hills flagship, Matsuhisa, short-listed among the world's top dining destinations. Hiding out alongside a New Age bookstore and a yogurt shop in the Malibu Country Mart is Matsuhisa's lower-key little sister, Nobu Malibu. Superb sushi, delectable sizzling plates, delicate bento box desserts, and many Matsuhisa-born innovations can be found here at bargain prices—comparatively speaking. On warmer nights, reserve a table on the enclosed garden patio. *Open Sun.–Thurs. 5:45–10 p.m., Fri.–Sat. 5:45–11 p.m.* $$$

One Pico

1 Pico Blvd., Santa Monica, 310-587-1717

Three walls of windows encase this elegant beachfront restaurant at Shutters, which on any given night hosts many more locals than it does hotel guests. The dining room's unbeatable seaside setting more than makes up for whatever excitement may be lacking in the broad "New American" menu, meant to keep everyone perfectly happy if not totally enthralled. Favorites include Brentwood corn and tortilla soup with lobster, seared scallops with arugula and mascarpone risotto, pan roasted Alaskan halibut with tomato, fennel, and basil, and a New York Steak with big, chunky Cowboy Fries. *Open daily for lunch 11:30 a.m.– 2:30 p.m.; dinner 6:30–10 p.m.; Sun. brunch 11 a.m.–2:30 p.m.* $$

Patrick's Roadhouse

106 Entrada Dr., Pacific Palisades, 310-459-4544

One look at this funky green building emblazoned with a shamrock, filled with all sorts of old junk lining the walls and you know there's a long story behind it. Patrick's is friendly, family-run, and full of character. Best of all, when you're craving fried, this place has it all in big, tasty portions. *Open Mon.–Tues. 8 a.m.–3 p.m., Wed.–Fri. 8 a.m.–9 p.m., Sat. 9 a.m.–10 p.m., Sun. 9 a.m.–9 p.m.* $

Pedals

1 Pico Blvd., Santa Monica, 310-587-1707

Casual meals at Shutters are taken downstairs at this wood-beamed Cal-Italian cafe. Choice tables are out on the 50-seat patio, just a lattice fence away from the Santa Monica beach promenade. *Open daily 6:30 a.m.–10 p.m.* $

Röckenwagner

2435 Main St., Santa Monica, 310-399-6504

A memorable culinary experience awaits guests of Hans Röckenwagner, whose double-feature in the Frank Gehry-designed Edgemar Center is unanimously praised by foodies and value-conscious fine-diners, lunchers, and brunchers alike. Recently revamped, the restaurant now includes an 80-seat brasserie for casual-elegant meals and an intimate 30-seat formal dining chamber (the Röckenwagner Room) where two prix fixe meals are offered Tues.–Sat. 6–9 p.m. The brasserie's German-inflected Cal-Continental menu includes originals like weisswurst with pretzel roll and sweet Bavarian mustard, veal goulash with spatzle, and seared striped bass with pea shoots and saffron sauce. For Sunday brunch, there are homemade pastries, sautéed bratwurst with eggs, and a delicious German apple pancake. *Open Sun.–Fri. 5:30–10 p.m., Sat. 5:30–10:30 p.m., Sun. brunch 10 a.m.–3 p.m.* $-$$

Sushi Roku

1401 Ocean Ave., Santa Monica, 310-458-4771

In short order, this stylin' Japanese chain became one of the hottest destinations with the in-crowd for straight-ahead premium sushi, cantaloupe martinis, rich desserts, and trendy Cal-Asian dishes like grilled yellowtail with cilantro sesame sauce, flash-fried striped bass with spicy ponzu sauce, and a pan-roasted Main lobster with shrimp, scallops, and garlic peppercorn sauce. The Santa Monica branch isn't quite as industry-saturated as its precursor in West Hollywood (323-655-6767), but the spacious dining room is just as sleek and patrons tend to wear black here too. If you're up in Pasadena, there's a Sushi Roku near you (626-683-3000). *Open for lunch Mon.–Fri. 11:30 a.m.–2:30 p.m.; dinner 5:30–11:30 p.m.; Sat. 11 a.m. –11:30 p.m.; Sun. 4:30–11:30 p.m.* $

Uncle Bill's Pancake House

1305 Highland Ave., Manhattan Beach, 310-545-5177

This sunny breakfast spot is at its craziest on Sundays when half of Manhattan Beach arrives to up their cholesterol count with huge portions of eggs, pancakes, hash browns, and cheddar-cheese-and-bacon waffles. The indoor tables turn over faster, but Uncle Bill's patio is really where you want to be—on a hill overlooking flower-lined cottages and the ocean. It's worth putting your name on the list and taking a longer walk. *Open Mon.–Fri. 6 a.m.–3 p.m., Sat.–Sun. 7 a.m.– 3 p.m.* $

Coastal L.A.: The Nightlife

Cameo Bar

1819 Ocean Ave., Santa Monica, 310-260-7500

The stylish lobby lounge in the new and very chic Viceroy Hotel saves a drive out to West Hollywood for hipsters and industry types who'd rather be schmoozing, posing, and sipping cosmopolitans near the ocean. Outfitted with bold custom furnishings, glass cocktail tables, Colonial green walls, and a shag-rug library area with angled bookshelves, the main draw is still the outside deck with its twin plunge pools and private cabanas starting at $500/day. While the hotel awaits a less restrictive liquor license, drinks must stay inside the building. *Open daily 11 a.m.–2 a.m.*

Chez Jay

1657 Ocean Ave., Santa Monica, 310-395-1741

If a tidal wave hit Santa Monica, this portholed survivor on Ocean Avenue would live to tell the tale. A veteran dive bar/restaurant strewn with peanut shells and filled with old-timers, bit-part actors, and the odd celeb, Chez Jay has chalked up some serious yarns in its 45 years. Owner Jay Fiondella would be happy to tell you about the time Steve McQueen rode in on his motorbike, or the one about Alan Shepard smuggling a Chez Jay peanut to the moon. Untuck your shirt and have a seat at the friendly bar. Or grab a private booth in the back for steaks and lobster tails. *Open Mon. 6 p.m. –2 a.m., Tues.–Fri. 12 p.m.–2 a.m., Sat.–Sun. 9 a.m.–2 a.m.*

Circle Bar

2926 Main St., Santa Monica, 310-450-0508

New ownership and a complete overhaul a few years ago transformed this former bad-boys beer bar into one of Santa Monica's top lounges. Tricked out with Bruce Lee posters and a Far East palette, the tight oval-shaped room gets packed on weekends when young Westside hipsters come here to prey on each other. The jukebox is loud, the drinks are tasty, and DJs spin on Tuesdays (white trash rock), Wednesdays (dance, techno, hip hop), and Sundays (trance, house). *Open nightly 9 p.m.–2 a.m. $*

Harvelle's

1432 4th St., Santa Monica, 310-395-1676

The Westside's oldest blues club (1931) has drawn an impressive roster of top performers onto a compact stage that might seem more at home in Chicago than a block above Santa Monica's Third Street Promenade. Weekend crowds can quickly make this slim, dark bar seem like an overstuffed phone booth, especially on its tight, checkered dance floor that's cheek-by-jowl with the musicians. On calmer nights, you'll hear some good local journeyman bands jamming blues, soul, and funk for an informed crowd of Westsiders and tourists. *Open nightly 8 p.m.–2 a.m.* $

McCabe's Guitar Shop

3101 Pico Blvd., Santa Monica, 310-828-4497

During the day, this hallowed guitar shop is a great place to test top-of-the-line Martins and Taylors without anyone getting on your case. After hours, the back guitar room serves as a makeshift concert floor that's best judged by the artists who've played on it, including Beck, Jackson Browne, Elizabeth Cotton, Charlie Haden, John Lee Hooker, Les Paul, and an assortment of international greats from Ali Farka Toure to the throat singers of Tuva. Just make sure you're not sitting behind a post. *For shows call the 24-hour concert hotline, 310-828-4403.* $

Side Door

900 Manhattan Ave., Manhattan Beach, 310-372-1684

An antivenom for all those South Bay alehouses, sports bars, and tube top patios blasting Bob Seger and Tom Petty, Manhattan Beach's littlest lounge has no sign, no front entrance, and best of all, a no flip-flops policy. It could be mistaken for a private party if there wasn't a line curving out the door on weekends. So what's all the fuss about? Half a dozen small tables, a few couches with silk pillows, a funky soundtrack, and a civilized dude tending bar who may or may not have a bottle of Viognier handy but at least knows what it is. *Open Sun.–Thurs. 5 p.m.–midnight, Fri.–Sat. 5 p.m.–1:30 a.m.* $

Temple Bar

1026 Wilshire Blvd., Santa Monica, 310-393-6611

Music is what sets this live venue apart from the usual dark sexy lounge filled with glowing candles and grinning Buddhas. House DJs trade sets with an eclectic mix of funk, hip hop, R&B, and Latin bands from down the street or across the globe. Theme nights include Jazz Mondays and a feast for Latin and African grooves on Thursdays called "Rhythm Room." Burgers, samosas, blackened shrimp tacos, and other good eats are accompanied by a tasty martini menu. *Open Sun.–Thurs. 8 p.m.–2 a.m., Fri.–Sat. 9 p.m.–2 a.m.* $

The Veranda at Casa del Mar

1910 Ocean Way, Santa Monica, 310-581-5533

A big deal in the 1920s and '30s, the immense lobby lounge at this restored waterfront landmark is back in business. Gawk for a moment from the Hotel Casa del Mar's front entrance, where a lavish sunken salon of plush velvet couches, rattan chairs, and a huge stone hearth leads to an equally grand bar area with floor-to-ceiling windows framing the Pacific. Martinis are a specialty here. There's also an excellent selection of wines by the glass and a light lounge menu which includes calamari fritters, chicken dumplings, grilled shrimp, and panini with buffalo mozzarella. Jazz and other live music is featured nightly. *Open Sun.–Thurs. 11 a.m.–11:30 p.m., Fri.–Sat. 11 a.m.–12:30 a.m.*

Zanzibar

1301 5th St., Santa Monica, 310-451-2221

The resident DJs at Zanzibar would be welcome at any dance club in town. The fact that they're spinning nu-jazz, future-soul, electro-dub, and afro-beat at a hot new lounge brought to you by the creators of Temple Bar means that Santa Monica must have a club scene worth knowing about—even if it's only at this stylish Indian/African dance mecca. *Open Wed.–Sun. 9 p.m.–2 a.m.* $

Coastal L.A.: The Attractions

Aqua Day Spa

1422 2nd St., Santa Monica, 310-899-6222

When at Aqua, do as the Romans did—hit the baths. Half a dozen soaking pools offer a road to recovery at this top day spa in downtown Santa Monica. Follow up with various scrubs, rubs, wraps, masks, vitamin peels, beauty treatments, or the very popular Stone Abhyanga massage, which uses heated rocks and aromatic oils to loosen all your knots. If your body needs it, this place probably offers it. *Open Mon. noon–10 p.m., Tues.–Thurs. 10 a.m. –10 p.m., Fri.–Sat. 9 a.m.–10 p.m., Sun. 10 a.m.–9 p.m.*

Bergamot Station

2525 Michigan Ave., Santa Monica, 310-829-5854

Get your art fix all in one place at this unique complex, an agglomeration of 33 local galleries, ten shops, and a museum. As the converted warehouses might indicate, this site did time as an industrial wasteland before becoming an eclectic forum for local painters, sculptors, photographers, jewelers, and a variety of other skilled artisans. Contemporary exhibits can be found at the Santa Monica Museum of Art in building G-1. When everything starts to look the same, it's time for a break at The Gallery Cafe, where tasty specials change daily. *Open Tues.–Fri. 10 a.m.–5 p.m., Sat. 11 a.m.–5 p.m. (most galleries).*

Escape on Horseback

2623 Old Topanga Canyon Rd., Topanga Canyon, 818-591-2032

The back yard of this friendly ranch high up in the Santa Monica Mountains is a vast chaparral-covered wilderness with miles of trails and dramatic views of the coast. Saddle up for a 90-minute ride with an experienced guide who'll let you canter if you can handle a horse. Groups rarely exceed six people, and intimate two-person rides can be arranged with advance notice. Romantic sunset rides in the hills with a gourmet dinner are also offered. $$$$

Leo Carillo State Beach

35000 Pacific Coast Highway, Malibu, 818-880-0350

Nearly 30 miles upcoast from Santa Monica at the county line, Malibu's last stop attracts surfers, sailboarders, and beachcombers to its one-and-a-half mile sandy beach speckled with sea caves and some nice tide pools. Hikers and campers can cross the highway to the adjoining state park filled with hilly trails and sycamore-sheltered campgrounds. Between December and April keep a lookout for gray whales.

Malibu Country Club

901 Encinal Canyon Rd., Malibu, 818-889-6680

Los Angeles has a ton of golf clubs open to the public, but none with names like this. High above the coast of Malibu, the gates of this William F. Bell-designed, par 72 course are surprisingly wide open to nonmembers. There aren't any ocean views on these canyon-encased fairways, but they are lovely, secluded grounds in their own right. There's no driving range either, so warm up in the shower before you come. *Open Mon. 6:30 a.m. –3:30 p.m., Tues.–Sun. 6:30 a.m.–7 p.m.*

Manhattan Beach

End of Manhattan Beach Blvd., Manhattan Beach

Hard-to-please visitors tend to cheer up when taken to this swell yuppie back yard in the South Bay—"Now, this is California." Even former squatters like the Beach Boys would gasp at the rents down here these days. Otherwise, it's still Endless Summer at this mecca for surfers, volleyball exhibitionists, rollerbladers, and bikini chasers. If you wove all the blond hair together on this sunny strand, it would reach Jupiter. For a lively happy hour, head one beach community south and take your pick of bars on the Hermosa Strand.

Marina del Rey Sportfishing

Dock 52, Fiji Way, Marina Del Rey, 310-822-3625

This 30-year-old company has built a sturdy reputation for finding the fish. Experienced and novice anglers alike can choose from a variety of open-party half- or three-quarter–day trips. Licensed vessels comb Santa Monica Bay for all seasonal gamefish including yellowtail, bass, barracuda, halibut, and bonita. Rods and tackle can be rented, bait is included, lunch is served on the longer excursions, and even fish cleaning and packaging is offered. During Gray Whale migration season (January–March), whale watching trips are also offered every morning during the week and twice daily on weekends. *Half-day fishing trips leave at 6:30 a.m. and noon, returning approximately five hours later. Three-quarter day trips depart at 7 or 8 a.m., returning at around 3 p.m.* $$-$$$

Marina Sailing

13441 Mindanao Way, Marina del Rey, 310-822-6617

One of six Marina Sailing locations scattered along the SoCal coast between Ventura and San Diego, this one lets you pull out of the world's largest manmade pleasure-craft marina on vessels ranging from a 20-foot Santana to a 42-foot Catamaran. Reasonably priced quarter-day, half-day, and full-day rentals are offered with or without skippers. Weekend sailing lessons can also be arranged. $$$$

Montana Avenue

From Seventh St. to 17th St., Santa Monica

Shabby Chic, Jill Roberts, Michael Stars, and A.B.S. are just a few of the 150 establishments lining this tree-lined stretch of boutiques, galleries, vintage furniture shops, cafes, and restaurants in Santa Monica's upscale north end.

Ocean Front Walk

From Rose Ave. to Washington St., Venice Beach

Venice Beach's carnivalesque Strand has received some clean-up funds over the last few years. Thankfully, it hasn't lost its essential grit. Buy some incense or ten pairs of sunglasses for a steal. Get a massage from a homeless chiropractor. Check out the dudes pumping iron, shooting hoops, banging drums, or spouting off on some nutty subject. Here, the circus is always in town.

Paradise Bound Yacht Charters

Ritz-Carlton Hotel, 4375 Admiralty Way, Marina del Rey, 310-578-7963

The "Silver Eagle," a 42-foot Catalina Sailing Yacht with three private double cabins and gourmet meal service, operates out of the Ritz-Carlton for luxury sunset cruises, marriage proposals, birthdays, and all other occasions. $$$$

Point Mugu State Park

9000 Pacific Coast Hwy., Point Mugu State Park, Malibu, 818-880-0350

More than 70 miles of hiking trails at this 15,000-acre retreat in the Santa Monica Mountains include five miles of varied Malibu coastline and a lofty backdrop of river canyons, sycamore-dotted valleys, and one of the last remaining examples of indigenous California grassland. The La Jolla Valley Loop Trail is a moderately strenuous but crowd-free ten-mile ramble that starts at the Ray Miller trailhead and passes seasonal waterfalls, oak groves, and bursts of sage, lavender, and wildflowers in the spring. Near the junction of these two trails, the La Jolla Valley Camp provides piped water, restrooms, and oak-shaded picnic tables. Bag a few more miles and find higher vista points on this day hike by cutting west from the Valley Loop Trail to the Mugu Peak Trail.

Pure Surfing Experience

524 14th St., Manhattan Beach, 310-546-4451

Now entering its seventh year, Manhattan Beach's official surf school has helped thousands of people learn how to safely ride the waves, including kids as young as five and as old as seventy. Founded by a former L.A. County lifeguard and run by pro-level instructors, the school offers private lessons (usually 90 minutes) as well as weekend group clinics at Manhattan Beach's Rosecrans break and at two other reliable spots nearby. Boards and wet suits are included, safety is emphasized, and nearly everyone stands up in the first or second class. $$$$

South Bay Bicycle Trail

From Will Rogers State Beach to Torrance County Beach

Spanning 22 miles from Pacific Palisades to the South Bay with a few detours along the way, this paved bicycle path lets you check off as many beaches, boardwalks, and piers as your leg muscles will allow. Have coffee in Santa Monica and brunch in Marina del Rey. Or do breakfast in Venice, late-lunch in Manhattan Beach, and happy hour in Hermosa. Just be back before the rental counter closes. Congestion is heaviest between Santa Monica and Venice, where the path is shared with walkers, joggers, bladers, skaters, wheelchair riders, three-wheel recumbent bikers, and people on other various contraptions. Keep going and it lightens to almost nothing on long open stretches at Dockweiler State Beach and El Segundo Beach before traffic picks up again at Manhattan Beach.

Temescal Gateway Park

Temescal Gateway Park, 15601 Sunset Blvd., Pacific Palisades, 310-454-1395

This accessible park right off of Sunset Blvd. in Pacific Palisades is one of the Westside's quickest and easiest escape hatches into the mountains, providing well-tended trails and some wonderful views of the coast at the top. Enter the parking lot from Sunset at Temescal Canyon Road (or save a few bucks by parking on the street). Temescal Ridge Trail and Temescal Canyon Trail form a five-mile loop up a moderate to steep grade—passing seasonal waterfalls, rocky outcrops, and sweeping ocean vistas. Watch out for poison oak (leaves grow three to a stem and each leaf contains three leaflets, which look like small oak leaves). Bring your own water.

Third Street Promenade

Between Broadway and Wilshire Blvd., Santa Monica

Developed in the late '80s, downtown Santa Monica's lively three-block pedestrian zone of restaurants, shops, cafes, theaters, kiosks, and nonstop street performances is one of the great models of civic revitalization. Friday and Saturday nights can be a zoo here, when extended store hours often run past midnight. Climbing rents have shoved out some of the smaller players, but Borders, Barnes & Noble, and Banana Republic haven't completely taken over. Other popular stops include the Broadway Deli, Arcana Books, Z Gallerie, Anthropologie, and a new Krispy Kreme donut stand.

Zuma Beach

30050 Pacific Coast Highway, Malibu

Malibu's best full-service beach borders quieter gems like Westward Beach and Point Dume's County Beach, which are slightly trickier to access. For a restful day on four miles of sand with restrooms, lifeguards, volleyball courts, gymnastic rings, and fry-shacks when you need them, start here. The water is clean, the surf's decent, the sand is beer-bottle-free, and Santa Monica is a relaxing 20 miles away. Save six bucks by parking for free on PCH.

Downtown & About L.A.

In Los Angeles on business? Who says you have to act like it the whole time? When the meeting adjourns, the convention's over, and the tie and name tag come off, you can get a lot more out of this town than free HBO and a decent night's sleep. From Downtown galleries and historic sights and Pasadena's top spas and fairways to some of the city's best retreats and culinary finds, Downtown & About L.A. helps you pack some off-hours L.A. punch into your next business trip.

Downtown & About L.A.: The Itinerary

Three Great Days and Nights

Your Hotel: **Millennium Biltmore Hotel Los Angeles**

Morning: Start your day at Smeraldi's, the Biltmore's handsome breakfast and dining room. Or up your cholesterol count at L.A.'s beloved 24/7 *greasy spoon*, the **Original Pantry Café,** where no one will bat an eye if you order a ribeye with your pancakes.

Take the morning to explore Downtown L.A.'s *architectural and historical wonders* that are hiding below, behind, and between the mandatory stack of bank towers. A tour of the newly opened, Frank Gehry–designed **Walt Disney Concert Hall** should be at the top of your list, if only just to see what $274 million buys these days. Then stroll down into the thick of Broadway on the lower end of Bunker Hill to the **Bradbury Building**, a five-story 19th-century masterpiece that you'd easily miss from the outside but may recognize once you're through the doors as a location in the movie *Blade Runner.* Across the street is L.A.'s oldest and largest *food and produce bazaar*, **Grand Central Market**. Whether you're looking for a quick fish taco, a refreshing cup of tamarindo, or five pounds of chicken feet or whatever—this is the place. Then, head north on Broadway into **Chinatown** and have a wander, or ramble a few blocks east to explore **Little Tokyo**, another compact cultural pocket in Downtown L.A.

Afternoon: Get a unique perspective of L.A. at one of several classic Downtown lunch stops. For a leisurely meal, dine out in the sunny courtyard at **Traxx** in L.A.'s *beautiful Union Station*. Nearby, **Philippe the Original** shares the honors of Oldest Restaurant in the City (1908) and Best French Dip Sandwich with its equally nostalgia-inducing rival Cole's P.E. Buffet, down on seedier Sixth St. But Philippe's wins for its ten-cent cup of coffee, its daring purple-pickled egg, and a surprisingly decent wine list. For a homey meal with outrageously kitschy decor, step inside **Clifton's Brookdale Cafeteria** and linger over ox tails or roast turkey with all the trimmings in an oddly feel-good setting. For a view of Downtown's artier side—and some good *bistro fare*—have a seat at the lively hide-away **410 Boyd**.

The **Los Angeles County Museum of Art** (LACMA) boasts one of the country's largest holdings of paintings, photos, sculptures, textiles, and other works dating back to the ancients—which would explain that gravitational pull you're experiencing as you head up Wilshire Blvd.'s *Museum Row* and into this huge facility. Another engaging afternoon option is the **Museum of Tolerance**, where you can view gripping exhibits about race and prejudice in America, many of them interactive, with a large segment devoted to the history of the Holocaust. Right Downtown on the edge of Little Tokyo, the unique **Japanese American National Museum** provides both triumphant and heartbreaking chronicles of Japanese American life over several generations.

If you're tired from too many meetings or weary from too much walking, loosen all your knots by booking a massage and "taking the waters" at the **Beverly Hot Springs**, a classic Korean-style spa that (you'd never guess) is sitting right on the city's only natural *thermal mineral water* spring.

Evening: Start with drinks and unbeatable views at **Windows**, perched on the 32nd floor of the TransAmerica Center. Then move on to **Patina**, superchef Joachim Splichal's *Cal-French flagship* and one of the city's most renowned dining rooms—now open inside the new Walt Disney Concert Hall. If reservations elude you here, another Splichal charmer is the nearby Italian restaurant, **Zucca**. For a real done-up Italian dining experience and a Russian novel–sized wine list, **Cicada** is your place. Or, for some of the best sushi and Japanese cuisine in the city, reserve at the stylish **R-23**, hiding out on the other side of the tracks.

Whether it's dinner and a show or a show then dinner, you can pair any of the above restaurants with *a pair of tickets* for a swell night Downtown. Nearby are the L.A. Philharmonic at the **Walt Disney Concert Hall**; big-name shows and musicals at the **Ahmanson Theater**; and award-winning dramas at the **Mark Taper Forum**. Between late spring and early fall, head up to Griffith Park's famous **Greek Theatre**, the place to hear your favorite bands jamming alfresco.

Close the night out on the festive **Rooftop Bar at The Standard Downtown**, one of L.A.'s hottest spots, featuring a studiously hip crowd and—what else?—private poolside cabanas.

Day 2

Morning: Enjoy a room service breakfast and then energize yourself for big day ahead at the Biltmore's *well-stocked health facility*, which includes a gorgeous Pompeii-themed natatorium.

Time to head out. No exploration of Downtown L.A. is complete without a visit to the **Museum of Contemporary Art** (MOCA). Half-buried in Bunker Hill, the building itself is an *impressive exhibit* and is home to one of the country's finest collections of American and European art. Admission includes entrance into **The Geffen Contemporary**, MOCA's cool offsite property, just five minutes away in Little Tokyo. Another illuminating art stop in the area is the smaller and lesser known **Museum of Neon Art** (MONA).

Afternoon: For lunch, you're in a great position to choose between two of Downtown's top restaurants. Just around the corner from the Standard, **Café Pinot** is a brasserie serving light Cal-Continental cuisine with wide-angle *skyscraper views*. **Water Grill** is commonly called the city's est seafood restaurant, featuring a phenomenal raw bar and the very freshest catches of the day.

Downtown may be where L.A. got started, but you may have noticed that the city has grown a bit since then. Pull out of the central business district and take an afternoon (at the very least) to get acquainted with another Los Angeles neighborhood or two (or three). Heading west: Cruise along *Hollywood Boulevard* to taste some of old Tinseltown and what's become of it (get your bearings by flipping through the Classic Hollywood itinerary, pp. 69–73). Carry on to West Hollywood's Sunset Strip and downtown Beverly Hills (the New Hollywood section provides ideas for this, pp. 91–111). Or go the distance, and hit the beaches and boardwalks of Santa Monica and Venice (see Coastal L.A., pp. 134–159).

Evening: Now that you're on the Westside, you've got a few hundred excellent restaurants to choose from. Top picks include **Matsuhisa**, one of the world's famous destinations for Japanese cuisine. **Alex** is a hot and haute Cal-French class act from celebrated young chef Alex Scrimgeour. Equally fresh and exciting is **Opaline**, a *chic modern bistro* serving inspired Cal-French cuisine. For the finest of fine French meals in L.A., **L'Orangerie** still takes top honors. Down the street is **Sona**, another serious foodie stop featuring a variety of rousing tasting-menus in a Zen-like atmosphere. If you're hungry for couscous, succulent squab, sweet b'stilla, or other Moroccan delights (like an on-call belly dancer) a feast at **Dar Maghreb** is something you won't soon forget.

Any bars around here? In fact, there are so many you'll have to pardon our exclusions. For the *real-deal martini* in old-school Hollywood, begin by seating yourself in one of the swivel chairs at the gorgeous bar at **Musso & Frank Grill**, the neighborhood's oldest restaurant. Carry on to the theme-y bars and hipster lounges lining Cahuenga Blvd. and Vine St., including **Beauty Bar** and **Daddy's**. For the velvet rope treatment on the Sunset Strip, try your luck at **Skybar** or **Barfly**. When you've had enough, retire to the elegant **Polo Lounge** in the Beverly Hills Hotel.

Day 3

Morning: Begin your day at whichever place you didn't go on day one, either Smeraldi's or the Original Pantry Café, and fuel up for a good walk. Choose one of the **Los Angeles Conservancy Walking Tours** in the Downtown area that highlight the historical and architectural treasures this nonprofit organization helps preserve. Then, take a number (bring along a paper) and experience Chinatown's most famous *dim sum brunch* at **Empress Pavilion**. Golfers can get a head start in Pasadena with 18 holes at **Brookside Golf Course**. Or go the distance and reserve a tee time at **Industry Hills Golf Club**, which boasts two of the finest courses in SoCal.

Afternoon: It's about time **Arnie Morton's of Chicago** got a downtown L.A. location. Enter this *classic steakhouse* for a wonderful midday meal that should tide you over until dinner—next week. For a marginally lighter but still tasty and satisfying lunch, Pasadena's best burgers and pies await you at—where else?—**Pie 'N Burger**.

If all you know about Pasadena is the Little Old Lady, you've got a lot to catch up on. Historic downtown Pasadena has a slower-paced charm that lets you step out of L.A.'s hubbub for a spell. Just minutes away, feast your eyes on one of the world's most remarkable *private art collections* at the **Norton Simon Museum**. Or wander through the 150-acre **Huntington Botanical Gardens** and have high tea at the **Rose Garden Tea Room**. Whatever you do, be sure to reserve an hour for rejuvenation on the massage table or in the Vichy shower—or both—at **Amadeus Spa**, an award-winning full-service facility in downtown Pasadena.

Evening: One of the best shows in Pasadena this evening is likely being performed at the **Pasadena Playhouse**, a lovingly restored *drama stage* and one of the city's proudest and oldest landmarks.

Though it feels a bit apart, Pasadena is still solidly a part of the L.A. scene. Dinner options can be as star-studded and foodie-friendly as in any other part of town. Dine late at **Madre's**, a hot restaurant under the J-Lo label that features Latin cuisine, live music on the weekends, and a *lively bar scene*. Or, savor a night of tasty Chinese-Malaysian cuisine at the lovely **Nonya**—one of the city's most delectably unique Asian-fusion kitchens. For a romantic evening, opt for a patio table at **The Raymond**, a homey retreat serving outstanding Cal-Continental dishes.

During the summer and early fall, another Saturday evening option is to head back Downtown and experience the popular **Los Angeles Neon Tour,** an open-air, double-decker road trip through *the neon-rich streets* of Downtown and Hollywood. Afterward, if you're still hungry, pull into the **Pacific Dining Car**, the only upscale restaurant in L.A. that never closes. This '20s-era classic is best known for its steaks, but they'll also happily serve you a great eggs Benedict after 11 p.m.

Cap off the night back at the Biltmore's stately **Gallery Bar**, one of the most *elegant lounges* on either side of town, and congratulate yourself on making a vacation out of what might have been just a business trip.

Downtown & About L.A.: The Hotels

Hilton Checkers Hotel

535 S. Grand Ave., Downtown, 213-624-0000 / 800-423-5798
www.checkershotel.com

While downtown Los Angeles doesn't offer as much obvious romance as Malibu, Beverly Hills, or Bel-Air, its palpable sense of history and its air of un-Hollywoodized refinement offers a distinctly different and in some ways grander view of the city. Nowhere will you find more charming evidence of this than at the Hilton (formerly Wyndham) Checkers Hotel, a 12-story boutique property and a historic monument, which remains one of the finest examples of Old World charm in Los Angeles (along with its neighbor across the street, the Millennium Biltmore). One hundred eighty-eight rooms and suites resonate with European style (though the standard deluxe rooms are a little on the small side). Suites provide plenty of extra space, including a full guest bathroom and a sunlit dining area. Highlights include a rooftop pool and Jacuzzi deck with unbeatable close-ups of the L.A. skyline. The famous Checkers Restaurant, once presided over by The French Laundry's Thomas Keller, remains a local favorite, serving exceptional Cal-Continental cuisine and offering pre-show dinner packages that include transportation to and from Downtown's Performing Arts Center. Weekend romance packages include deluxe accommodations, sparkling wine, and a full room-service breakfast. $$

Millennium Biltmore Hotel-Los Angeles

506 S. Grand Ave. Downtown, 213-624-1011 / 800-245-8673
www.millenniumhotels.com

Since 1923, L.A.'s grand dame of hotels has hosted kings, presidents, dignitaries, the Beatles, generations of celebrities, and businessmen milking their corporate expense accounts for all they're worth. A treasured landmark right in the heart of Downtown's central business district, this 11-floor Italian Renaissance–style beauty is the only hotel in town with its own separate walking tour hosted by the Los Angeles Conservancy. It has also received more facelifts over the years than Joan Rivers, the latest being in 2002 from new owners Millennium Hotels and Resorts. In a city where urban improvement has often meant tearing something old and in-the-way down only to replace it with a monstrosity or parking lot, the Biltmore, with its frescoed lobby and 683 stately guest rooms, remains the city's most reliable Old World fixture. Classic Rooms, occupying the third through ninth floors, feature warm gold, cream, and ivory color schemes with rich woods, plush drapery, French shutters, and rather small but well-appointed marble bathrooms. Newly modeled Club Rooms on the tenth and eleventh floors offer extra space, personalized butler service, and access to the exclusive Club Lounge, where a complimentary continental breakfast is served. Two restaurant options at the hotel include Sai Sai for sushi, tempura, and traditional Japanese kaiseki meals and Smeraldi's for casual Cal-Italian cuisine. Just past the lobby, the handsome Gallery Bar is downtown's most dignified retreat for a premium cocktail. One floor down, the Biltmore's venerable health club is also something to see, offering full spa facilities and a gorgeous Roman-style pool. $$

St. Regis Los Angeles

2055 Avenue of the Stars, Century City, 310-277-6111 / 800-325-3589 www.stregis.com

Staying out in Century City may not have as much cachet as lodging next door in Beverly Hills or up in West Hollywood—with a few outstanding exceptions. The latest is this extravagant property, a sure candidate for Best New Hotel, occupying the former tower annex of the Century Plaza (after a $43 million renovation, of course). As sumptuous as any guest room on the "in" side of the hills, the floor-to-ceiling views, stretching from Downtown to the Hollywood Hills and to the coast are, if anything, even more commanding from this luxurious high-rise. Done up in rich chocolate and mustard shades, the 297 well-appointed rooms provide huge California king beds with Frette linens, full marble and mahogany bathrooms with deep soaking tubs and separate showers, comfy sitting areas, and private balconies with those views. Classic high tea and light meals are served in the elegant St. Regis Lounge, and fine Cal-French dining is enjoyed inside or outside at the hotel's restaurant, Encore. There's also a full European spa and health club with a heated outdoor pool. If you still need it, Beverly Hills is just a mile away. $$$$

The Standard Downtown

550 S. Flower St. Downtown, 213-892-8080 www.standardhotel.com

What's life without risks? The Standard, which already had such a good thing going at its trendy West Hollywood flagship, took a big leap in reimagining this former Superior Oil company headquarters as a haven for young, hip suits stuck down in the financial district. Has it paid off? We haven't looked at the books, but the Rooftop Bar crowds alone seem to indicate yes. The hotel's 207 guest rooms are playfully grouped into nine Standard-esque subcategories, ranging from "Cheap" (260 sq. ft/$95) to "Huge" (420 sq. ft./$205), "Gigantic" (460 sq. ft./$225), "Humongous" (580 sq. ft./$275), and "Wow!" (710 sq. ft./$325). All of them come with multipurpose "Living" Platform Beds, designed for every other imaginable bed-friendly activity besides sleeping; oversized down pillows and duvets; cordless two-line speaker phones with data ports; fully-loaded stereos; stocked mini bars; and welcome little details like extra-strength travel candles and a full supply of aromapharmacy products. Entry-level digs are on the lower floors, with queen-sized beds, big glass-enclosed showers (no tub), and little else to write home about. Medium rooms get you farther off the ground and large rooms provide some extra space and a king-sized bed. Guests who want a tub have to go up to at least XL ($185) and can spring an extra $20–40 for a vanity area and extra closet space. What do the Wow! rooms have that the others don't? Emperor-sized beds, separate lounging areas, and big-screen TVs. There's also a Big Penthouse ($450) and Bigger Penthouse ($500). Hotel facilities include a 24-hour restaurant, a fully-equipped fitness center, and an indoor lobby lounge with billiard tables. $$

Downtown & About L.A.: The Restaurants

Alex

6703 Melrose Ave., Los Angeles, 323-933-5233

Ultratalented toque Alex Scrimgeour presides over this outstanding Cal-French newcomer, featuring gourmet cuisine and inventive prix fixe meals in a class of their own. Menus are seasonal and might include such rich offerings as grilled langoustine accented with anchovy butter, sea bass swaddled in pancetta, and a goat cheese soufflé. The setting is as sophisticated as the food, a cathedral of dark mahogany furnishings, stained glass, and moss-green walls. *Open Mon.–Sat. 6–10 p.m.* $$$

Arnie Morton's of Chicago

735 S. Figueroa St., Downtown, 213-553-4566

Branches of this first-class steakhouse stretch from Hackensack to Kowloon, so it's about time Downtown made it onto Morton's map. Until a few years ago, anyone craving the Morton's experience (which includes the whole tableside treatment) had to journey west to La Cienega Blvd. Now you can sit in this rough-hewn boy's club and enjoy first-rate chops just three blocks north of the Staples Center. Fresh fish, lobster, and chicken entrées are nice but come in second to the signature beef cuts, including the house specialty, a 24-ounce porterhouse. Save room the chocolate velvet cake or the hot upside-down apple pie. *Open Mon.–Fri. 11:30 a.m.–11 p.m., Sat. 5:30 –11 p.m., Sunday 5–10 p.m.* $$$

Café Pinot

700 W. Fifth St., Downtown, 213-239-6500

Part of the distinguished Pinot restaurant group run by über-chef Joachim Splichal, this small brasserie is known for its lighter interpretations of Cal-French cuisine—a relative term that still includes duck leg confit and a bowl of French onion soup dripping in cheese if you require it. The leafy patio and canopied sky room overlooking the Central Library's lovely Maguire Gardens provides the perfect oasis beneath all the bank towers for business lunches or pre-theatre dining, and welcomes a fairly eclectic mix of week-end downtowners. *Open for lunch Mon.–Fri. 11:30 a.m.–2:30 p.m.; dinner Sun. 4:30–9 p.m., Mon.–Tues. 5–9 p.m., Wed.–Thurs. 5–9:30 p.m., Fri.–Sat. 5–10 p.m.* $

Cicada

617 S. Olive St., Downtown, 213-488-9488

Any more gold leaf on the ceiling of this eye-popping Deco dining room and it would have to be moved from the historic Oviatt Building to Fort Knox. One of Downtown L.A.'s classic formal dining destinations, Cicada is a favorite venue for weddings, corporate dinners, and any other events requiring chenille sofas and a 600-label wine list that's difficult to lift. Antipastis at this elegant Nouvelle Northern Italian spot include seared foie gras with caramelized mango, microgreens in vanilla coulis, or tarragon-scented crab cake on a bed of white coleslaw in a dijon mustard remoulade. This might be followed by duck ravioli with shitake mushrooms, sweet peas, and shallots, or tornedos of sesame salmon with skinned red potatoes, baby carrots, and Swiss chard in a pinot noir sauce. *Open for lunch Mon.–Fri. 11:30 a.m. –2 p.m.; dinner Mon.–Sat. 5:30–9 p.m.* $$

Clifton's Brookdale Cafeteria

648 S. Broadway, Downtown, 213-627-1673

Smack in the middle of Broadway, you can escape to the back woods. The redwood wilderness theme in this beloved depression-era cafeteria includes a stuffed moose, a 20-foot waterfall, lots of fake boulders, and a chapel built inside a fake tree. Don't come here for the lamb shank and the Jell-O (like we need to tell you that), but for the amazingly atmospheric nourishment in this five-story L.A. kitsch-fest. *Open Mon.–Fri. 6:30 a.m.–6 p.m., Sat.–Sun. 6:30 a.m.–7 p.m.* $

Dar Maghreb

7651 W. Sunset Blvd., Hollywood, 323-876-7651

You'll find this exotic 27-year-old venue on a relatively quiet patch of Sunset Boulevard in Hollywood. Enter through large doors into a compact greeting area where monastic robed hosts lead you into a dark dining room that might be a set from *The Arabian Nights*. Seat yourself at a cushioned knee-high table, where a bowl of water is brought for a traditional hand-washing. Choose from one of several prix fixe meals and prepare for a course-by-course Moroccan-style feast that you eat with your hands (hence the mandatory hand-washing). Specials of the evening include couscous and sweet eggy b'stilla, savory lamb and squab dishes, and frequent appearances by a young, writhing belly dancer who appreciates having bills tucked into her apparel. Gape for a few moments at the bill, then remember that part of what you're paying for here is the experience. *Open Mon.–Fri. 6–11 p.m., Sat.–Sun. 5:30–11 p.m.* $$$

Empress Pavilion

Bamboo Plaza, 988 N. Hill St., Chinatown, 213-617-9898

The weekend dim sum experience at this classic Cantonese banquet hall at the top of Chinatown is its strong suit (ignore the forgettable decor and perfunctory service, which you didn't come here for in the first place, so don't bother sweating the small stuff). Crowds are heaviest in the early afternoon, when a good portion of the city seems to be here waiting for their carts of steamed prawns, delectable dumplings, stewed chicken feet, and fried turnip cakes. Bring the Sunday paper along and take a number. Or, come in the off-hours for a variety of excellent Hong Kong–style seafood dishes and a garlicky steamed Dungeness crab worth driving miles for. *Open Mon.–Fri. 9 a.m.–10 p.m. (dim sum 'til 3 p.m.), Sat.–Sun. 8 a.m.–10 p.m. (dim sum 'til 2 p.m.)* $

410 Boyd

410 Boyd St., Downtown, 213-617-2491

Live slightly on the edge by venturing into a mildly intimidating pocket of Downtown and reward your palette at this cool, New American bistro. Highlights include the grilled ahi club sandwich, blackened chicken salad, an assortment of excellent pasta dishes, and the signature one-pound gorgonzola-crusted New York steak. The lively art bar scene here feels about as New York as downtown L.A. gets, with revolving local art exhibits to boot. Closed on the weekend. *Open Mon. 11:30 a.m.–2:30 p.m., Tues.–Fri. 11:30 a.m.–10 p.m.* $

L'Orangerie

903 N. La Cienega Blvd., West Hollywood, 310-652-9770

Recognized as the top French restaurant in Los Angeles (and one of only two kitchens in the city bearing the Relais Gourmand plaque), L'Orangerie offers one of the most refined dining experiences anywhere. Recent accolades include a 2003 Award of Excellence from the *Wine Spectator* and a Chef of the Year nod to new toque Christopher Eme, whose nightly prix fixe menus are an eight-course gastronomic event. Signature *amuse bouches* like egg in the shell with Petrossian Sevruga caviar might be followed by a perfectly presented roasted squab breast in wine sauce with macaroni gratin and tomato confit, or John Dory with crispy potatoes and greens. Slightly less intimidating than the opulent main dining room is the elegant patio, with a roof that slides open on moonlit nights. Wherever you sit, this is definitely special-occasion terrain. Reservations are strongly recommended. *Open Tues.–Sun. 6 –11 p.m.* $$$

Madre's

897 Granite Dr., Pasadena, 626-744-0900

You may not see owner Jennifer Lopez at her hot new addition to Pasadena's dining scene, but she's sat in at least a few of these chairs. The formal main dining room suggests old-school Havana, with lace tablecloths, fine china, and enough chandeliers to open a lighting store. The meaty Latin menu has a marked Cuban accent. Live Latin bands play Thursday through Saturday after 9 p.m. If you're not in the mood for braised oxtail, pounded steak *empanizado*, or skirt steak drizzled with *mojo criollo*, you can always just come for some of the best mojitos in town—priced accordingly. *Open Tues.–Sun. 11 a.m.–3 p.m., 5–11 p.m.* $$

Matsuhisa

129 N. La Cienega Blvd., Los Angeles, 310-659-9639

Only a few top chefs in Los Angeles have been granted celebrity status, and only one of them is a sushi master. At the founding location of his empire of destination Japanese restaurants (which now stretches from Aspen to Milan) Nobu Matsuhisa runs what many foodies continue to call the best restaurant in the city. There's lobster ceviche with lime stone lettuce, halibut cheeks with pepper sauce, and about a hundred more special plates to choose from. Just say "omakase" (chef's choice) to let Nobu's staff spare you the hassle of figuring it all out. *Open for lunch Mon.–Fri. 11:45 a.m.–2:15 p.m.; dinner daily 5:45–10:30 p.m.* $$$

Nonya

61 N. Raymond Ave., Pasadena, 626-583-8398

Nonya's cuisine is a delicate blend of Chinese, Indonesian, and Malaysian influences. The Asian garden-style dining room is a study in good feng shui, with rich dark woods, flickering candles, high ceilings, groves of potted bamboo, and a koi pond. Guests can warm-up with Asian cocktails at the bar during happy hour (*Mon.–Fri. 4–7 p.m.*) and continue with a savory selection of Southeast Asian–fusion delicacies. Start with a pungent satay or the signature salad ikan mangga, a refreshing medley of mango, halibut, and red onion lightly dressed in a lemongrass lime vinaigrette. Best-sellers include crispy Szechwan duck and a charbroiled lamb loin marinated with garlic, lemongrass, soy sauce, and chili. *Open for lunch Sun.–Fri. 11:30 a.m. –2:30 p.m.; dinner Sun.–Thurs. 5–10 p.m., Fri.–Sat. 5–11 p.m.* $

Opaline

7450 Beverly Blvd., Los Angeles, 323-857-6725

"Opaline," the term Oscar Wilde used to describe the color of absinthe, matches the yellow-green color palette in this hot new inventive Cal-French addition to Beverly Blvd.'s soaring dining scene. Like absinthe, it's a palette you take to or you don't. Fortunately, Opaline's "honest" wine list and its seasonal entrees, which might include rosemary-rubbed guinea hen, pan-seared loup de mer, and an out-of-this-world double-cut grilled pork chop, rise above any debates about restaurant design. An adjacent bar called "The Den" serves bargain small-plates of tapas and pressed sandwiches. *Open for lunch Mon.–Fri. 11:30 a.m.–2:30 p.m.; dinner Mon.–Sat. 5:30 –11:30 p.m.* $$

Original Pantry Café

875 S. Figueroa St., Downtown, 213-972-9279

There may be more facts and figures attached to this classic 24-hour steak and slaw greasepit than any other restaurant in the city—including that it's owned by a former L.A. mayor, that it grinds through about twenty cows a day, and that it's been keeping cardiologists in business since 1935. Of course, none of these stats much matter when you're buzzed and craving short ribs and a mountain of corn niblets at 3 a.m. (definitely the most sensible time to line up for a table or fryer-facing counter stool). Cash only. *Open daily 24 hours.* $

Pacific Dining Car

1310 W. 6th St., Downtown, 213-483-6000

You'd think a railcar-themed restaurant on the edge of Downtown that never closes would frighten most people away. Not so at this classy 83-year-old icon, which features USDA Prime Eastern corn-fed, dry-aged, mesquite-grilled beef and a wine list that would be tough to bench press. Get here around 5 p.m. for one of L.A.'s best happy hour spreads—baby back ribs, broiled chicken wings, and shrimp. Attention eggs benedict fans—y'all come back for breakfast, y'hear? *Open daily 24 hours.* $$$

Patina

Walt Disney Concert Hall, 141 S. Grand Ave., Downtown, 213-972-3331

Celebrated chef Joachim Splichal launched a restaurant and catering empire starting with this 14-year-old dining destination, one of only two Relais Gourmand kitchens in the city. The playful yet stunning Cal-French and prix fixe menus and impeccable waitstaff are now in a new location inside the Walt Disney Concert Hall. A private behind-the-scenes Chef's Table can accommodate two to six guests for a special seven-course meal with wine pairings. *Open daily for lunch 11:30 a.m.–2 p.m.; dinner 5–11 p.m.* $$$

Philippe the Original

1001 N. Alameda St., Downtown, 213-628-3781

Nostalgia at this 1908 landmark comes in the form of warm 'n' chubby French rolls packed with a lean pile of pork, ham, beef, lamb, or turkey, dipped in jus, and set on a plastic tray with a ten-cent cup-a-joe (and a purple pickled egg, if you like). Yes, there's sawdust on the floor and a slew of L.A. memorabilia on the walls. There's spicy homemade mustard on the family-style tables and one of the most varied lunch crowds you'll find anywhere. Cash only. *Open daily 6 a.m.–10 p.m.* $

Pie 'N Burger

913 E. California Blvd., Pasadena, 626-795-1123

One Formica counter, a few token tables, and reliably perfect heartland food. That's good enough for the motley crew of suits, Pasadena soccer moms, and Cal Tech physics majors that have been keeping this place going for the last 40 years. Lovingly created burgers are spiked with homemade Thousand Island dressing. Sodas are handmixed from syrup and soda water, just like in the old days. And of course, pies are made right here. *Open Mon.–Fri. 6 a.m.–10 p.m., Sat. 7 a.m.–10 p.m., Sun. 7 a.m.–9 p.m.* $

R-23

923 E. Second St., Downtown, 213-687-7178

The hard part's over once you actually find this hip sushi hideaway tucked into a stylishly converted warehouse between Little Tokyo and the L.A. River. Have a seat in a corrugated cardboard chair (designed by Frank Gehry) and feast on some of the best sushi in the city. Other winning dishes from a long list of chef's specials include Dungeness crab salad, lobster tempura, grilled yellowtail collar, steamed bay scallops, and for vegetarians, a dish of sautéed shimeji mushroom with chili peppers. *Open for lunch Mon.–Fri. 11:30 a.m.–2 p.m.; dinner Mon.–Sat. 5:30–10 p.m.* $$

The Raymond

1250 S. Fair Oaks Ave., Pasadena, 626-441-3136

This unique converted bungalow in Pasadena has launched a thousand wedding anniversary traditions, exuding romance with its polished homey interior and tiny patios filled with flowers and fruit trees. The short straightforward menu changes weekly but might include a tender rack of lamb with Grand Marnier sauce, a perfectly grilled sea bass topped with fresh papaya, pineapple, kiwi and jalapeno relish, or a chicken Normandy with cream sauce, apples, and apple brandy. Desserts include rich old favorites like bananas foster, pecan tart, the guilt-inducing sour-cream chocolate cake, and the divinely creamy Raymond cheesecake. *Open for lunch Tues.–Fri. 11:30 a.m.–2:30 p.m., Sat. 11 a.m.–2:30 p.m.; dinner Tues.–Thurs. 6–9:30 p.m., Fri.–Sat. 5:45–10 p.m.; brunch Sun. 10 a.m.–2:30 p.m.* $$

Rose Garden Tea Room

Huntington Gardens, 1151 Oxford Rd., San Marino, 626-683-8131

Traditional English tea at the Huntington estate is served every day except Monday in a quaint cottage nestled next to three acres of roses. Warm scones and a bottomless pot of fresh-brewed tea are brought to your table in either the sunny main room or the more intimate Herb Room, overlooking the property's herb garden. There's a nice spread of finger sandwiches—cucumber and mint, watercress with horseradish, smoked salmon, chicken walnut with tarragon—plus fresh fruit and homemade sweets. On weekends especially, reserve at least a week in advance. *Open Tues.–Fri. noon–4:30 p.m., Sat.–Sun. 10:45 a.m.–4:30 p.m. (last seatings are at 3:30 p.m.).* $

Sona

401 N. La Cienega Blvd., West Hollywood, 310-659-7708

One look at the minimalist decor and the six-ton wine-decanting stone centerpiece and you know it's all about the food here—which lives up to the meditative atmosphere. A la carte menus and an assortment of prix fixe meals from classically-trained executive chef/pastry chef duo David and Michelle Myers change almost nightly at this one-year-old gourmet hotspot. A recent *Food & Wine* Best New Chef, David is known for creations like pickled papaya soup, confit of salmon with braised oxtail, and creamy macaroni with crispy sweetbreads. Michelle's wildly creative chocolate beignet is the famous dessert here—ambrosial and vaguely Tim Burton–ish. On weekends, a late-night, small-plate *kappo* menu takes over after 11 p.m., when chefs from other top restaurants tend to swing by for bite-sized tastes. *Open Tues.-Thurs. 6–10 p.m., Fri.-Sat. 5:30 p.m.–2 a.m.* $$$

Traxx
800 N. Alameda St., Union Station, Downtown, 213-625-1999

You don't need Amtrak tickets in your back pocket to enjoy a wonderful meal in L.A.'s Union Station. Set in the concourse of this stunning Mission-style building (arguably one of the most beautiful train stations in the U.S.), Traxx redefines whistle-stop cuisine with entrée salads and winning sandwiches at lunch and a wonderful New American menu in the evening. When the sun's out, grab a serene courtyard table in the back. *Open for lunch Mon.–Fri. 11:30 a.m.–2:30 p.m.; dinner 5:30–9 p.m., Sat. 5–9:30 p.m.* $$

Water Grill
544 S. Grand Ave., Downtown, 213-891-0900

Welcome to L.A.'s seafood mecca. The oyster and roe selections alone in this formal wood, leather, and brass dining room will move any raw bar aficionado to tears. New American–style entrees like steamed Mahi Mahi with peppercorns and roasted Blue Fin Tuna are subtly prepared without much aid from heavy crusts or sauces—no need when you've reeled in the best raw materials in town. A perfect choice before an evening at the Performing Arts Center, a few blocks up the street. *Open Mon.–Tues. 11:30 a.m.–9 p.m., Wed.–Fri. 11:30 a.m.–10 p.m., Sat. 5–10 p.m., Sun. 4:30–9 p.m.* $$$

Zucca
801 S. Figueroa St., Downtown, 213-614-7800

Joachim Splichal's charming Tuscan villa-style dining room, patio, and sculpture garden is shortlisted among the city's top Italian restaurants—and not just for its amazing looks. Pre-theatre or–Laker crowds (the restaurant's just two blocks from the Staples Center) are drawn to homemade pastas, fresh fish, and fine cheeses from the old country, paired with an equally tantalizing Italian wine list. *Open for lunch Mon.–Fri. 11:30 a.m.–2:30 p.m.; dinner Sun.–Thurs. 5–9 p.m., Fri.–Sat. 5–10 p.m.* $$

Downtown & About L.A.: The Nightlife

Ahmanson Theater
135 W. Grand Ave., Downtown, 213-628-2772

After a four-year-run of *Phantom of the Opera* in the early '90s, the Ahmanson formally apologized with a $17.1 million renovation and a grand reopening with Bernstein's *Candide*. A mix of big-name dramas and musical imports as well as productions from the resident Center Theater Group are presented in this large space, seating up to 2,000 people. Sightlines and acoustics have been improved, but it's still best to avoid the back half of the room. $$$$

Barfly
8730 Sunset Blvd., West Hollywood, 310-360-9490

See New Hollywood, p. 106 for listing.
Open Mon.–Sat. 7:30 p.m.–2 a.m. $

Beauty Bar
1638 Cahuenga Ave., Hollywood, 323-464-7676

See Hipster L.A., p. 126 for listing.
Open Sun.–Wed. 9 p.m.–2 a.m., Thurs.–Sat. 6 p.m.–2 a.m.

Daddy's
1610 N. Vine St., Hollywood, 323-463-7777

See Hipster L.A., p. 127 for listing.
Open Mon.–Sat. 8 p.m.–2 a.m., Sun. 9 p.m.–2 a.m.

Gallery Bar at the Millennium Biltmore Hotel
Millennium Biltmore Hotel, 506 S. Grand Ave., Downtown, 213-624-1011

Passing through this classic hotel's frescoed galleria and sipping an exorbitant 5 p.m. cocktail in its hushed, Prohibition-era lounge with gold walls and headshots of Lucille Ball and friends smiling at you may be the most regal part of your day—and, let's face it, you deserve it. For a notch of rowdiness with your next highball, head over to the property's Grand Avenue Sports Bar. *Open daily 4 p.m.–1 a.m.*

Greek Theatre

2700 N. Vermont Ave., Griffith Park, 323-665-1927

Rock, R&B, classical, Kenny G.—everything under the stars has been played at the Greek over the last 70-odd years. Nestled in the foothills of Griffith Park, the legendary 6,162-seat amphitheater has recently hosted The Black Crowes, The Gipsy Kings, Elton John, Patti LaBelle, Pearl Jam, the Russian National Ballet, Sting, and many other big-ticket shows that people will gladly navigate one of the worst parking bottlenecks in the city for. Acoustics are a distant second to the open-air ambience. *Season runs May –October.* $$$$

Los Angeles Neon Tour

Museum of Neon Art, 501 W. Olympic Blvd., Downtown, 213-489-9918

Every Saturday night throughout the summer and early fall, three dozen people gather at the Museum of Neon Art (MONA) for wine or beer and cheese. They then board a bright red open-air double-decker bus for an evening's exploration of L.A.'s coolest, brightest neon signs—rolling through Downtown, Chinatown, midtown, and Hollywood with an informative, entertaining host who knows his neon and his L.A. cultural history. If this sounds like your kind of party, book ahead. It's regularly ranked as L.A.'s top tour and gets booked up long in advance. Don't forget to bring a jacket—it can get cold up there. *Tours run from 7–10 p.m.* $$$$

Mark Taper Forum

135 W. Grand Ave., Downtown, 213-628-2772

For more than 35 years, this distinguished drama stage has chalked up just about every theatrical award in the book and launched many a play bound for Broadway and beyond. With just under 800 seats, the Taper is by far the smallest venue in downtown's four-part Performing Arts Center, which includes the Ahmanson Theatre, the Dorothy Chandler Pavilion, and the Walt Disney Concert Hall. Along with the Ahmanson, the Taper is operated year-round by the Center Theatre Group, one of the country's largest and most active theatre production companies. *The box office is open Tues.–Sun. noon–8 p.m., closed Mon.* $$$$

Musso & Frank Grill

6667 Hollywood Blvd., Hollywood, 323-467-7788

See Classic Hollywood, p. 79 for listing.
Open Tues.–Sat. 11 a.m.–11 p.m.

Pasadena Playhouse

39 S. El Molino Ave., Pasadena, 626-356-7529

This beautiful Spanish Colonial Revival theatre dates back to an earlier era when it was dubbed the official State Theatre of California. It was the first U.S. stage to present all of Shakespeare's plays and considered "Hollywood's Talent Factory" for helping to launch the careers of Dustin Hoffman and Gene Hackman, among other notables. Shuttered in 1969, the theatre sat empty for nearly two decades before re-emerging as one of the nation's top stages, garnering numerous awards under artistic director Sheldon Epps. The theatre headlines a year-round season of six plays and hosts more than 300 performances annually. $$$

Polo Lounge

9641 Sunset Blvd., Beverly Hills, 310-276-2251

See Classic Hollywood, p. 80 for listing.
Open daily until 1:30 a.m.

Rooftop Bar at The Standard Downtown

550 S. Flower St., Downtown, 213-892-8080

Leave it to The Standard to transform an abandoned Superior Oil building in L.A.'s grim financial district into one of the city's trendiest spots. Head straight to the top where the hotel's roof bar is stealing thunder from all those fancy pool decks on the Sunset Strip. The pool, the city views, the hot DJ rotation, the vibrating space-pod waterbed cabanas, the candy-apple-red bar, the see-and-be-seen crowd—it's all here. On summer weekends, "Beautiful Sunday" pool parties kick off just aboout as early as you might want to start guzzling champagne and booking a poolside massage. Showing up on a weeknight saves you a twenty-dollar cover and the lethal post-7 p.m. weekend lines. *Open daily from 11 a.m.–2 a.m. Cover charge Thurs.–Sun.* $

Skybar

8440 Sunset Blvd., West Hollywood, 323-848-6025

See New Hollywood, p. 108 for listing.
Open daily 11 a.m.–2 a.m.

Walt Disney Concert Hall

111 S. Grand Ave., Downtown, 213-972-7211

In 1988, renowned L.A. architect Frank Gehry turned in his winning design for what would become one of the world's most ambitious (and trouble-ridden) modern architectural projects. After a decade of feuding egos, budget fiascos, and construction stalemates followed by another three full years just to build the thing, the monumental new home of the L.A. Philharmonic and Master Chorale opened in October 2003 to nearly unanimous praise. And at a price tag of $274 million—phew! A swirl of facts and figures surround this eye-popper on Bunker Hill, described by Gehry as "a living room for the city," though one that required 30,000 pages of diagrams, a million square feet of wood, 12,500 unique shapes of structural steel, painstaking acoustical considerations and reconsiderations, and so on. Just how accessible this 2,265-seat "living room" will be to most of the city is another matter, but even outsiders will find it hard not admire this venue's arcing, looping, and soaring steel shell. Visitors can explore the hall's gardens and multilayered interior (though not the actual auditorium where rehearsals are usually in progress) on a guided group tour arranged through the Music Center (213-972-4399). Concert tickets can be reserved by contacting the Los Angeles Philharmonic Box Office (323-850-2000). *Box Office open Tues.–Sun. noon–6 p.m.* $$$$

Windows

1150 S. Olive St., 32nd Floor, Downtown, 213-746-1554

Choose from more than sixty martinis (one at a time, please) and follow up with a red-meat chaser on the 32nd floor of downtown's TransAmerica Center. Delve into your expense account in the sedate dining room, or do the cheese-stick thing in a cozy lounge area that provides the same marvelous cityscape views. Weekday happy hours (4–7 p.m.) feature half-price drinks and lots of bar menu specials. *Open for lunch Mon.–Fri. 11 a.m. –1:30 p.m.; dinner Tues.–Sat. 5–10 p.m.* $$

Downtown & About L.A.: The Attractions

Amadeus Spa

799 E. Green St., Pasadena, 626-578-3404

This award-winning spa chain is popular enough for two locations in Pasadena, offering a creative lineup of body, skin, and beauty treatments. Sessions might include a full one-hour massage under a Vichy shower, a synchronized rub from two therapists working in unison, or a complete head-to-toe multitreatment overhaul called "Carpe Diem" that lasts ten hours (and costs $515). Romantics can double their pleasure at the newer, smaller branch a few blocks away in Paseo Mall (280 E. Colorado Blvd.) which offers joint couples' massages. *Open Sun.–Mon. 9 a.m.–6 p.m., Tues. 8 a.m.–8 p.m., Wed. 9 a.m.–6 p.m., Thurs.–Fri. 8 a.m.–9 p.m., Sat. 7:30 a.m.–8 p.m.*

Beverly Hot Springs

308 N. Oxford Ave., Los Angeles, 323-734-7000

An errant oilman once struck hot mineral water at this unlikely sybaritic site, which now houses L.A.'s only natural thermal baths. Steamy soaks, scrubs, and shiatsus are rejuvenating experiences at this traditional Korean-style spa adorned with rock waterfalls and a soothing soundtrack of chimes, hissing steam, and easy-listening Brahms. Treatment rooms are only semi-private, but after a few minutes that won't matter. Call ahead for frequent promo specials. *Open daily 9 a.m.–9 p.m.*

Bradbury Building

304 S. Broadway, Downtown, 213-626-1893

Looking at the unremarkable exterior of this 19th-century architectural masterpiece—L.A.'s oldest commercial building, built by a rookie one-hit-wonder architect—you'll wonder yourself what all the fuss is about. Then enter its shocking iron, oak, and marble core bathed in sunlight and suddenly you've been transported into a sort of Sam Spade–themed Escher painting. There's nothing like that first time—and saying any more here would spoil the surprise.

Brookside Golf Course

1133 Rosemont Ave., Pasadena, 626-796-0177

Pasadena's lush Arroyo Seco grounds—home of the Rose Bowl—are also home to the neighborhood's most sophisticated public course, a distinguished former host of the Los Angeles Open. Pros and well-heeled amateurs flock to the Koiner course, a 7,037-yard, par 72 endurance test designed by Bobby Bell. The E.O. Nay course (or "Course Two") is a thousand yards shorter and easier to book. *Open daily 6 a.m.–7 p.m.* $$$$

Chinatown

Just north of the financial district, L.A.'s rather small and sedate Chinatown isn't New York's or San Francisco's, but a closer look reveals some great finds. Survey the first contemporary American Chinatown planned, built, and run by the local Chinese community by wandering north along its main thread, Broadway between Ord St. and Bernard St., and back down through Hill St., Spring St., and New High St., where all the curio shops, galleries, jewelry stores, ginseng counters, and tempting eateries can easily fill up a few hours. It's hard to miss Central Plaza (947 N. Broadway), Chinatown's pedestrian court with its handful of shops and multitiered pagoda. Other attractions along the way include Wing Hop Fung Ginseng and China Products Center (727 N. Broadway) a clearinghouse of Asian herbs, teas, crafts, and tableware. Farther north, the Chinese Historical Society of Southern California (411 and 415 Bernard St.) houses a bookstore and gallery open to visitors on Sunday from noon–5 p.m. Nearby Empress Pavilion (988 N. Hill St.) is dim sum headquarters, and the venerable Phoenix Bakery (969 N. Broadway) has been serving dessert since 1938.

The Geffen Contemporary

152 N. Central Ave., Downtown, 213-621-2766

See Hipster L.A., p. 131 for listing.
Open Tues.–Sun. 11 a.m.–8 p.m. (Thurs. until 8 p.m.). $

Grand Central Market

317 S. Broadway, Downtown, 213-624-2378

Unlike the pricey Farmers Market at Third and Fairfax, the true bazaar experience is still going strong at L.A.'s oldest and largest open air-market. In its 87th year, Grand Central is still bursting with cheap produce, meat, poultry, pupusas, warm tortillas, ceviche, fish tacos, chow mein, mango concoctions, fruit drinks you can't pronounce, and some of the best people-watching this side of the L.A. River.

Huntington Botanical Gardens

1151 Oxford Rd., San Marino, 626-405-2100

Founded by railroad and real estate tycoon Henry Huntington, the 150-acre grounds include three art galleries and a library filled with rare stuff. But unless a really old volume of *The Canterbury Tales* excites you, head for the gardens. An array of more than 15,000 plant species is immaculately arranged into a variety of themed landscapes, including Japanese, Australian, palm, desert, jungle, and subtropical, plus a separate rose garden with about 1,500 varieties of plants. *Open Tues.–Fri. noon–4:30 p.m., Sat. –Sun. 10:30 a.m.–4:30 p.m.* $

Industry Hills Golf Club

1 Industry Hills Parkway, Industry, 626-810-4653

If you thought there was no reason at all to schlep yourself (and your clubs) 20 miles east to the City of Industry in L.A.'s Inland Empire, this award-winning pair of William F. Bell championship courses provides two very good ones. Set on the rolling 650-acre grounds of the Pacific Palms Conference Resort, The Eisenhower (or "Ike") and Zaharias (or "Babe") courses are ranked among California's finest and most complex layouts for their long fairways, 160 sand bunkers, 8 lakes, and large, bent grass and Poa greens. Ike, a 6,735-yard, par 72 that's played host to the U.S. Open Qualifying, requires some serious brute force on its wide-open fairways. The Babe, a 6,600-yard, par 71, is known for its narrower fairways and strategically placed bunkers. Top facilities include a practice area and 64-station driving range, two restaurants, and a friendly staff full of PGA pros. *Open sunrise to sunset.* $$$$

Japanese American National Museum

369 E. 1st St., Little Tokyo, 213-625-0414

The world's largest collection of its kind is housed in this beautiful modern building dedicated to preserving the history, culture, and chilling WWII experiences of Japanese Americans. A permanent exhibit entitled "Common Ground: The Heart of Community" is the museum's stirring focal point, chronicling 130 years of Japanese American life through photos, documents, relics, and most notably an original WWII relocation camp structure from Wyoming's brutal Heart Mountain barracks camp. Pewter rice grain frames, spirit stones, sushi sets, and "Shiitake Happens" mugs can be purchased at one of L.A.'s most unique museum stores. *Open Tues.–Sun. 10 a.m.–5 p.m., Thurs. 10 a.m.–8 p.m., closed Mon. Admission is free every Thurs. 5–8 p.m. and every third Thursday of the month all day.* $

Little Tokyo

Fitted between First and Third Sts. (to the north and south) and Alameda and Main Sts (to the east and west), this condensed cultural pocket was first settled by Japanese immigrants in the late 19th century, and effectively wiped out during the mass internments of WWII. While the majority of L.A.'s Japanese population has spread to the 'burbs, these blocks remain a firm socio-economic and cultural hub for the community at large. It doesn't take much time to explore the area on foot. Highlights include an assortment of craft and earthenware shops, ramen and sushi counters, and the excellent Japanese American National Museum (369 E. First St.).

Los Angeles Conservancy Walking Tours

523 W 6th St., Suite 1216, Downtown, 213-623-2489

Hook up with volunteer guides from this large nonprofit organization for one of several excellent Saturday morning Downtown walking tours. The Broadway Theaters walk is a runaway favorite, showcasing the ornate remains of Movietown's first Main Street before Hollywood Blvd. took over in the '20s. A rotation of ten other tours includes closeups of Union Station, the Biltmore Hotel, and Little Tokyo. $

Los Angeles County Museum of Art (LACMA)

5905 Wilshire Blvd., Los Angeles, 323-857-6000

When you want to see a Winslow Homer, a Rembrandt, a Diego Rivera, and a Chinese sculpture from the Tang Dynasty all in one go, this big gray edifice on Wilshire Blvd.'s Miracle Mile is the place to do it. Permanent exhibits at LACMA—one of the country's largest art museums with over 250,000 holdings—cover a huge scope of American, European, and Asian works from the moderns to the ancients. Major traveling exhibitions almost always wind up here too. The facility includes a cafe, a Rodin sculpture garden, and a lecture hall and special screening theatre, plus extensive grounds shared with the oozing La Brea Tar Pits. Free outdoor jazz concerts on the museum's open-air plaza are a Friday evening ritual between April and December (5:30–8:30 p.m.). Free chamber concerts are held in the Leo S. Bing Theater on Sunday evenings (6 p.m.). *Open Mon., Tues., Thurs. noon–8 p.m., Fri. noon–9 p.m., Sat.–Sun. 11 a.m.–8 p.m., closed Wed.* $

Museum of Contemporary Art (MOCA)

250 S. Grand Ave., Downtown, 213-626-6222

See Hipster L.A. p. 132 for listing.
Open Tues.–Sun. 11 a.m.–5 p.m., Thurs. until 8 p.m. $

Museum of Neon Art (MONA)

501 W. Olympic Blvd., Downtown, 213-489-9918

See Hipster L.A., p. 132 for listing.
Open Wed.–Sat. 11 a.m.–5 p.m. $

Museum of Tolerance

9786 W. Pico Blvd., Los Angeles, 310-553-8403

In its ten years, this unique educational arm of the Simon Wiesenthal Center has welcomed nearly four million people, including nine heads of state and the Dalai Lama. Visits begins with a brief orientation, during which guests are prompted to choose between two doors, labeled "Prejudiced" and "Unprejudiced," which lead to the main exhibition room. Self-guided tours in the Tolerancenter lead through a floor of interactive exhibits that provoke self-examination while offering an objective exploration of contemporary and historic issues centering on race and prejudice in America, from the Civil Rights movement to the L.A. riots. Reserve an hour and five minutes for the extensive Holocaust Section, which takes visitors back in time and walks them room-by-room through a pre-taped chronicle of events during World War II. The museum also houses a multimedia learning center and a temporary exhibition gallery, and offers daily seminars hosted by Holocaust survivors. *Open Mon.–Thurs. 11:30 a.m.–6:30 p.m. (last entry 4 p.m.), Fri. 11:30 a.m.–3 p.m.(last entry 1 p.m.), Sun. 11 a.m.–7:30 p.m. (last entry 5 p.m.), closed Sat.* $

Norton Simon Museum

411 W. Colorado Blvd., Pasadena, 626-449-6840

The late industrialist Norton Simon ranks among the world's greatest art patrons and collectors in history. His staggering collection is best known for its European holdings, which showcase over five centuries of masterpieces, from Botticelli and Raphael to Toulouse-Lautrec and Picasso. A huge cache of French Impressionist work includes an entire gallery devoted to Degas. Simon's later art interests leaned toward India and Southeast Asia, and are represented here by a remarkable Asian sculpture collection spanning some 2,000 years. A recent $6-million renovation by Frank Gehry has brightened the place up and improved the lovely gardens, which are modeled after Monet's Giverny. For a look at the man behind the museum, Norton Simon's life is encapsulated in a half-hour documentary, screening daily in the museum's theater. Award-winning audio tours highlight more than a hundred works and allow you to view them in whatever order you choose. *Open daily noon.–6 p.m. except Fri. (until 9 p.m.) and Tues. (closed).* $

THE LOS ANGELES REGION

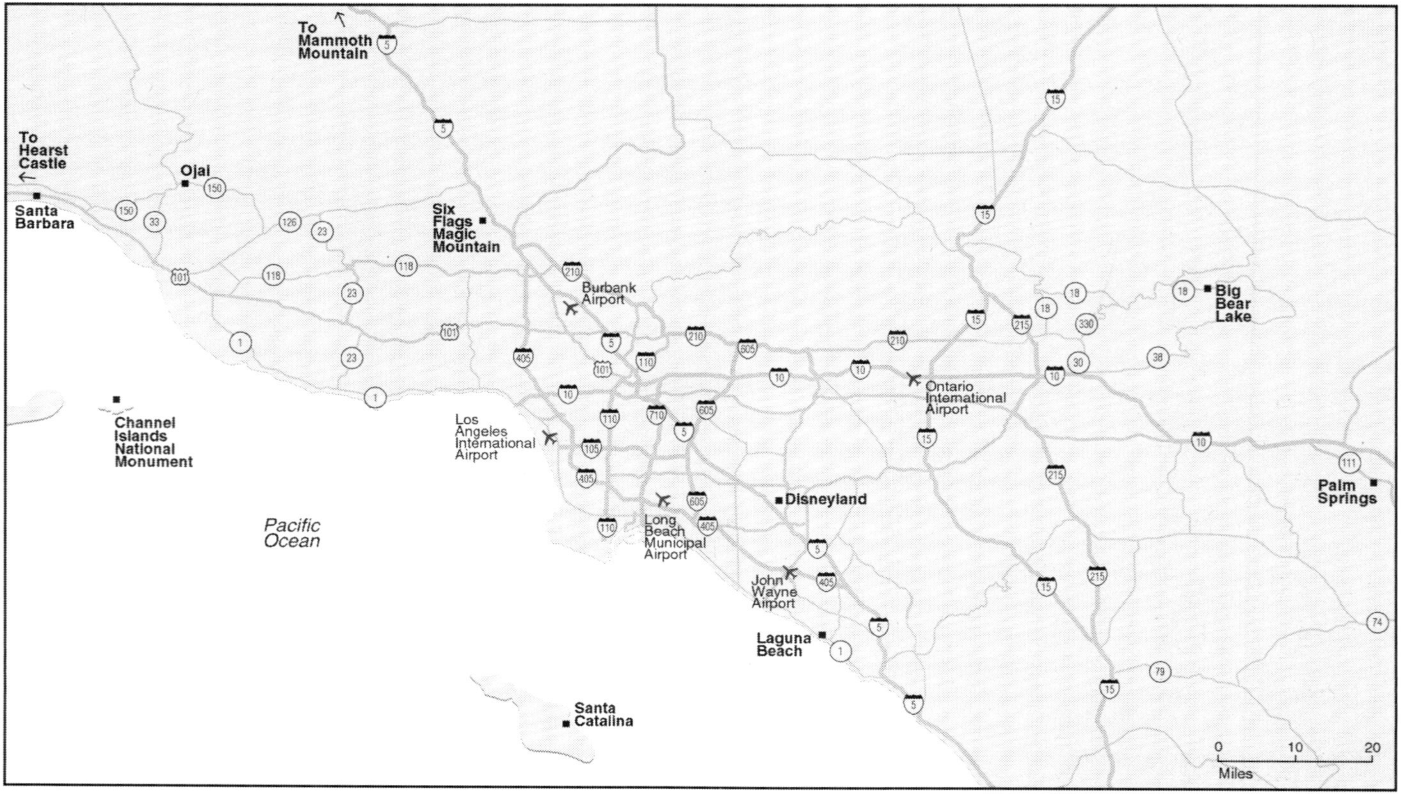

Leaving Los Angeles

The best thing about Los Angeles is that it's smack-dab in the middle of one of the most beautiful and varied areas on God's green earth. In just a few hours you can be skiing at a top resort, golfing in a desert oasis, or flopping on a lonely beach. If you've got days to spare (or if you've seen enough of the scene and want a change of pace), take our advice and get out of town. Just because you've visited L.A. doesn't mean you've seen California.

Big Bear Lake

The Lowdown: It's L.A. cottage country up at this convenient mountain resort area a few hours east in the San Bernardino Mountains. Dotted with cabins, B & Bs, and a wide array of outdoor draws, this retreat has been reeling in weekenders since Gable and Lombard honeymooned here back in the '30s. Aspen it ain't, but unless you want to schlep up to Mammoth or—yeesh—to Tahoe, Big Bear is the city's most obvious alpine escape for a getaway crowd of skiers, hikers, bikers, anglers, and romantic-cabin-in-the-woods renters. The teddy-bearish village and its namesake lake are a merciful 7,000 feet above the neighboring Mojave Desert and the inland cities of Riverside and San Bernardino. Summer temperatures hang pleasantly in the low 70s during the day, dropping to the mid 40s at night. Winter brings around 120 inches of snowfall. Rates drop and crowds disappear midweek.

Doing It: There are more than a dozen B & Bs in the Big Bear area, including Gold Mountain Manor (where Clark and Carole stayed), and several resorts, lodges, and cabins that run the gamut from bargain to luxury. Contact the Big Bear Lake Resort Association for a list. Skiers and snowboarders hit the slopes of the area's two alpine resorts, Bear Mountain and Snow Summit, and are followed by mountain bikers during the warmer months. Summer crowds are drawn to Big Bear Lake, an eight-mile-long freshwater oasis. Big Bear's forested slopes offer some of the best hiking trails south of the Sierras. Passes are required for parking at the trailheads. Contact the Big Bear Discovery Center for more information.

Getting There: Take I-10 East. Exit at Hwy. 30 North and continue north on Hwy. 330, which turns into Hwy. 18. Follow Hwy. 18 East and turn right across the Big Bear Lake dam and into Big Bear.

Big Bear Lake Contacts

Big Bear Discovery Center: 909-866-3437

Big Bear Lake Resort Association: 800-424-4232

Snow Summit: 909-866-5766

Bear Mountain: 909-585-2519

Gold Mountain Manor: 909-585-6997

Catalina Island

20 miles

The Lowdown: Southern California may not have a Martha's Vineyard, but there's always Catalina. Officially part of the remote Channel Islands chain, this very accessible offshore resort got off the ground when chewing gum baron William Wrigley Jr. purchased the land in 1919 and built a hilltop mansion here. By the 1940s, Cecil B. DeMille and Winston Churchill were pulling into Avalon Bay to go fishing and Glenn Miller was performing in the landmark Casino Ballroom. Mediterranean-style Avalon, Catalina's single port town, is now sprinkled with hotels, B & Bs, restaurants, boutiques, spas, and dive shops catering to a slightly broader clientele, albeit with a whiff of family money still in the air. The rest of the island is largely a wilderness preserve overseen by the Santa Catalina Island Conservancy. Crowds thin and rates drop midweek and outside the summer peak season.

Doing It: Catalina is as restful as you want to make it. Avalon boasts some of Southern California's most romantic retreats, including the Inn on Mount Ada (the old Wrigley Mansion) and an assortment of private villas and cottages managed by Catalina Island Vacation Rentals. The island's many activities include scuba diving, snorkeling, deep-sea fishing, and even mini-submarining through the rich marine world of Catalina's surrounding reefs. On land, there's a scenic nine-hole golf course (the oldest in Southern California), a heritage museum, botanical gardens, and hiking, horseback riding, and bus touring opportunities through the island's wild interior.

Getting There: Four ferry lines serve Catalina Island with several daily departures leaving from San Pedro, Long Beach, Newport Beach, and Dana Point. Catalina Express makes the trip in about an hour from San Pedro or Long Beach. Island Express Helicopter Service lifts off from the boat terminals in Long Beach and San Pedro, getting you there in about 15 minutes.

Catalina Island Contacts

Catalina Island Chamber of Commerce: 310-510-1520

Catalina Island Conservancy: 310-510-2595

Catalina Island Vacation Rentals: 310-510-2276

Catalina Express: 310-519-1212

Inn on Mount Ada: 310-510-2030

Island Express Helicopter Service: 800-228-2566

Channel Islands National Park

12–60 miles

The Lowdown: Floating off the coast of Southern California like a Club Med for pinnipeds, sea birds, and more than 2,000 species of plants and animals (including 150 found nowhere else on the planet), Channel Islands National Park has been called America's Galapagos. Five islands—Anacapa, San Miguel, Santa Barbara, Santa Cruz, and Santa Rosa—comprise this scattered offshore preserve, which is believed to have risen out of the Pacific as a result of volcanic activity some 14 million years ago. Since then, the islands have hosted Chumash Indians, European explorers, Mexican prisoners, cattle ranchers, and, above all, a highly protected ecosystem that remains as wild, isolated, and undeveloped as the nearby Southern California coast is not. Marine life ranges from microscopic plankton to the world's largest animal—the endangered blue whale. Climate on the islands is mild year-round, though high winds, fog, and sea spray are common. Park headquarters and an interpretive visitors center are located on the mainland, 70 miles north of Los Angeles (and 30 miles south of Santa Barbara) in the town of Ventura.

Doing It: All five islands are accessible by boat from Ventura and Santa Barbara harbors year-round, offering unique, offshore hiking, kayaking, tide-pooling, diving, and camping opportunities. Summer is the most popular time to visit the park, but the times to see migrating gray whales and the best wildflower shows are in the winter and spring respectively. Anacapa is the most accessible island and is a good introduction to the park, featuring dramatic cliffs, hundreds of birds, barking sea lions, hiking trails, a picnic area and lighthouse, excellent diving sites, and remote caves once frequented by Chumash Indians. Squeezing a campground, plenty of wildlife, and six miles of hiking trails into its one square mile, Santa Barbara is the smallest island in the park and also the hardest to get to. Santa Rosa offers secluded beach campgrounds, sweeping grasslands, oak- and ironwood-filled canyons, old Indian village sites, and a few ranger-led hikes. The westernmost island, San Miguel, is a true offshore wilderness experience for campers, with miles of ranger-led hiking trails and an estimated 15,000 seals and sea lions during mating season. The largest of the islands, Santa Cruz, did time as a Mexican penal colony and cattle ranch before joining the park. Tours here are offered by the Nature Conservancy and provide some of the most varied hiking, beachcombing, and wildlife-spotting opportunities in the island group. Allow a full day at least to visit the Channel Islands. There is a $10 fee for camping, otherwise, entrance is free. Bring all your own food and water supplies, plus a hat, sunscreen, and sturdy hiking shoes.

Getting There: Follow U.S. 101 North to Ventura, 70 miles north of L.A. on the coast. Take the Victoria Ave. exit, turning left onto Victoria Ave., then right onto Olivas Park Dr. to Harbor Blvd., where Olivas Park Dr. runs straight into Spinnaker Drive. The Channel Islands National Park Visitor Center (free parking at the beach parking lot) is located at the very end of Spinnaker Drive. Island Packers provides boat service to all of the Channel Islands from Ventura Harbor, offering a variety of half-day and multi-day trips. Truth Aquatics is the park's concessionaire for boat travel to the islands from Santa Barbara Harbor (90 miles north of L.A. on U.S. 101). Trips to the islands take anywhere from 90 minutes to 5 hours. For the quickest commute to Santa Rosa Island, Channel Islands Aviation runs flights from Camarillo airport (50 miles north of L.A. on U.S. 101). Trips vary from one-day to multi-day camping excursions. Call for prices, schedules, reservations, and specific directions.

Channel Islands Contacts

Channel Islands Aviation: 805-987-1301

Island Packers: 805-642-1393

Channel Islands National Park Visitor Center: 805-658-5730

Truth Aquatics: 805-962-1127

Disneyland

30 miles

The Lowdown: Approaching its 50th anniversary, in 2005, the world's most famous theme park pre-celebrated a few years ago with a $1.5 billion expansion. Disneyland is now joined by new attractions Disney's California Adventure, Downtown Disney, and the resort's most upscale digs, the 751-room, Arts & Crafts–style Grand Californian Hotel. There's more to see and do—and buy—than ever before. Start with a Disneyland Resort Hopper ticket which includes back-and-forth admission to both parks all day. Don't forget to use the FastPass service included with all park entrance tickets to cut your wait time at the parks' most popular rides. Summers and weekends are the busiest times. Avoid long lines in the hot sun by visiting midweek or off-season.

Doing It: Disneyland is divvied up into eight theme lands teeming with rides, shows, and all those happy, fuzzy creatures smiling on the outside and suffering heatstroke on the inside. Honorable mentions include Adventureland, home of the popular Indiana Jones Adventure thrill ride, an audio-animatronic-enhanced Jungle Cruise, the Polynesian-themed Enchanted Tiki Room, and the straight-out-of-Africa attraction, Tarzan's Treehouse. Tomorrowland is Disney's homage to the future, where you'll find 3-D shows, techno-spectacles and, most importantly, a handful of zippy rides including Astro Orbiter, Autopia, and that old interplanetary favorite, Space Mountain. New Orleans Square is a faux French Quarter setting and home of the Haunted Mansion, the Pirates of the Caribbean ride, and enough Dixieland music pumped into its mini courtyards and winding streets to fill your ears with their annual quota. Everyone's favorite flume ride, Splash Mountain, is in Critter Country. The Mark Twain Riverboat, the Columbia Sailing Ship, the Big Thunder Mountain Railroad, and the Golden Horseshoe Stage are all in Frontierland, celebrating America's glorious pioneer past—at least as seen from this side of the fence.

Disney's California Adventure Park honors its home state—and the natives, explorers, immigrants, aviators, entrepreneurs, and entertainers who built it—with three separate theme lands: The Golden State, the Hollywood Pictures Backlot, and Paradise Pier. Celebrating (and, okay, idealizing to some degree) California's many lovely faces, The Golden State includes the Grizzly River Run, a double-waterfall white-water rafting ride, and Soarin' Over California, a movie journey through California's natural wonders in seats that actually move and "fly" along with the image. The Hollywood Pictures Backlot celebrates movie culture with its 2000-seat Hyperion Theater, which presents live stage versions of classic Disney animated features. Also here is the Art Deco Disney Animation building featuring half a dozen interactive galleries and Jim Henson's MuppetVision 3-D spectacle. The nostalgia-soaked Paradise Pier pays homage to California's old seaside amusement pier days. Top attractions here include an old-style roller coaster with a wicked loop, called California Screamin', and the enormous Sun Wheel, a one-of-a-kind Ferris wheel with sliding gondolas that whip in and out of the center as they revolve.

Between the two theme parks, the 300,000-square-foot Downtown Disney quarter (no admission fee required) is the resort's new dining, shopping, and entertainment complex. You'll find several stores here, a 12-screen Art Deco–inspired multiplex theater with stadium-style seating, more than a dozen restaurants including all-star chef Joachim Splichal's Mediterranean-inspired Catal Restaurant & Uva Bar, and a handful of evening venues, including the latest branch of the House of Blues.

Getting There: Take I-5 South from Los Angeles to the city of Anaheim in Orange County. Exit at Disneyland Drive and turn left. Proceed south and look for signs directing you to Theme Parks. Disneyland is open every day of the year with extended operating hours during the summer and holiday periods.

Disneyland Contacts

Anaheim/Orange County Visitor and Convention Bureau: 714-765-8888

Disneyland Recorded Information: 714-781-4565

Disneyland Customer Service: 714-781-7290

Disneyland Tickets and Reservations: 714-781-4400

Disney's Grand Californian Hotel: 714-635-2300

Hearst Castle San Simeon

245 miles

The Lowdown: Built over a span of nearly 30 years (and never quite finished), Hearst Castle exemplifies the power of the almighty dollar, the effects of unchecked megalomania, and the total inadequacy of the phrase "it's big" when describing certain real estate properties. Hearst and architect Julia Morgan began work on this amazing Mediterranean Revival compound looming above the village of San Simeon at the south end of Big Sur in 1919, stuffing it over the years with more priceless acquisitions than this 165-room pad could ever fully assimilate. And that's not even counting the pools and gardens and grounds. Deeded to the state after the family could no longer keep it up, Hearst Castle is now one of California's busiest tourist attractions, annually hosting more than a million visitors—none of whom will ever quite have it this good.

Doing It: Several small hotels, motels, and B & Bs serve Hearst Castle in neighboring coastal villages just south of San Simeon. For something wildly different, check into the Madonna Inn, a famous kitsch castle in San Luis Obispo featuring more than a hundred uniquely themed quarters. From there, it's a 40-mile drive north to Hearst Castle, where four separate two-hour walking tours are offered several times daily between 8:20 a.m. and 3:20 p.m. during the winter (with slightly longer summer hours). Reservations are strongly recommended for all of them.

Getting There: Follow U.S. 101 North about 200 miles from Los Angeles to San Luis Obispo. Then take the Pacific Coast Highway (Hwy. 1) another 40 miles north to San Simeon and Hearst Castle. Parking is in the visitor-center lot. Five miles up the hill is the Hearst estate, accessible only by tour buses.

Hearst Castle Contacts

California Reservations:
800-444-4445

Madonna Inn:
800-543-9666
805-543-3000

Laguna Beach

60 miles

The Lowdown: Southern California's "Riviera" finds its nucleus in this prosperous seaside village lined with galleries, beaches, a boardwalk, and a half-dozen miles of premium ocean-facing property. The plein-air painters who founded Laguna's thriving artist colony back in the early 20th century would be appalled by today's summer weekend traffic inching into town along the coast. Otherwise, the same balmy postcard setting that inspired them is still basking in the sun here—but on four-star hotel balconies, leafy restaurant patios, and a squeaky clean beach in the heart of downtown. Most of the action in Laguna is concentrated in the Village, a quarter-mile stretch of cafes, bars, antique shops, boutiques, and art studios huddled on the north side of the Pacific Coast Highway (PCH). Directly across the street is Main Beach, the most central of Laguna's 30 beaches and coves running north and south. Among Laguna's many renowned events is the summer's biggest draw, The Festival of Arts & Pageant of the Masters (see Calendar section).

Doing It: For a list of hotels, inns, and cottage rental companies serving Laguna Beach, contact the Visitors and Conference Bureau. Or simply check into the Surf & Sand Resort and Spa, the town's most elegant beach property, with balconies right above the waves. Top landmarks include the Laguna Art Museum and the award-winning Laguna Playhouse, the oldest continuously operating theatre company on the West Coast. Beyond the Village's cluster of shops and galleries, Laguna boasts nearly 20,000 acres of coastal wilderness and marine preserves overseen by Laguna Coast Wilderness Park. Several local tour operators show hikers, horseback riders, divers, kayakers, and whale-watchers a good time in Laguna's great outdoors.

Getting There: Take I-405 South to Hwy. 133 South and follow it to the Pacific Coast Highway and Laguna Beach. Turn left on PCH into the Village.

Laguna Beach Contacts

Laguna Art Museum: 949-494-8971

Laguna Playhouse: 949-497-2787

Laguna Coast Wilderness Park: 949-855-7275

Laguna Beach Visitors and Conference Bureau: 949-497-9229

Ritz-Carlton Laguna Niguel: 949-240-2000

Surf & Sand Resort: 949-497-4477

Mammoth Mountain

The Lowdown: This one's a drive, but well worth it if you can afford to spend a few days at a top alpine resort in the Sierra Nevada mountains. Just 30 miles south of Yosemite National Park and five miles from the tourism-fed town of Mammoth Lakes, Mammoth Mountain's 11,053-foot summit and 3,500 acres of ski terrain have opened up considerably since the first chair-lift was built 50 years ago. Mammoth now boasts 29 state-of-the-art lifts, a new gondola, and a surge of lodges, condos, restaurants, and shops sprouting around its brand new Village at the base of the mountain. Also part of the Mammoth operation is June Mountain, a smaller boutique resort about 20 miles to the north. Perched above 7,000 feet, Mammoth enjoys a mild summer climate in the mid-70s during the day and rarely dips below 40 degrees at night. Sunny winters range from 10-40 degrees. The mountain gets an average of 385 inches of snow per year.

Doing It: A wide range of hotels, B & Bs, and cabins serve Mammoth Mountain, including several luxury options right in the Village. Contact Mammoth Resort or the Mammoth Lakes Visitors Bureau for a full list of options. Primarily known as a major ski destination, Mammoth draws all forms of outdoors enthusiasts during the warmer months too, including fly-fishermen, hikers, mountain bikers, and golfers flocking to the Sierra Star Golf Club's stunning 18-hole championship course. Mountain bikes can be rented in the Village from the Adventure Center, where a U.S. Forest Service window provides information and shuttle service to backcountry trails.

Getting There: Take I-5 North. Exit onto Hwy. 14 North, pass through the town of Mojave and continue to Hwy. 395 North. Head west on Hwy. 203 (Mammoth Lakes Junction) and into the town of Mammoth Lakes. For a quicker commute by air, L.A. Excursions offers flight service from LAX.

Mammoth Mountain Contacts

Adventure Center and U.S. Forest Service: 760-934-0706

June Mountain: 760-648-7733

L.A. Excursions: 310-937-9543

Mammoth Lakes Visitors Bureau: 760-934-2712

Mammoth Resort: 800-626-6684

Mammoth Mountain Ski Information: 760-934-2571

Sierra Star Golf Club: 760-924-4653

Ojai

65 miles

The Lowdown: Back in the 1930s, Frank Capra chose this lovely hideaway to represent mythical Shangri-la in the movie *Lost Horizon*. Generations of artists, Hollywood recluses, spiritual leaders, environmentalists, and ardently community-oriented folks have all had a hand in preserving the tiny town of Ojai and its surrounding valley on the edge of Los Padres National Forest. A quick, pleasant drive from L.A., Ojai's unflashy five square miles remain the smallest and slowest-growing city in Ventura County—by choice—sprinkled with galleries, spas, New Age-y shops, cafes, and spiritual retreats. Best known for its arts events held throughout the year, including the very popular two-day Studio Artists Tour in October, Ojai's small-town feel and serene woodland surroundings are still the best draw of all.

Doing It: Guests of Ojai can choose from B & Bs, vacation houses, meditation compounds, and a pair of time-honored resorts: The distinguished Ojai Valley Inn & Spa features an 18-hole championship golf course and horseback riding; The Oaks at Ojai is a down-to-earth health retreat offering a wealth of treatments and fitness classes. Antiquing, gallery-hopping, and latte-sipping are among the more popular activities in and around the Arcade, the town's Mission Revival–style nerve center. Outdoor recreation in the surrounding Ojai Valley includes long walks or bicycle rides along the Ojai Valley Trail leading into the coastal town of Ventura; camping, boating, and bass fishing at nearby Lake Casitas; and hiking the back-country trails of the vast Los Padres National Forest. Contact the Ojai Ranger Station for maps, guidebooks, brochures, and wilderness permits.

Getting There: Take I-5 North past Valencia to Hwy. 126 West. Head north on Rt. 150 to Ojai. Or take U.S. 101 North to Ventura; exit onto Hwy. 33 East and follow the signs into Ojai.

Ojai Contacts

The Oaks At Ojai:
805-646-5573

Ojai Ranger Station:
805-646-4348

Ojai Valley Chamber of Commerce and Visitor's Bureau:
805-646-8126

Ojai Valley Inn & Spa:
805-646-5511

Palm Springs

110 miles

The Lowdown: The rehabilitation of Palm Springs from a washed-up desert convention site to a hot retro playground for college kids, gays, gamblers, golfers, hipsters, retired folks, and spirituality seekers is one of the more remarkable recoveries in the resort world. This arid strand of leisure communities (collectively known as Palm Springs Desert Resorts) hugging chocolate-brown mountains in the Coachella Valley is back in a major way. And why not? It's Palm Springs, which means perfect weather (when you're not boiling or freezing) and as wild, restful, or enlightening a scene as you want.

Doing It: Nearly 7,000 hotel rooms and 150 hotels serve greater Palm Springs, ranging from bargain bungalows and quaint desert inns to full-service luxury resort and spa retreats. The Palm Springs Visitor Center offers a free hotel reservation service and can also assist in finding the right place. Besides shopping, lounging at the pool, and beelining to top local spas like Two Bunch Palms for a heavenly soak and a 90-minute rub, a wide array of outdoor recreation activities includes hiking and horseback riding through the desert outback, exploring the reopened Tahquitz Canyon and other sacred Indian sites just south of town, and even taking a guided tour of the area's vast windmill fields. Golf fanaticism is palpable here, with more than 100 courses gracing the valley. When blistering summer days are breaking the thermometer, cool off up at 8,500 feet by riding the Palm Springs Aerial Tramway up Mount San Jacinto for some great views aboard the world's largest rotating tramcars. Top draws in town include the Fabulous Palm Springs Follies (featuring seasoned showgirls over the age of 50) and the Cahuilla Indian-run Spa Resort Casino.

Getting There: Take I-10 East. Exit at Hwy. 111 exit which leads into Palm Springs along N. Palm Canyon Drive.

Palm Springs Contacts

Palm Springs Aerial Tramway: 760-325-1391

Palm Springs Visitor Center: 760-778-8418

Spa Resort Casino: 760-325-1461

Tahquitz Canyon: 760-416-7044

Two Bunch Palms: 760-329-8791

Santa Barbara

90 miles

The Lowdown: This moneyed city of fewer than a hundred thousand people holds its own as the easy seaside choice for weary Angelenos who need to get away but don't have the time or cash to do Napa or Hawaii. If red-tiled roofs, cute shops, and Spanish heritage properties are your passion, you'll find downtown Santa Barbara very exciting. The rest of us will be happy to give State Street a few slow laps before heading to more than a dozen quality beaches lining the shore, exploring the satellite coastal communities of Carpinteria, Goleta, and Montecito, or wine tasting in the neighboring Santa Ynez and Santa Maria Valleys. Originally settled by Chumash Indians and redecorated by Spanish missionaries, Mexican ranchers, American robber barons, and Hollywood celebs, it's easy to see the draw of this relaxed place with its artsy undertones and perfect Mediterranean climate.

Doing It: Accommodation options include historic B & Bs, family-run inns, guest ranches, cottage rentals, and palatial beachside resorts like the Four Seasons Biltmore in celebrity-studded Montecito. Coastal Escapes is a local reservation service that can help steer you to the right place. Santa Barbara's architectural heritage can be best experienced along downtown's Red Tile Walking Tour, covering a dozen blocks of landmarks. Sailing, kayaking, windsurfing, deep-sea fishing, beach-bumming, and day-tripping out to Channel Islands National Park are all popular activities around the coast. On land, the area boasts eight championship golf courses and more than sixty vineyards in the city's neighboring Wine Country. Hikers can escape even farther, along miles of trails in the surrounding Santa Ynez Mountains.

Getting There: Take U.S. 101 North from Los Angeles straight into downtown Santa Barbara. For a more scenic drive along the coast, take Hwy. 1 north through Malibu which hooks up with U.S. 101 in Oxnard.

Santa Barbara Contacts

Coastal Escapes: 800-292-2222

Four Seasons Biltmore: 805-969-2261

Santa Barbara Visitor Center: 805-965-3021

Santa Barbara Conference & Visitors Bureau: 805-966-9222

Six Flags Magic Mountain

35 miles

The Lowdown: Southern California's hair-raising branch of the Six Flags empire has come a long way from its humble beginnings in the early 1970s. It now features more than one hundred rides, games, and attractions and—if you can ignore all the Valley youths and the odd street-gang daytrip here—several are unlike anything you've ever experienced. Once just a one-roller-coaster stop, the 260-acre theme park is now an Xtreme coaster nirvana, with 16 of them (the most in any park in the world) looping, corkscrewing, and cobra-rolling their way into several world titles. There's the world's tallest roller coaster (Superman: The Escape/415 feet), the world's tallest and fastest stand-up roller coaster (The Riddler's Revenge/156 feet, 65 mph), and the world's tallest and fastest suspended looping boomerang coaster (Déjà vu/ 196 feet, 65 mph) among others. Magic Mountain's nine themed lands offer several more lunch-churners with names like Freefall, Goliath, and Colossus (the tallest wooden coaster west of the Rockies). The latest addition is Scream, an aptly-named floorless coaster with more than seven 360-degree inversions. Right next door to Magic Mountain is Six Flags' tropical-themed aqua park, Hurricane Harbor.

Doing It: A General Use Admission ticket ($44.99) includes all rides, shows, and attractions at Magic Mountain. Combo tickets also get you into Hurricane Harbor on the day of your visit or on any other day during the season. Magic Mountain is open daily between April and early September, Fridays and weekends through September and October, and weekends and holidays the rest of the year.

Getting There: Take I-5 North (or I-405 North to I-5 North) to the Magic Mountain Parkway exit just past Valencia.

Six Flags Magic Mountain Contacts

Six Flags Magic Mountain and Hurricane Harbor: 661-255-4100

The L.A. Calendar

Every city has its big events, but when you live in the place that hosts both the Oscars and the Rose Bowl, well...forgive us if we're a little smug. Here's a month-by-month breakdown of some of the biggest events in the greater Los Angeles area to help you plan your trip. From the Venice Art Walk to the L.A. Marathon, there's something for everyone here all year long.

The L.A. Calendar

January	February	March
Tournament of Roses Parade and Rose Bowl Game* L.A. Auto Show	Academy Awards* Chinese New Year Parade L.A. Open Golf	L.A. Marathon

April	May	June
Long Beach Grand Prix	Cinco de Mayo Venice Art Walk	Playboy Jazz Festival

July	August	September
Festival of the Arts and Pageant of the Masters*	U.S. Open of Surfing and Beach Games* Japanese Festival Long Beach Blues Festival	L.A. County Fair Watts Towers Day of the Drum

October	November	December
AFI Fest Halloween Carnaval*	Catalina Island Triathlon Doo Dah Parade Hollywood Christmas Spectacular	Hollywood Lights Festival

* *The Fun Seeker's Top Five Events*

January

Tournament of Roses Parade and Rose Bowl Game*

On January First at 8 a.m., Pasadena ushers in the New Year with its world-famous parade of floral floats, followed by one of the biggest football games of the year (in the top four of Bowl games, with teams chosen by computer ranking). The Rose Bowl is "The Granddaddy of Them All," and isn't sponsored by FedEx, Nokia, or Tostitos like some of the other big college bowls out there. Kick-off is usually at 2 p.m.

Contact: *626-449-7673, www.tournamentofroses.com*

Greater L.A. Auto Show

Car culture was practically invented in Los Angeles, so it's no surprise that this city hosts one of the world's biggest and coolest auto expos. For more than a week in early January, the L.A. Convention Center is a car-, truck-, and SUV-lover's fantasy, featuring about 1,000 hot new rides including futuristic models and more than two dozen world and North American debuts. Keep an eye out for special guests like Mario Andretti. Avoid the mobs by attending a special sneak preview, usually hosted two or three days before the show.

Contact: *213-741-1151, www.laautoshow.com*

February

The Academy Awards*

Formerly in March, Hollywood's biggest tribute to itself has been pushed forward to late February when dolled-up celebs congregate at Hollywood & Highland's new Kodak Theatre for Oscar Night. Don't expect to get anywhere near the entrance of this private, high-security event, but crowds will always flock here to catch a glimpse of their favorite stars outside. Bleacher seats, if set up, are traditionally offered on a lottery basis. But most importantly, there is no hotter weekend in L.A., especially for restaurants and nightlife in *New Hollywood.*

Contact: *310-247-3000, www.oscars.org*

Chinese New Year and Golden Dragon Parade

L.A.'s Chinese community throws its own New Year's party on a Saturday afternoon in late January or early February. Floats, marching bands, and 100-foot dragons parade down North Broadway into the heart of Chinatown amidst some 50,000 celebrants and a steady eruption of firecrackers. Famous guests of honor have included Bruce Lee, Dr. Haing Ngor from *The Killing Fields*, Kieu Chinh from *The Joy Luck Club*, and actress Ming-Na. The good times carry on into the evening, so stick around for dinner in Chinatown.

Contact: *213-617-0396, www.lagoldendragonparade.com*

Nissan L.A. Open Golf Tournament

It's the oldest civic-sponsored golf competition on the PGA Tour. More important, this 76-year-old event is the Tour's only stop in Los Angeles—and an excellent place to spy on celebrity golf fans. The ritzy Riviera Country Club in Pacific Palisades has been hosting the tournament for the last four decades.

Contact: *800-752-6736, www.nissanopen.pgatour.com*

March

Los Angeles Marathon

While New York and Boston wait for the ice to thaw, L.A. hosts the nation's first big city marathon (and the world's fourth largest) on the first Sunday in March. The 26.2-mile course starts and ends Downtown, looping past 25 entertainment sites and about a million cheering spectators. The race usually begins just after 8 a.m., starting with the world-renowned Wheelchair Division. More than twenty thousand marathoners are expected. Other events held on this day include a 5K (3.1 mile) run/walk and a non-competitive Bike Tour along the marathon route.

Contact: *800-444-5544, www.lamarathon.com*

April

Toyota Grand Prix of Long Beach

Southern California's most anticipated street race roars to life in mid-April on the coast of Long Beach. The big races of this three-day motorsporting tradition are held on Sunday, when the pros burn up a 1.97 mile course winding along Shoreline Drive. Saturday is when drivers like Clint Eastwood, Jay Leno, and Cameron Diaz take to the streets for the celebrity laps. One-, two-, and three-day ticket packages are available.

Contact: *888-827-7333, www.longbeachgp.com*

May

Cinco de Mayo

May 5th (which, by the way, is not Mexico's Independence Day) marks Mexico's miraculous victory over French invaders during the Battle of Puebla (1862). Celebrations are scattered throughout the city all week, but the main event is held Downtown around historic Olvera Street, where mariachis, dancers, food stalls, and plenty of other festive offerings are in full swing for three days.

Contact: *213-628-1274, www.cityofla.org/elp*

Venice Art Walk

This annual art crawl, food fair, and local fundraiser is your ticket to Venice's thriving art scene. More than 60 private studios open their doors to visitors, who can enjoy several one-time exhibits as well as meetings with emerging and famous painters, sculptors, photographers, cartoonists, and graphic artists. Don't miss the silent auction, where bids are placed for hundreds of contemporary works.

Contact: *310-392-9255, www.venicefamilyclinic.org*

June

Playboy Jazz Festival

In mid-June, Hugh Hefner puts on a respectable two-day show at the Hollywood Bowl, featuring an eclectic range of fully-clothed jazz legends, international musicians, and hot newcomers hosted by longtime Master of Ceremonies Bill Cosby. Past performers at this music event, now celebrating its 25th year, include the Blind Boys of Alabama, Herbie Hancock, Dave Holland, Poncho Sanchez, and Boz Scaggs.

Contact: *310-449-4070, www.playboy.com*

July

Festival of Arts and Pageant of the Masters*

Laguna Beach hosts one of California's largest, longest-running, and—at times—oddest summer art shows during the months of July and August. Works from more than 150 artists in this six-acre canyon setting near the coast run the gamut from paintings, sculptures, and photographs to weavings, handcrafted furniture, musical instruments, and model ships. Several workshops, hands-on demonstrations, and docent-led tours are offered throughout the day. Evening guests can enjoy the weirdly beautiful Pageant of the Masters, a surreal 90-minute tableaux series featuring real-life reenactments of classic works of art accompanied by live narration and an orchestral score.

Contact: *800-487-3378, www.foapom.com*

August

U.S. Open of Surfing and Beach Games*

Huntington Beach is a surfer-dude and bikini-filled hotbed on any day of the summer. During the annual U.S. Open of Surfing in late July and the first week of August, it's ground zero—attracting many of the world's best big-wave riders and more than two hundred thousand tanned fans. Running alongside the main event are the Beach Games, which include no-less-extreme competitions in BMX biking and skateboarding. Women's surfing finals are usually held on the second last day of the event (Saturday), followed by the men's finals on Sunday. Music, food, and entertainment are all included.

Contact: *714-969-3492, www.hbvisit.com*

Nisei Week Japanese Festival

One of the oldest Japanese-American celebrations has been held in downtown's Little Tokyo district since the 1930s. The seven-day cultural festival in mid-August includes art exhibits, Ondo dance performances, martial arts demonstrations, fashion shows, a parade, traditional tea ceremonies, the crowning of a kimono-clad Queen, and some of the best Karaoke this side of Honshu.

Contact: *213-687-7193, www.niseiweek.org*

Long Beach Blues Festival

This top two-day blues fest, held over Labor Day weekend on the Long Beach State University campus, marks its 25th year this year. A thinning supply of old-school blues legends has forced the annual concert to widen its parameters somewhat, with recent "blues" headliners including Joe Cocker, Al Green, and the Allman Brothers. It's still the biggest and best blues festival in the West. Wine, beer, and food are served.

Contact: *562-985-5566, www.jazzandblues.org*

September

Los Angeles County Fair

This ain't your average hot-dog-on-a-stick county fair (although you certainly can get one here—along with a fried Snickers Bar for dessert). More than 80 years old, this 17-day happening set in Pomona, about 35 miles east of downtown L.A., has grown into one of the world's largest events of its kind. Throughout most of September, the expansive Fairplex grounds teem with livestock and agricultural displays, a giant botanical section, art exhibits, quilting and cooking competitions, entertainment stages, heaps of food stands, and 72 carnival rides, including the largest portable Ferris Wheel in the western hemisphere.

Contact: *909-623-3111, www.fairplex.com*

Watts Towers Day of the Drum

Percussion traditions from around the world are celebrated at this full-day drumfest in the Watts Art Center Amphitheater—adjacent to the amazing towers built by folk art legend Simon Rodia. A jazz concert is hosted here on the following day. Both events are free.

Contact: *213-847-4646, www.wattstowers.net*

October

AFI Fest

If you can't make it to Cannes or Sundance, this prestigious event hosted by the American Film Institute gives you a taste of Hollywood festival hype—right in Hollywood, of all places. More than 140 films from emerging filmmakers around the world are screened throughout late October and early November. Filmmaker/audience receptions, cultural events, and live entertainment are all part of the scene as well. And, yes, celebrities do come out for this one, particularly at gala showings held in the ArcLight's Cinerama Dome. Book ahead.

Contact: *323-856-7600, www.afi.com*

Halloween Carnaval*

All persuasions except the overly timid are welcome to participate or gape at this flamboyant Halloween street party thrown by West Hollywood's gay community. The spectacle takes place, of course, on October 31st along a small portion of Route 66 where folks are definitely getting their kicks—Santa Monica Blvd. between La Cienega Blvd. and LaPeer St. Various stages and booths line the cordoned-off blocks, but the night's best, spookiest draw is the parade of outrageous costumes.

Contact: *800-368-6020, www.visitwesthollywood.com*

November

Catalina Island Triathlon

In early November, L.A.'s favorite offshore escape is also one of the world's most beautifully situated triathlon sites. If you can bear the mid-60-degree water in Avalon Bay and the unpaved roads and hills of Catalina Island—or if you just want to check into a charming inn and watch others stumble through this half-mile swim, 10-mile cycle, and 3.1-mile run—be sure to make your reservations long in advance.

Contact: *714-978-1528, www.pacificsportsllc.com*

Doo Dah Parade

Pasadena's most colorful event was inspired by the Rose Bowl Parade—in the most lampoonish sense. The Doo Dah Parade (a.k.a. "the other parade") is as wacky as its older sibling is wholesome. Offbeat participants include the West Hollywood Cheerleaders, The BBQ and Hibachi Marching Grill Team, and The Howlelujah Chorus. The parade usually starts at 11:30 a.m., heading south on Raymond Ave. (from Holly St.) to Colorado Blvd., and turning west to Pasadena Ave.

Contact: *626-440-7379, www.pasadenadoodahparade.com*

Blockbuster Hollywood Christmas Spectacular

Never mind the new corporate sponsor and mouthful of a title for this event, it's still the good old Hollywood Christmas Parade. Back in the 1920s, the draw consisted of a few pine trees and a young starlet sitting with a guy dressed up as Santa Claus in a reindeer-pulled sleigh. Now, every Sunday after Thanksgiving, more than a million spectators come to see some 100 celebrities parading along the streets of Hollywood. Live performances, marching bands, equestrians, and a pageant of star-studded floats run east on Hollywood Blvd. and West on Sunset Blvd. between Highland Ave. and Vine St. Santa Claus is somewhere in there too. The parade is at 6 p.m., but get there by 4 p.m. if you want to see anything.

Contact: *323-469-2337, www.hollywoodchristmas.com*

December

Holiday Light Festivals

Griffith Park's holiday light show is one of the largest and most impressive of its kind on the West Coast. Cars and leisurely foot traffic are drawn nightly to this illuminated mile along Crystal Springs Drive from early December until the day after Christmas. Another bright spot during the holiday season is on the coast at Marina del Rey, where boats of all shapes and sizes are adorned in strands of light.

Contact: *888-527-2757, www.laparks.org*

The L.A. Black Book

Quick—where was that restaurant you were just reading about? Or that club—you know, the one with the sushi? Nobody should have to get along without a Black Book of all the important names and numbers at their fingertips. Ours is also cross-referenced to help you find in a flash which "L.A. Experience" it's in and all its details.

Hotels

NAME	ADDRESS	AREA	PHONE	EXPERIENCE PERFECT	PAGE PAGE
Argyle, The	8358 W. Sunset Blvd. www.argylehotel.com	WH	323-654-7100 800-225-2637	New	96
Avalon Hotel	9400 W. Olympic Blvd. www.avalonbeverlyhills.com	BH	310-277-5221 800-535-4715	Hipster	118
Beach House at Hermosa	1300 The Strand www.beach-house.com	HB	310-374-3001 888-895-4559	Coastal	140
Beverly Hills Hotel & Bungalows	9641 Sunset Blvd. www.beverlyhillshotel.com	BH	310-276-2251 800-283-8885	Classic Hotel Pools	74 47
Casa del Mar	1910 Ocean Way www.hotelcasadelmar.com	SM	310-581-5533 800-898-6999	Coastal	140
Chateau Marmont	8221 W. Sunset Blvd. www.chateaumarmont.com	WH	323-656-1010 800-242-8328	Classic	74
Four Seasons Hotel Los Angeles at Beverly Hills	300 S. Doheny Dr. www.fourseasons.com	BH	310-273-2222 800-332-3442	New	96
Hilton Checkers Hotel	535 S. Grand Ave. www.checkershotel.com	HW	213-624-0000 800-423-5798	Downtown	166
Hollywood Roosevelt Hotel	7000 Hollywood Blvd. www.hollywoodroosevelt.com	WH	323-466-7000 800-950-7667	Classic	74
Hotel Bel-Air	701 Stone Canyon Rd. www.hotelbelair.com	BA	310-472-1211 800-648-4097	Classic	74
Inn at Playa del Rey	435 Culver Blvd. www.innatplayadelrey.com	PDR	310-574-1920	Coastal	141
Luxe Hotel	360 N. Rodeo Dr. www.luxehotels.com	BH	310-273-0300 800-468-3541	New	97
Maison 140	140 S. Lasky Dr. www.maision140.com	BH	310-281-4000 800-432-5444	Classic	76
Malibu Beach Inn	22878 Pacific Coast Hwy. www.malibubeachinn.com	MA	310-456-6444 800-462-5428	Coastal	141
Millennium Biltmore Hotel- Los Angeles	506 S. Grand Ave. www.millenniumhotels.com	DT	213-624-1011 800-245-8673	Downtown Hotel Pools	166 47
Mondrian	8440 W. Sunset Blvd. www.mondrianhotel.com	WH	323-650-8999 800-525-8029	New Hotel Pools	97 47
Peninsula Beverly Hills, The	9882 S. Santa Monica Blvd. www.peninsula.com	BH	310-551-2888 800-462-7899	New Presidential Ste.	98 56
Raffles L'Ermitage Beverly Hills	9291 Burton Way www.lermitagehotel.com	BH	310-278-3344 800-323-7500	New	98
Regent Beverly Wilshire Hotel	9500 Wilshire Blvd. www.regenthotels.com	BH	310-275-5200 800-427-4354	Classic	76
Shutters on the Beach	1 Pico Blvd. www.shuttersonthebeach.com	SM	310-458-0030 800-334-9000	Coastal Presidential Ste.	142 56
St. Regis Los Angeles	2055 Avenue of the Stars www.stregis.com	CC	310-277-6111 877-787-3452	Downtown Presidential Ste.	167 56

* AH=Agoura Hills; AV=Atwater Village; BA=Bel-Air; BB= Burbank; BH=Beverly Hills; CC=Century City; CU=Culver City; DT=Downtown Los Angeles; GP=Griffith Park; HB=Hermosa Beach; HW= Hollywood; ID=Industry; LA=Los Angeles; LF=Los Feliz; MA=Malibu; MB=Manhattan Beach; MDR= Marina del Rey; MP=Moorpark; PA= Pasedena; PP=Pacific Palisades; PDR=Playa del Rey; SC=Studio City; SL=Silver Lake; SM=Santa Monica; SMo=San Marino; TC=Topanga Canyon; UC=Universal City; VE=Venice; WH=West Hollywood; WLA= West Los Angeles; WW=Westwood

Hotels (cont.)

NAME	ADDRESS	AREA	PHONE	EXPERIENCE PAGE / PERFECT PAGE
Standard Downtown, The	550 S. Flower St. www.standardhotel.com	DT	213-892-8080	Downtown 168
Standard Hollywood, The	8300 W. Sunset Blvd. www.standardhotel.com	WH	323-650-9090	Hipster 118
Sunset Marquis Hotel & Villas	1200 N. Alta Loma Rd. www.sunsetmarquishotel.com	WH	310-657-1333 800-858-9758	Hipster 119
Viceroy	1819 Ocean Ave. www.viceroysantamonica.com	SM	310-260-7500 800-622-8711	Coastal 143
W Los Angeles Westwood	930 Hilgard Ave. www.whotels.com	WW	310-208-8765 888-625-4988	Hipster 119

Restaurants

NAME	ADDRESS	AREA	PHONE	EXPERIENCE PAGE / PERFECT PAGE
A.O.C.	8022 W. Third St.	LA	323-653-6359	New 99
Ago	8478 Melrose Ave.	WH	323-655-6333	New 99 Celebrity-Owned 37
Alegria on Sunset	3510 W. Sunset Blvd.	SL	323-913-1422	Hipster 120
Alex	6703 Melrose	LA	323-933-5233	Downtown 169
Apple Pan, The	10801 W. Pico Blvd.	WLA	310-475-3585	Cheeseburger 38
Arnie Morton's of Chicago	735 S. Figueroa St.	DT	213-553-4566	Downtown 169
Asia de Cuba	8440 W. Sunset Blvd.	WH	323-848-6000	New 100 Always Trendy 34
Back on the Beach	445 Pacific Coast Hwy.	SM	310-393-8282	Coastal 144
Barney Greengrass	9570 Wilshire Blvd., 5th Fl.	BH	310-777-5877	New 100 Power Lunch 55
Blueberry	510 Santa Monica Blvd.	SM	310-394-7766	Coastal 144
Brighton Coffee Shop	9600 Brighton Way	BH	310-276-7732	Classic 77
Café Pinot	700 W. Fifth St.	DT	213-239-6500	Downtown 169
Campanile	624 S. La Brea Ave.	LA	323-938-1447	Classic 77
Canter's	419 N. Fairfax Ave.	LA	323-651-2030	Hipster 120 Late-Night Eats 48
Capo	1810 Ocean Ave.	SM	310-394-5550	Coastal 144
Cha Cha Cha	7953 Santa Monica Blvd.	WH	323-848-7700	Hipster 120
Chaya Venice	110 Navy St.	VE	310-396-1179	Coastal 145 Cheeseburger 38
Chez Mimi	246 26th St.	SM	310-393-0558	Coastal 145
Chinois on Main	2709 Main St.	SM	310-392-9025	Coastal 146
Cicada	617 S. Olive St.	DT	213-488-9488	Downtown 170
Clafoutis	8630 W. Sunset Blvd.,	WH	310-659-5233	New 100
Clifton's Brookdale Cafeteria	648 S. Broadway	DT	213-627-1673	Downtown 170
Cobras & Matadors	7615 W. Beverly Blvd.	LA	323-932-6178	Hipster 120
Crustacean	9646 Little Santa Monica Blvd.	BH	310-205-8990	New 100 Ethnic Dining 41
Dan Tana's	9071 Santa Monica Blvd.	WH	310-275-9444	Classic 77 Steakhouses 61

Restaurants (cont.)

NAME	ADDRESS	AREA	PHONE	EXPERIENCE PERFECT	PAGE PAGE
Dar Maghreb	7651 W. Sunset Blvd.	HW	323-876-7651	Downtown Ethnic Dining	170 41
Dolce	8284 Melrose Ave.	WH	323-852-7174	New Celebrity-Owned	101 37
Du-Pars	12036 Ventura Blvd.	SC	818-766-4437	Classic Late-Night Eats	77 48
Duke's Malibu	21150 Pacific Coast Hwy.	MA	310-317-0777	Coastal	146
EM Bistro	8256 Beverly Blvd.	LA	323-658-6004	New	101
Empress Pavilion	Bamboo Plaza, 988 N. Hill St.	CH	213-617-9898	Downtown	171
Fenix at The Argyle	8358 W. Sunset Blvd.	WH	323-848-6677	New	102
Fonz's	1017 Manhattan Ave.	MB	310-376-1536	Coastal	146
410 Boyd	410 Boyd St.	DT	213-617-2491	Downtown	171
Fred 62	1850 N. Vermont Ave.	LF	323-667-0062	Hipster	121
Geoffrey's	27400 Pacific Coast Hwy.	MA	310-457-1519	Coastal	147
Grace	7360 Beverly Blvd.	LA	323-934-4400	New Of-the-Moment	102 53
Granita	23725 W. Malibu Rd.	MA	310-456-0488	Coastal	147
Grill on the Alley, The	9560 Dayton Way	BH	310-276-0615	New Power Lunch	102 55
Highland Grounds	742 N. Highland Ave.	HW	323-466-1507	Hipster	121
Hollywood Hills Restaurant	1745 N. Vermont Ave.	LF	323-661-3319	Hipster	122
Hotel Bel-Air Restaurant	701 Stone Canyon Rd.	BA	310-472-1211	Classic Romantic Dining	78 58
House of Blues	8430 W. Sunset Blvd.	WH	323-848-5100	Hipster	122
Il Cielo	9018 Burton Way	BH	310-276-9990	Classic Romantic Dining	78 58
Inn of the Seventh Ray	128 Old Topanga Canyon Rd.	TC	310-455-1311	Coastal	148
Ivy at the Shore	1541 Ocean Ave.	SM	310-393-3113	Coastal	148
Ivy, The	113 N. Robertson Blvd.	BH	310-274-8303	New Power Lunch	102 55
Jer-ne	4375 Admiralty Way	MDR	310-574-4333	Coastal	148
Jones Hollywood	7205 Santa Monica Blvd.	HW	323-850-1727	Hipster	122
Katana	8439 W. Sunset Blvd.	WH	323-650-8585	New Sushi	103 63
Kate Mantilini	9101 Wilshire Blvd.	BH	310-278-3699	New	103
King's Road Cafe	8361 Beverly Blvd.	LA	323-655-9044	Hipster	123
Koi	730 N. La Cienega Blvd.	LA	310-659-9449	New Sushi	103 63
L'Orangerie	903 N. La Cienega Blvd.	WH	310-652-9770	Downtown	171
La Scala	434 N. Canon Dr.	BH	310-275-0579	Classic	78
Le Dome	8720 W. Sunset Blvd.	WH	310-659-6919	Classic	78
Le Pain Quotidien	9630 Little Santa Monica	BH	310-859-1100	New	104
Linq	8338 W. Third St.	LA	323-655-4555	Hipster Always Trendy	123 34

Restaurants (cont.)

NAME	ADDRESS	AREA	PHONE	EXPERIENCE PAGE PERFECT PAGE
Little Door, The	8164 W. Third St.	LA	323-951-1210	New 104 Romantic Dining 58
Lobster, The	1602 Ocean Ave.	SM	310-458-9294	Coastal 149
Lucques	8474 Melrose Ave	WH	323-655-6277	Hipster 123
Madame Matisse	3536 W. Sunset Blvd.	SL	323-662-4862	Hipster 124
Madre's	897 Granite Dr.	PA	626-744-0900	Downtown 172 Celebrity-Owned 37
Mangiamo	128 Manhattan Beach Blvd.	MB	310-318-3434	Coastal 149
Matsuhisa	129 N. La Cienega Blvd.	LA	310-659-9639	Downtown 172 Sushi 63
Miceli's	1646 N. Las Palmas St.	HW	323-466-3438	Classic 79
Morton's	8764 Melrose Ave.	WH	310-276-5205	Classic 79
Musso & Frank Grill	6667 Hollywood Blvd.	HW	323-467-7788	Classic 79 Steakhouses 61
Newsroom Café	120 N. Robertson Blvd.	WH	310-652-4444	New 104
Nobu Mailbu	3835 Crosscreek Rd.	MA	310-317-9140	Coastal 149
Nonya	61 N. Raymond Ave.	PA	626-583-8398	Downtown 172 Ethnic Dining 41
One Pico	1 Pico Blvd.	SM	310-587-1717	Coastal 150
Opaline	7450 Beverly Blvd.,	LA	323-857-6725	Downtown 173
Original Pantry Café	877 S. Figueroa St.	DT	213-627-6879	Downtown 173
Pacific Dining Car	1310 W. Sixth St.	DT	213-483-6000	Downtown 173 Steakhouses 61
Paladar	1651 Wilcox Ave.	HW	323-465-7500	New 105 Of-the-Moment 53
Patina	Walt Disney Concert Hall, 141 S. Grand Ave.	DT	213-972-3331	Downtown 174
Patrick's Roadhouse	106 Entrada Dr.	PP	310-459-4544	Coastal 150
Pedals	1 Pico Blvd.	SM	310-587-1707	Coastal 150
Philippe the Original	1001 N. Alameda St	DT	213-628-3781	Downtown 174
Pie 'N Burger	913 E. California Blvd.	PA	626-795-1123	Downtown 174 Cheeseburger 38
Pig 'N Whistle	6714 Hollywood Blvd.	HW	323-463-0000	Classic 80
Polo Lounge	9641 Sunset Blvd.	BH	310-276-2251	Classic 80
R-23	923 E. Second St	DT	213-687-7178	Downtown 174
Raymond, The	1250 S. Fair Oaks Ave.	PA	626-441-3136	Downtown 175
Röckenwagner	2435 Main St.	SM	310-399-6504	Coastal 150
Rose Garden Tea Room	1151 Oxford Rd.	SMo	626-683-8131	Downtown 175
Sanamluang Café	5176 Hollywood Blvd.	HW	323-660-8006	Hipster 124 Late-Night Eats 48
Smoke House	4420 Lakeside Dr.	BB	818-845-3731	Classic 80
Sona	401 N. La Cienega Blvd.	WH	310-659-7708	Downtown 175
Spago	176 N. Cañon Dr.	BH	310-385-0880	New 105 Always Trendy 34
Sushi Roku	1401 Ocean Ave.	SM	310-458-4771	Coastal 151

Restaurants (cont.)

NAME	ADDRESS	AREA	PHONE	EXPERIENCE PERFECT	PAGE PAGE
Toast	8221 W. Third St.	LA	323-655-5018	Hipster	124
Traxx	800 N. Alameda, Union Station	DT	213-625-1999	Downtown	176
24/7 Restaurant at The Standard	8300 W. Sunset Blvd	WH	323-650-9090	Hipster	125
Uncle Bill's Pancake House	1305 Highland Ave.	MB	310-545-5177	Coastal	151
Vermont	1714 N. Vermont Ave.	LF	323-661-6163	Hipster	125
Vert	6801 Hollywood Blvd., 4th Fl.	HW	323-491-1300	Hipster	125
Water Grill	544 S. Grand Ave.	DT	213-891-0900	Downtown	176
White Lotus	1743 Cahuenga Blvd.	HW	323-463-0060	New Of-the-Moment	105 53
Yamashiro	1999 N. Sycamore Ave.	HW	323-466-5125	Classic	80
Zucca	801 S. Figueroa St.	DT	213-614-7800	Downtown	176

Nightlife

NAME	ADDRESS	AREA	PHONE	EXPERIENCE	PAGE
Acme Comedy Theatre	135 N. La Brea Ave.	LA	323-525-0202	Hipster	126
Actor's Gang Theatre	6209 Santa Monica Blvd.	HW	323-465-0566	Hipster	126
Ahmanson Theatre	135 W. Grand Ave.	DT	213-628-2772	Downtown	177
Bar at Hotel Bel-Air	701 Stone Canyon Rd.	BA	310-472-1211	Classic Hotel Bars	81 39
Barfly	8730 W. Sunset Blvd.	WH	310-360-9490	New See-and-Be-Seen	106 59
Bar Marmont	8171 W. Sunset Blvd.	WH	323-650-0575	New	106
Beauty Bar	1638 Cahuenga Ave.	HW	323-464-7676	Hipster Theme Bars	126 64
Bigfoot Lodge, The	3172 Los Feliz Blvd.	AV	323-662-9227	Hipster Theme Bars	127 64
Burgundy Room, The	1621 1/2 Cahuenga Blvd.	HW	323-465-7530	Hipster	127
Cameo Bar	1819 Ocean Ave.	SM	310-260-7500	Coastal	152
Chez Jay	1657 Ocean Ave.	SM	310-395-1741	Coastal	152
Circle Bar	2926 Main St.	SM	310-450-0508	Coastal Meet Markets	152 49
Club Bar at The Peninsula Beverly Hills	9882 S. Santa Monica Blvd.	BH	310-551-2888	New Hotel Bars	106 39
Conga Room, The	5364 Wilshire Blvd.	LA	323-938-1696	Classic Nightclubs	81 52
Daddy's	1610 N. Vine St.	HW	323-463-7777	Hipster Meet Markets	127 49
Deep	1707 N. Vine St.	HW	323-462-1144	New Nightclubs	107 52
Derby, The	4500 Los Feliz Blvd.	LF	323-663-8979	Hipster	127
Dresden Room, The	1760 N. Vermont Ave.	LF	323-665-4294	Hipster	128
Egyptian Theatre	6712 Hollywood Blvd.	HW	323-466-3456	Classic Movie Theaters	81 50
El Carmen	8138 W. Third St.	LA	323-852-1556	Hipster	128

Nightlife (cont.)

NAME	ADDRESS	AREA	PHONE	EXPERIENCE PERFECT	PAGE PAGE
El Coyote	7312 Beverly Blvd.	LA	323-939-2255	Hipster	128
Formosa Café	7156 Santa Monica Blvd.	WH	323-850-9050	Classic	82
Forty Deuce	5574 Melrose Ave.	LA	323-465-4242	New	107
4100 Bar	4100 W. Sunset Blvd.	SL	323-666-4460	Hipster	128
Gallery Bar at the Millennium Biltmore Hotel	506 S. Grand Ave.	DT	213-624-1011	Downtown Hotel Bars	177 39
Good Luck Bar	1514 Hillhurst Ave.	LF	323-666-3524	Hipster Theme Bars	129 64
Grauman's Chinese Theatre	6925 Hollywood Blvd.	HW	323-464-8111	Classic	82
Greek Theatre	2700 N. Vermont Ave.	GP	323-665-1927	Downtown	178
Harvelle's	1432 Fourth St.	SM	310-395-1676	Coastal	153
Hollywood Bowl	2301 N. Highland Ave.	HW	323-850-2000	Classic	82
House of Blues	8430 W. Sunset Blvd.	WH	323-848-5100	Hipster Music Venues	122 51
Ivar	6356 Hollywood Blvd.	HW	323-465-4827	New Nightclubs	107 52
Joya	242 N. Beverly Dr.	BH	310-274-4440	New	107
Jones Hollywood	7205 Santa Monica Blvd.	WH	323-850-1727	Hipster Meet Markets	122 49
Lobby Lounge at The Standard	8300 W. Sunset Blvd.	WH	323-650-9090	Hipster	129
Lola's	945 N. Fairfax Ave.	LA	213-736-5652	New	108
Los Angeles Neon Tour	Museum of Neon Art, 501 W. Olympic Blvd.	DT	213-489-9918	Downtown Guided Tours	178 45
Lucky Strike Lanes	6801 Hollywood Blvd.	HW	323-467-7776	Hipster	129
Mark Taper Forum	135 W. Grand Ave.	DT	213-628-2772	Downtown	178
McCabe's Guitar Shop	3101 Pico Blvd.	SM	310-828-4497	Coastal	153
Nacional	1645 Wilcox Ave.	HW	323-962-7712	New	108
Pantages Theatre	6233 Hollywood Blvd.	HW	323-468-1700	Classic	82
Pasadena Playhouse	39 S. El Molino Ave.	PA	626-356-7529	Downtown	179
Polo Lounge	9641 Sunset Blvd.	BH	310-276-2251	Classic	80
Rooftop Bar at The Standard Downtown	550 S. Flower St.	DT	213-892-8080	Downtown See-and-Be-Seen	179 59
Roost, The	3100 Los Feliz Blvd.	AV	323-664-7272	Hipster	130
Side Door	900 Manhattan Ave.	MB	310-372-1684	Coastal	153
Silent Movie Theatre	611 N. Fairfax Ave.	HW	323-655-2520	Classic Movie Theatres	88 50
Sixteen-Fifty	1650 Schrader Ave.	HW	323-465-7449	Hipster	130
Skybar	8440 W. Sunset Blvd.	WH	323-848-6025	New Hollywood See-and-Be-Seen	108 59
Spaceland	1717 Silver Lake Blvd.	SL	323-661-4380	Hipster Music Venues	130 51
Temple Bar	1026 Wilshere Blvd.	SM	310-393-6611	Coastal	154
Troubadour	9081 Santa Monica Blvd.	WH	310-276-6168	Classic Music Venues	83 51

Nightlife (cont.)

NAME	ADDRESS	AREA	PHONE	EXPERIENCE PERFECT	PAGE PAGE
Veranda at Casa del Mar, The	1910 Ocean Way	SM	310-581-5533	Coastal	154
Walt Disney Concert Hall	111 S. Grand Ave.	DT	213-628-2772	Downtown	180
Well, The	6255 W. Sunset Blvd.	HW	323-467-9355	Hipster	130
Whiskey Bar	1200 Alta Loma Rd.	WH	310-657-0611	New	108
White Lotus	1743 Cahuenga Blvd.	HW	323-463-0060	New	105
Wiltern, The	3790 Wilshire Blvd.	LA	213-388-1400	Classic	83
Windows	1150 S. Olive St.	DT	213-746-1554	Downtown	180
Zanizibar	1301 Fifth St.	SM	310-451-2221	Coastal	154

Attractions

NAME	ADDRESS	AREA	PHONE	EXPERIENCE	PAGE
Angeles Crest Highway				Rides on Harley	57
Autry Museum of Western Heritage	4700 Western Heritage Way	GP	323-667-2000	Hipster	131
Bergamot Station	2525 Michigan Ave.	SM	310-829-5854	Coastal Art Spaces	155 35
Beverly Hills Trolley Tour	Rodeo Dr. and Dayton Way	BH	310-285-2438	Classic	84
Bouquet Canyon to Lake Castaic				Rides on Harley	57
Bradbury Building	304 S. Broadway	DT	213-626-1893	Downtown	181
Catalina Island				Views of L.A.	66
Chinatown		DT		Downtown	182
Farmers Market	6333 W. Third St.	LA	323-933-9211	Classic	85
Frederick's of Hollywood Lingerie Museum	6608 Hollywood Blvd.	HW	323-466-8506	Classic	85
Geffen Contemporary, The	152 N. Central Ave.	DT	213-621-2766	Hipster	131
Getty Center, The	1200 Getty Center Dr.	LA	310-440-7300	New Museums	109 40
Greystone Park & Mansion	905 Loma Vista Dr.	BH	310-550-4796	Classic	85
Hollywood Entertainment Museum	7021 Hollywood Blvd.	HW	323-465-7900	Classic Museums	85 40
Hollywood Forever Cemetery	6000 Santa Monica Blvd.	HW	323-469-1181	Classic Graveyards	86 44
Hollywood Walk of Fame	Hollywood Blvd.	HW		Classic	86
Holy Cross Cemetery	5835 W. Slauson Ave.	CU	310-670-7697	Graveyards	44
Huntington Botanical Gardens	1151 Oxford Rd.	SMo	626-405-2100	Downtown	183
Japanese American National Museum	369 E. First St.	DT	213-625-0414	Downtown	183
Kodak Theatre	6801 Hollywood Blvd.	HW	323-308-6300	Classic	86
Leo Carillo State Beach	35000 Pacific Coast Hwy.	MA	818-880-0350	Coastal	156
Little Tokyo		DT		Downtown	184
Los Angeles Conservancy Walking Tours	523 W. Sixth St., Ste. 826	DT	213-623-2489	Downtown Guided Tours	184 45
Los Angeles County Museum of Art (LACMA)	5905 Wilshire Blvd.	LA	323-857-6000	Downtown	184
Manhattan Beach		MB		Coastal Beaches	156 36

Attractions (cont.)

NAME	ADDRESS	AREA	PHONE	EXPERIENCE PAGE PERFECT PAGE
Mann's Village Theatre	961 Broxton Ave.	WW	310-248-6266	Movie Theaters 50
Montana Avenue		SM		Coastal 157 Fashion Districts 42
Mulholland Drive		BH		Views of L.A. 66
Mulholland Highway		LA		Hipster 132 Rides on Harley 57
Museum of Contemporary Art (MOCA)	250 S. Grand Ave.	DT	213-626-6222	Hipster 132 Art Spaces 35
Museum of Neon Art (MONA)	501 W. Olympic Blvd.	DT	213-489-9918	Hipster 132
Museum of Television & Radio	465 N. Beverly Dr.	BH	310-786-1000	New 110 Museums 40
Museum of Tolerance	9786 W. Pico Blvd.	LA	310-553-8403	Downtown 185
NBC Studios	3000 W Alameda Ave.	BB	818-840-3537	New 110 Studio Tours 62
Norton Simon Museum	411 W. Colorado Blvd.	PA	626-449-6840	Downtown 185 Art Spaces 35
Ocean Front Walk		VE		Coastal 157
Paramount Pictures	5555 Melrose Ave.	HW	323-956-5000	Classic 87
Paramount Ranch	Paramount Ranch Rd.	AH	818-597-9192	Classic 87
Petersen Automotive Museum	6060 Wilshire Blvd.	LA	323-930-2277	Hipster 133
Point Mugu State Park	9000 Pacific Coast Hwy.	MA	818-880-0350	Coastal 158 Hikes 46
Red Line Tours	6773 Hollywood Blvd.	HW	323-402-1074	Classic 87 Guided Tours 45
Rodeo Drive		BH		New 91 Fashion Districts 42
Runyon Canyon Park	2000 N. Fuller Ave.	HW	213-485-5111	New 111 Hikes 46
South Bay Bicycle Trail		LA		Coastal 158
Southwest Museum	234 Museum Dr.	LA	323-221-2163	Hipster 133
Sunset Strip		WH		New 94 Fashion Districts 42
Temescal Gateway Park	15601 Sunset Blvd.	PP	310-454-1395	Coastal 159 Hikes 46
Third Street Promenade		SM		Coastal 159
Universal Studios Hollywood	100 Universal City Plaza	UC	818-508-9600 818-622-3801	New 111 Studio Tours 62
Venice Beach		VE		Beaches 36
Walt Disney Concert Hall	111 S. Grand Ave.	DT	213-628-2772	Downtown 180
Warner Brothers Studios	4301 W. Olive Ave.	BB	818-972-8687 818-954-1744	Classic 89 Studio Tours 62
Westwood Village Memorial Park	1218 Glendon Ave.	WW	310-474-1579	Graveyards 44
Will Rogers State Historic Park	1501 Will Rogers, State Park Rd.	PP	310-454-8212	Classic 89
Zuma Beach	30050 Pacific Coast Hwy.	MA		Coastal 159 Beaches 36

Golf Courses

NAME	ADDRESS	AREA	PHONE	EXPERIENCE / PERFECT	PAGE
Brookside Golf Course	1133 Rosemont Ave.	PA	626-796-0177	Downtown Golf Courses	182 43
Industry Hills Golf Club	1 Industry Hills Parkway	ID	626-810-4653	Downtown	183
Los Feliz Municipal Golf Course	3207 Los Feliz Blvd.	LF	323-663-7758	Hipster	132
Malibu Country Club	901 Encinal Canyon Rd.	MA	818-889-6680	Coastal	156
Rancho Park Golf Course	10460 W. Pico Blvd.	LA	310-838-7373	New Golf Courses	111 43
Rustic Canyon Golf Course	15100 Happy Camp, Canyon Rd.	MP	805-530-0221	Classic	88
Wilson/Harding Golf Courses	4730 Crystal Springs Dr.	GP	323-664-2255	Hipster Golf Courses	133 43

Services and Shops

NAME	ADDRESS	AREA	PHONE	EXPERIENCE / PERFECT	PAGE
Beverly Hills Rent-a-Car	9220 S. Sepulveda Blvd.	LA	310-337-1400	Rent Wheels	54
Book City	6627 Hollywood Blvd.	HW	323-466-2525	Classic	84
Cristophe Salon	348 North Beverly Dr.	BH	310-274-0851	New	109
Crunch Fitness	8000 W. Sunset Blvd.	WH	323-654-4550	Hipster	131
EagleRider	11860 S. La Cienega Blvd.	LA	310-320-3456	Rent Wheels	54
Epicurean School of Culinary Arts	8759 Melrose Ave.	WH	310-659-5990	Classic	84
Escape on Horseback	2623 Old Topanga, Canyon Rd.	TC	818-591-2032	Coastal	155
Grand Central Market	317 S. Broadway	DT	213-624-2378	Downtown	182
Heli USA	16303 Waterman Dr.	VN	818-994-1445	New Views of L.A.	109 66
Hollywood & Highland	6801 Hollywood Blvd.	HW	323-960-2331	Classic	86
Marina del Rey Sportfishing	Dock 52, Fiji Way	MDR	310-822-3625	Coastal	156
Marina Sailing	13441 Mindanao Way	MDR	310-822-6617	Coastal	157
Necromance	7220 Melrose Ave.	LA	323-934-8684	Unusual Shopping	65
Paradise Bound Yacht Charters	4375 Admiralty Way	MDR	310-578-7963	Coastal	157
Pure Surfing Experience	524 14th St.	MB	310-546-4451	Coastal	158
Rent-A-Wreck	12333 W. Pico Blvd.	WLA	310-659-3277	Rent Wheels	54
Skeletons in the Closet	1104 N. Mission Rd.	DT	323-343-0760	Unusual Shopping	65
Soap Plant/Wacko	4633 Hollywood Blvd.	LF	323-663-0122	Unusual Shopping	65
3rd Street Dance	8558 W. Third St.	LA	310-275-4683	Classic	88

Spas

NAME	ADDRESS	AREA	PHONE	EXPERIENCE / PERFECT	PAGE
Amadeus Spa	799 E. Green St.	PA	626-578-3404	Downtown	181
Aqua Day Spa	1422 Second St.	SM	310-899-6222	Coastal	155
Beverly Hot Springs	308 N. Oxford Ave.	LA	323-734-7000	Downtown Spas	181 60
Burke Williams Day Spa	8000 W. Sunset Blvd.	WH	323-822-9007	Hipster	131
Ole Henriksen Face/Body	8622-A W. Sunset Blvd.	WH	310-854-7700	New Spas	110 60
Spa Mystique	2025 Avenue of the Stars	CC	310-551-3251	Classic Spas	88 60

Index

Key to page number styles: Roman—description in theme chapter, Leaving and Calendar; *Italic*—listing within Itinerary; **Bold**—description in Perfect L.A. section

Key to page number styles: Roman—description in theme chapter, Leaving and Calendar; *Italic*—listing within Itinerary; **Bold**—description in Perfect L.A. section

I

J

K

L

M

Key to page number styles: Roman—description in theme chapter, Leaving and Calendar; *Italic*—listing within Itinerary; **Bold**—description in Perfect L.A. section

Key to page number styles: Roman—description in theme chapter, Leaving and Calendar; *Italic*—listing within Itinerary; **Bold**—description in Perfect L.A. section